PEOPLE'S BIBLE COMMENTARY

JOSHUA

ADOLPH L. HARSTAD

PBC

CONCORDIA PUBLISHING HOUSE · SAINT LOUIS

CONTENTS

ILLUSTRATIONS

EDITOR'S PREFACE

The *People's Bible Commentary* is just what the name implies—a Bible and commentary for the people. It includes the complete text of the Holy Scriptures in the popular New International Version. The commentary following the Scripture sections contains personal applications as well as historical background and explanations of the text.

The authors of the *People's Bible Commentary* are men of scholarship and practical insight gained from years of experience in the teaching and preaching ministries. They have tried to avoid the technical jargon which limits so many commentary series to professional Bible scholars.

The most important feature of these books is that they are Christ-centered. Speaking of the Old Testament Scriptures, Jesus himself declared, "These are the Scriptures that testify about me" (John 5:39). Each volume of the *People's Bible Commentary* directs our attention to Jesus Christ. He is the center of the entire Bible. He is our only Savior.

We dedicate these volumes to the glory of God and to the good of his people.

The Publishers

INTRODUCTION TO JOSHUA

The book's place in the Bible

The book of Joshua swings open the door to part two of God's Old Testament library. English Bibles call this section the 12 historic books. They follow the five books of Moses and consist of Joshua through Esther. These historic books cover about a thousand years of history: from Joshua's time at about 1400 B.C. to the time of Nehemiah, approaching 400 B.C.

Hebrew Bibles place Joshua first among the books called the prophets. That placement says something about the kind of history we read in Joshua. *Prophetic history,* scholars often call it. Prophetic history is not just the story of ancient Israel told for the sake of historical facts. Rather, it offers us selected slices of Israel's history chosen by a prophet to inspire faith by his God-breathed message.

The prophetic history in Joshua touches each of us in a personal way. The book of Joshua is an exciting early portion of the story of our salvation that features God's background work for Jesus' cross and empty tomb. A candle needs a candlestick. The Light of the world needed a setting when he took on our flesh. We see in the book of Joshua how the Lord gave Israel the land he promised and thus provided the setting for the saving acts of Jesus.

The background from the Bible

The five books of Moses (the Pentateuch) give the background for the book of Joshua. We prize the message of

1

fulfillment in Joshua when we hold in mind the Lord's promise of the land of Canaan.

The Lord first made the promise of the land to Abraham. After Abraham had traveled through Canaan to its approximate center at Shechem, the Lord said: "To your offspring I will give this land" (Genesis 12:7).

God's promise had meaning far beyond giving turf to one nation. The very words that promised the land also guaranteed the world its Savior. The "offspring" who received the land were not just Abraham's countless descendants. The particular offspring is one person: Jesus (Galatians 3:16). The land was his workplace for constructing our salvation. The Lord therefore tied the promise of the land to the promise of the Savior and sealed all he said by the covenant of circumcision (Genesis 17). He repeated the same promise to Isaac (Genesis 26:3,4) and to Jacob (Genesis 28:13,14).

Years passed without fulfillment of the promise. Abraham owned "not even a foot of ground" in Canaan (Acts 7:5). He had to *purchase* land from a Hittite of Hebron to bury his wife Sarah (Genesis 23:19,20). When a Philistine demanded that Isaac move from a place in Canaan where he had planted crops and dug wells, Isaac moved (Genesis 26:16,17). The Land of Promise was still in the firm grasp of others.

Jacob and the Israelites even became physically separated from the Promised Land. A famine in Canaan forced them to migrate to Egypt where they settled in the region of Goshen (Genesis 46). Four hundred thirty years passed in Egypt. The Israelites became slaves. The stubbornness of Pharaoh and the hostile environment of the Sinai Peninsula cut them off from their God-promised land.

But through the hand of Moses, the Lord led Israel past both obstacles. The Lord shepherded them in their desert trek. At Mount Sinai he made a second covenant with them. That covenant governed Israel's life in the Promised Land until the coming of the Savior.

At Kadesh Barnea Moses sent out 12 spies to explore Canaan (Numbers 13). The Israelites rebelled when they heard the spies' report of powerful people and fortified cities. Their faithless conclusion: "We should choose a leader and go back to Egypt" (Numbers 14:4). Only Joshua and Caleb urged marching on to enter the land because, they said, "the LORD is with us" (Numbers 14:9). God punished the grumbling Israelites. The whole rebellious generation—everyone over 20 years old—died in the desert. For 38 years they wandered until the body of the last grumbler dropped in the sand. Of that generation only Joshua and Caleb were allowed to enter Canaan.

The Lord even barred Moses from the land. His harsh words and rash action at the rock at Meribah cost him entrance. The Lord told him: "Because you did not trust in me enough to honor me as holy in the sight of the Israelites, you will not bring this community into the land I give them" (Numbers 20:12). God let Moses lead Israel only to the doorstep of Canaan in Trans-Jordan. Two and a half tribes of Israel settled there. But Canaan proper lay across the Jordan River.

As the Pentateuch closes, God gives Moses a bird's-eye view of the Promised Land from the top of Mount Nebo. There he dies without crossing the Jordan (Deuteronomy 34). The new leader, Joshua, and the new generation of Israelites are poised in the plains of Moab awaiting God's instructions. They are to be his cutting edge to conquer and distribute the land. The Lord makes no empty promises! The scene is set for the book of Joshua.

Author and time of writing

Jewish and early Christian traditions say that Joshua is the author of the book that bears his name. But neither the book itself nor any other part of the Bible names the book's author. We can only speculate.

The book of Joshua itself contains some hints that may lead us to opinions about authorship and point us to a general time of writing.

1. Joshua's death is recorded in the book (24:29). If there is a single author, he seems to be someone who lived after Joshua's time.
2. In 5:1 the author writes in the first person about crossing the Jordan and says, "We had crossed over." This leads some to think that the author was an eyewitness of the book's events. Others explain the *we* as a corporate term that means the same as "our nation Israel." In the same way, an American might write "We landed on the moon in 1969."
3. The author writes before King David dislodged the Jebusites from Jerusalem (Joshua 15:63). The book therefore could not have been written during the time of the later kings. (David ruled at about 1000 B.C.)
4. The phrase "to this day," repeated often in Joshua, suggests that the author wrote at a time somewhat separated from the events he relates.

In *Introduction to the Old Testament,* R. K. Harrison says that Joshua was written "perhaps about 1045 B.C., and thus within the lifetime of Samuel, who may actually have contributed in some manner to its compilation." Marten H. Woudstra in his commentary, *The Book of Joshua,* notes the "joyful optimism" evident in the book and favors a time of writing when this optimism was evident: during "the life-

4

time of Joshua and of the elders who outlived him" (Joshua 24:31). Edward J. Young, in *An Introduction to the Old Testament,* leans toward the same time of writing as Woudstra and says that the author was "possibly an elder, who had been an eyewitness to most of the events recorded in the book."

The man Joshua

The book of Joshua is named after its central character, Joshua son of Nun. Joshua was from the tribe of Ephraim and thus from Joseph's line. He was born during the bitter bondage years in Egypt.

His original name was Hoshea, which means "salvation." Moses expanded his name to Joshua, "the LORD saves" (Numbers 13:16). A thousand years later in the book of Nehemiah, his name is spelled J-e-s-h-u-a. In the Greek Old Testament, that form of his name became Jesus. His name and our Savior's are identical. To eliminate confusion, the NIV calls him Joshua rather than Jesus in the two New Testament passages that name him, Acts 7:45 and Hebrews 4:8.

Joshua's name first appears in the Bible in Exodus chapter 17. Moses gave him the order to choose some men and fight the Amalekites. Joshua acted precisely "as Moses had ordered" (Exodus 17:10). Without excuses, in obedience and trust in the Lord, he tackled the job. The Lord provided an overwhelming victory. We may remember that battle at Rephidim for the scene of Moses holding up his hands while Aaron and Hur supported his tired arms to secure victory. The one orchestrating the battle was the obedient general Joshua.

Later in Exodus we see Joshua as Moses' faithful aide-de-camp who accompanied Moses at Mount Sinai and guarded his special tent of meeting (Exodus 24:13; 33:11). Joshua's steady, God-trusting character shines during the episode of the spies' mission into Canaan (Numbers 13 and 14). He and Caleb were insistent that the Israelites stop their blasphemous words about returning to Egypt and press on into the land. Even threats of stoning did not intimidate him. The minority of two was not afraid to stand up against the majority of thousands when the two stood with the Lord's promise.

Joshua "followed the LORD wholeheartedly" (Numbers 32:12) and was "a man in whom is the spirit" (Numbers 27:18). That was God's own appraisal of Joshua. This man with a valuable mix of gifts—deeply spiritual and highly practical—was God's choice for Moses' successor.

At the time of Moses' death, Joshua was an old man, perhaps in his 80s. Yet he was just starting the greatest work of his life. Spiritual and physical vigor, wholehearted trust in God's promises, willingness to be in a moral minority, obedience, bravery, leadership by personal example—the work ahead called for a man with these kinds of qualifications. The Lord blessed Joshua with these qualities, honed his skills, strengthened his faith, and made him the man to lead the people of promise at a critical period of salvation history.

The date of the conquest

The accounts of Joshua cover about 30 years. But where do those years fit in the pages of world history? A continuing debate among Bible scholars centers on that question. It has not always been a debate of the meek. Opinions place them within the Late Bronze Age (ca. 1550–1200 B.C.), but about 150 years separate them. Should the conquest under Joshua be dated about 1400 B.C. (the early date), about 1250 B.C. (the late date), or somewhere in between?

When it comes to determining many Old Testament dates, we are not just guessing. A big help for Old Testament dating came with the discovery of some Assyrian lists of

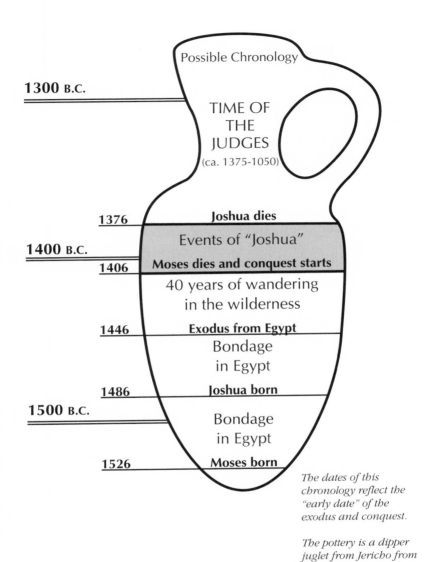

Possible Chronology

1300 B.C.

TIME OF
THE
JUDGES
(ca. 1375-1050)

1376 — Joshua dies

Events of "Joshua"

1400 B.C.

1406 — Moses dies and conquest starts

40 years of wandering
in the wilderness

1446 — Exodus from Egypt

Bondage
in Egypt

1486 — Joshua born

1500 B.C.

Bondage
in Egypt

1526 — Moses born

*The dates of this
chronology reflect the
"early date" of the
exodus and conquest.*

*The pottery is a dipper
juglet from Jericho from
the Late Bronze Age
(1550-4200 B.C.).*

Chronological chart

names. These lists name each year from 893 B.C. to 666 B.C. after the Assyrian prime minister for that year. Scholars have dubbed these lists *eponym* lists, a word that means "named after." One list mentions a solar eclipse. Astronomers have computed that this eclipse occurred in 763 B.C. With that year established as a reference point, scholars could assign an exact year to all the Assyrian officials mentioned in the lists. An Assyrian inscription provided the link to the Old Testament through the mention of King Jehu. Jehu, probably in the first year of his reign, is named and pictured with Assyrian King Shalmaneser III. Since Shalmaneser's dates are known through the eponym lists, a date can be assigned to Old Testament King Jehu. The books of Kings and Chronicles fill in the rest of the dates with their chronological information.

Archaeology, astronomy, and the Bible have therefore worked together to determine dates for many Old Testament characters and events. But how can we use these dates to determine the time of Joshua's conquest?

First Kings 6:1 says that King Solomon began to build the temple in the fourth year of his reign and that this was 480 years after the exodus from Egypt. Through the dating process sketched above, we can determine that the fourth year of Solomon's reign is in or about 966 B.C. Since this was 480 years after the exodus, the exodus took place in or about 1446 B.C. Take into consideration the 40 years of desert wandering after the exodus, and we calculate that Joshua's conquest started about 1406 B.C. Through a literal reading of 1 Kings 6:1, we arrive at the early date for Joshua's conquest.

While we do not pretend that the 1406 B.C. date is absolutely certain, it is based on Scripture and the best available chronological material. It serves as a convenient peg on which to hang the conquest events.

Despite the clear testimony of Scripture, however, many Old Testament scholars prefer the late date of about 1250 B.C. for the conquest. They claim that the archaeological record favors their position. Evidence of destruction to Canaan's cities is said to be scant for the early date and more abundant for the late date. But who caused the destruction in 1250 B.C.? Could it have been other Canaanites or the later judges rather than Joshua? And didn't Joshua, with only a few exceptions, leave Canaanite cities intact for habitation by the Israelites? Could this account for scant evidence of destruction in 1400 B.C.? Little fuel for debate has been unearthed in recent years. Yet the debate goes on.

Ancient texts from Joshua's time

Archaeology has opened three windows on the world of Joshua.

The Amarna Letters

These writings from about 1400–1350 B.C. shed light on political, religious, and social life in Canaan. They were discovered in 1887 when an Egyptian woman was pulverizing clay tablets to fertilize her garden. She had found the tablets while digging in the ruins of Tell El Amarna. The site later yielded more than three hundred diplomatic letters between the Egyptian pharaoh and other heads of state and vassals. Some of the letters came from the pharaoh's vassals in Canaan at Joshua's time (according to the early date). In one letter the ruler in Jerusalem begs the pharaoh for military help because the "Habiru" are closing in. While there is much debate over who the Habiru were, the term here may have referred to the invading Hebrews under Joshua. The general picture we get of Joshua's world from the Amarna Letters is that Egypt's grip on Canaan was weakening. City-states with their kings were filling the power vacuum left by a weakening Egypt. This picture of Canaanite city-states and their turmoil is in harmony with what we observe in the pages of Joshua.

The Ugaritic Writings

In 1928 a whole library of ancient tablets was unearthed on the Syrian coast. The site known today as Ras Shamra was known at Joshua's time as Ugarit. The writings are from about 1400–1365 B.C. They are in a language closely related to Old Testament Hebrew. The Ugaritic tablets are especially fascinating because of the light they cast on Canaanite religion. They record bloodthirsty gods and goddesses and sensual worship with ritual prostitution. The book of Joshua reveals God's judgment on the horrible religion and immorality practiced in ancient Canaan and pictured in the library of Ugarit.

The Nuzi Tablets

These writings, about 20,000 clay tablets in all, illuminate the customs of the Mideast during the 15th century and earlier. We get a detailed picture of ancient life through legal documents covering such subjects as inheritance laws, the apportioning of land by casting lots, adoption, wills, and deathbed utterances made before witnesses. We find parallels for many of these customs in the book of Joshua.

The book's message

The pages of Joshua echo with the sounds of collapsing walls, the clash of swords, the roar of fires, and the booming *amen* of God's grateful nation. But through all these sounds, the author sustains this clear message: The Lord has fulfilled his promise of the land, and we can trust him to fulfill all his promises.

Outline

Theme: The Lord fulfills his promise of the land

I. Preparations for taking the land (1:1–5:12)
   A. The Lord encourages Joshua (1:1-9)
   B. All Israel will participate (1:10-18)
   C. Rahab and the spies (2:1-24)
   D. Crossing the Jordan (3:1-17)
   E. Two memorials (4:1-24)
   F. Circumcision and Passover renewed (5:1-12)

II. The land is captured (5:13–12:24)
   A. The fall of Jericho (5:13–6:27)
   B. Achan's sin (7:1-26)
   C. Ai destroyed (8:1-29)
   D. The covenant renewed at the two mountains (8:30-35)
   E. The Gibeonite deception (9:1-27)
   F. The sun stands still (10:1-15)
   G. Five Amorite kings killed (10:16-28)
   H. Southern cities conquered (10:29-43)
   I. Northern cities defeated (11:1-15)
   J. Victories reviewed (11:16–12:24)

III. The land is allotted (13:1–21:45)
   A. Land still to be taken (13:1-7)
   B. Division of the land east of the Jordan (13:8-33)
   C. Division of the land west of the Jordan (14:1–19:51)
   D. Cities of refuge (20:1-9)
   E. Towns for the Levites (21:1-45)

IV. The heirs of the land respond (22:1–24:33)
   A. A misunderstanding settled (22:1-34)
   B. Joshua's farewell to the leaders (23:1-16)

PART ONE

Preparations for Taking the Land
(1:1–5:12)

The first five books of the Bible end as an unfinished story. At the close of Deuteronomy, the Israelites were still camped east of the Jordan, on the plains of Moab. The Lord's covenant people could only fix a longing gaze across the Jordan toward the Promised Land. Moses, the leader for 40 years, has died in Moab. Israel has mourned for 30 days. What now?

The book of Joshua reads like a sequel to Moses' books. The common thread is the Lord's covenant promise to give the land of Canaan to Israel. When he made this promise to Abraham, the Lord had added an even greater promise of a special heir who would come to bless all people (Genesis 22:18; Galatians 3:16).

How will the Lord fulfill his promise of the land now that Moses lies buried in Moab? The answer unfolds.

The Lord encourages Joshua

1 **After the death of Moses the servant of the LORD, the LORD said to Joshua son of Nun, Moses' aide: ²"Moses my servant is dead. Now then, you and all these people, get ready to cross the Jordan River into the land I am about to give to them—to the Israelites. ³I will give you every place where you set your foot, as I promised Moses."**

The Lord's promise is alive, even though Moses is dead. The days of waiting are about to give way to God-directed action. But first the Lord inspires Israel's new leader with courage.

The Lord *speaks* to Joshua. We are not told just how he spoke. But by communicating with Joshua, he shows himself to be a personal God in touch with his people. He is not some far-removed being, like an African "high god." Nor is he just a speechless "force" or "energy" in the universe, as in New Age religion.

By speaking to Joshua as he once spoke to Moses, the Lord shows that Joshua now stands in the sandals of Moses as the God-appointed leader. While Moses was still alive, Joshua had been commissioned as Moses' successor (Numbers 27:18-23). Now Joshua is in charge.

The author does not need to identify Joshua in detail. We know him quite well from Exodus, Numbers, and Deuteronomy, in which his name appears 26 times. Now the author simply calls him the son of Nun and Moses' aide. This is the man we know as the competent general, the spy who gave the optimistic report, Moses' right-hand man, the Spirit-filled man of wholehearted obedience (Exodus 17:13; 33:11; Numbers 14:6-9; 27:18; 32:12).

God was not taking a chance on a new leader. For 40 years Joshua had been trained, tested, and proved faithful. The task ahead was critical. It called for a proven leader. So does Jesus' kingdom work today. Leadership roles belong with people "known to be full of the Spirit and wisdom" (Acts 6:3); and "they must first be tested" (1 Timothy 3:10). But at the same time that a progressive church selects tested and trusted leaders, it also provides training for the unproven so that new "Joshuas" are waiting in the wings.

At this time of change in leaders, the Lord makes a fond parting reference to Moses. The closing verses of Deuteronomy speak a glowing eulogy of this incomparable man "whom the LORD knew face to face" (Deuteronomy 34:10-12).

The Lord himself calls Moses "my servant." That tiny word *my* shows Moses' greatest honor. He belongs to the Lord in life and in death—for eternity! And the Lord has accepted his service, imperfect though it was.

Here is concrete comfort for us. Through Christ we belong to God forever. He counts us his very own and is not ashamed to call us his servants.

The Lord's way of speaking about Moses also shows us how to speak about one another in positive terms that reflect our status under God's grace.

Why does the Lord state to Joshua the obvious, that "Moses . . . is dead"? After all, Israel had known that fact for at least 30 days, though his grave site was God's secret (Deuteronomy 34:6). Mention of Moses' death serves as some reminders for us and as a special signal for Israel:

1. Moses' death is a reminder of his disobedience and the Lord's judgment on it (Numbers 20:12). He deprived himself of a blessing and died outside the Land of Promise. For our own joy, the Lord insists on obedience. Let his new leader and us readers take notice!

2. Moses' death is a reminder that the Lord controls the life and time of death of his people. Moses died a healthy man (Deuteronomy 34:7). The Lord's people die when he calls them. Old age, accident, sickness, act of war—one of these may be listed on a certificate as the cause of death. But the final cause of a believer's death is the Father's call (Psalm 31:15). Joshua would be putting his life on the line in battle after battle. The reminder that our times are in the hands of the Lord gives comfort.

3. Moses' death is a reminder to do God's work on earth with all vigor while we are still able (Ecclesiastes 9:10). Seize the day!

4. Moses' death also reminds us that the Lord's kingdom does not rest on the shoulders of one mere man. Even Moses, a great servant of the Lord, was dispensable. He died. But the Lord's kingdom did not topple. That fact does not belittle Moses. It magnifies the Lord who continues to provide workers for his church. He does not fail to supply new servants like Joshua, Paul, Luther, and today's pastors, missionaries, teachers, and lay leaders (Ephesians 4:11-13). That reminder to Israel's new top man is a guard against conceit. It also ensures that no matter who the servant is, God's work will get done. The Lord's servants enjoy the privilege of working for him. But at God's chosen time they are dispensable to his church on earth.

The Lord's immediate purpose in calling attention to Moses' death is to sound a signal. Moses would not enter the land. Neither would God make him watch while the nation entered without him. His death removed the last obstacle to entrance and served as a trumpet blast for Israel to get ready. The Lord's very words show that he speaks of Moses' death as a reveille. "Now then"—in light of the death of Moses—"get ready." There is a time to mourn at the death of a great leader. And there is a time to dry tears, roll up sleeves, and get ready to carry out the Lord's exciting plans. Now is that time!

Think of the excitement at this moment in Israel's history! For centuries God had spoken in the future tense about giving Canaan to Israel. To Abraham, Isaac, and Jacob he had prophesied: "I *will* give this land." Now on this day early in the month of Nisan (March/April), perhaps in 1406 B.C., he changes his tense to the *immediate* future and commands Joshua and Israel to enter "into the land I am about to give." These exciting words also introduce the theme of the whole book of Joshua. The promise of the land is to be fulfilled!

Just how the Lord will give the land is made clear when he says, "I will give you every place where you set your foot." The land is an outright gift for Israel to step up and take by faith. The Israelites did not deserve it or earn it (Deuteronomy 9:5,6). Their fighting will not be the underlying cause of their possessing it. It will only appear as the visible cause. And sometimes not even that, as the first "battle" at Jericho will soon show! Israel will inherit the land because of the Lord's covenant promise, repeated most recently to Moses.

The "outright gift" emphasis of the Lord may also be felt in the words "to the Israelites." The term *Israelites* often brings up thoughts of the grumbling people of Israel in the desert, defying their Lord. Even their gross ingratitude could not deter the Lord from fulfilling his promise in the eyes of their children. He is about to give the land to the Israelites because he made a covenant promise!

The Lord's undeserved love is obvious in the land gift to Israel. But it would be even more plain when the special heir of that land would die to redeem the whole world. "While we were still sinners, Christ died for us" (Romans 5:8). *The gift of the land to one nation* was designed to set the stage for *the gift of redemption for all nations* through Jesus, the land's ultimate heir.

Israel will receive the land gift. But as the Lord speaks to Joshua, an imposing barrier still blocks the Israelites from Canaan. The Lord calls attention to this obstacle when he commands: "Get ready to cross the Jordan River."

That is a big command! Just how big sinks in when we note that the Jordan and its valley are part of the Great Rift that stretches all the way from Turkey down into Malawi and Mozambique in southeast Africa. This rift is such a deep gash down the face of the earth that it can be seen from the moon.

From the census figures recorded in Numbers chapter 26, we can project that Israel was a nation of at least two million people. That massive assembly would have to descend from the plains of Moab into this chasm near the earth's lowest point at 1,296 feet below sea level. Then they would have to cross the river at flood stage (3:15) and penetrate a land filled with hostile nations. Israel's new leader would need a heart made bold by the Lord. God gave Joshua the encouragement he needed in the form of a visual display with commentary. The Lord holds before Joshua's eyes the inviting land just beyond the Great Rift.

4"Your territory will extend from the desert to Lebanon and from the great river, the Euphrates—all the Hittite country—to the Great Sea on the west. 5No one will be able to stand up against you all the days of your life. As I was with Moses, so I will be with you; I will never leave you nor forsake you."

The Lord frames the Promised Land with the natural borders of antiquity in the Middle East—an expansive desert, a snowcapped mountain range, a dominant river, and the Great Sea that would later be called the middle of the earth (Mediterranean). The appeal of the land already known by Israel to be flowing with milk and honey is heightened by the frame God places around it. Other boundary descriptions of the Land of Promise are found in Genesis 15:18-21; Exodus 23:31; Numbers 34:1-12; and Deuteronomy 1:7; 11:24.

It may be difficult to tell exactly from where to where the Lord draws his lines on an imaginary map. But the general territory is evident. If we take Deuteronomy 11:24 as our cue, the Lord is here sketching a rough X.

The first line of the Lord's X stretches from the Arabian Desert in the southeast to Lebanon in the northwest. It is likely that "the desert" is the Arabian Desert since it is the most imposing desert of the Middle East. "Lebanon," which means "white," refers to the Lebanon mountain ranges. Their snowcapped peaks or white limestone cliffs provide the name. In Hebrew the Lord says, "this Lebanon." On a clear day, Joshua can see the mountain peaks far to the northwest as the Lord speaks to him in Moab.

The second line of the Lord's X runs from the Euphrates River in the northeast to the shores of the Mediterranean Sea in the southwest. The Lord may be summarizing all of Israel's promised turf when he refers to "all the Hittite country." An alternate view is that "all the Hittite country" refers only to the northern part—from Lebanon to the Euphrates.

On display with these wide boundaries is God's more-than-generous way of dealing with his people. The one who is about to give Israel "a good and *spacious* land" (Exodus 3:8) often gives us not just bare needs but "immeasurably more than all we ask or imagine" (Ephesians 3:20). His people have good reason to say, "The boundary lines have fallen for me in pleasant places; surely I have a delightful inheritance" (Psalm 16:6).

The Lord does not promise that all this territory will be in the hands of the Israelites at once. He will give it "little by little," according to his promise in Exodus 23:29,30. Remember also that retaining possession of the land is tied to obedience to the Sinai Covenant. (See Deuteronomy 11:22-25;

30:17,18.) The Lord will not force his gift on people who despise the giver.

The Lord does not want Joshua to think that the holders of this land will surrender without a fight. Israel will be facing off against "nations larger and stronger" than itself (Deuteronomy 11:23). That is the stark reality. But the Lord's promise makes it clear that no matter how impressive the opponents, Joshua will not die on the battlefield. When the dust and smoke of battle clear, he will be standing firm. The Lord assures Joshua that "no one will be able to stand up against you all the days of your life." Hinted at in those words to an already old man is the promise of a very long life. Joshua may already be in his 80s as the Lord speaks to him. But the gray-bearded general will not die in his 80s or even his 90s (24:29).

Throughout Joshua's long life, the Lord promises to be with him in the same way he was with Moses. How was the Lord with Moses? Remember the walk on dry land through the Red Sea, the water from the rock, and the manna and quail. Recall the personal conversations between the Lord and Moses. That is the gracious way the Lord will now be with Joshua. Matthew Henry, in an almost 300-year-old commentary, makes a catching comment on the Lord's promise to be with Joshua as he was with Moses. Henry says that Joshua may not have had the same presence of mind as Moses, but he had the same presence of God. That is all he needed.

The Lord's promise does not mean that Joshua should retire all his natural talents. That would be putting the promise to a sinful test. As Israel's general he would need to use every bit of strategy he could muster. At the same time, he would know that only God's promise and presence guarantees success. Faith in God's promises and confident actions go together naturally. Only a person who wants to tempt

God sits down and dares God to prove his promise in the face of laziness.

Because of Joshua's unique role, the Lord directs some of his promises to him alone. But at least one promise—the most reassuring one—belongs to God's people of all times: "I will never leave you nor forsake you." These words are an echo of Deuteronomy 31:1,6-8, where the promise applies to all Israel. The writer of Hebrews repeats these words for New Testament Christians. He applies this promise so that we do not become obsessed with piling up material goods for security. "Keep your lives free from the love of money and be content with what you have, because God has said, 'Never will I leave you; never will I forsake you'" (Hebrews 13:5). A cornucopia cluttered with cars, cash, and credit cards does not ensure a full life. The Lord's gracious presence does.

Joshua's success is the Lord's aim as he heaps up further encouragement:

⁶"Be strong and courageous, because you will lead these people to inherit the land I swore to their forefathers to give them. ⁷Be strong and very courageous. Be careful to obey all the law my servant Moses gave you; do not turn from it to the right or to the left, that you may be successful wherever you go. ⁸Do not let this Book of the Law depart from your mouth; meditate on it day and night, so that you may be careful to do everything written in it. Then you will be prosperous and successful. ⁹Have I not commanded you? Be strong and courageous. Do not be terrified; do not be discouraged, for the LORD your God will be with you wherever you go."

Of all the Israelites, Joshua is God's choice to fulfill his promise. When God says, "You will lead these people to inherit the land," he emphasizes *you* in the Hebrew. What a privilege to be the Lord's unique agent at this exciting hour of fulfillment!

But the responsibility that comes with the privilege must land heavy on Joshua's shoulders as he gazes across the chasm to the land filled with enemies. A mere mortal with a divine task carries a heavy load. Then there is the nation he is to lead—that infamous nation that exasperated Moses until his emotions spilled over. A broken Moses sobbed before the Lord: "Why have you brought this trouble on your servant? I cannot carry all these people by myself; the burden is too heavy for me. If this is how you are going to treat me, put me to death right now" (see Numbers 11:10-15).

The Lord wants Joshua to be "prosperous and successful," not to feel frustrated and discouraged as Moses did. So he lavishes on him heavy doses of encouragement. Three times he bolsters Joshua's faith by urging him to "be strong and courageous." For the second time in the span of a few moments, God promises to be with him wherever he goes.

The repetition of the Lord's encouragement is both striking and significant. Does the repetition show that a clumsy editor spliced together some similar documents to form the book of Joshua and failed to remove the overlaps? Some critics make this claim. But there are better reasons for the repetition.

First, repetition plays a big part in Hebrew writing style. In his speaking, the Lord accommodates himself to this style of his people. Second, the repetition is for emphasis. He wants Joshua to be sure that he can conquer Canaan. Joshua is no different from us. To be firm in our faith, we need to hear God's uplifting words again and again.

At the very core of his encouragement, the Lord insists that Joshua cling to the written Word. His Bible reading is to be *thorough* so that he will know and obey all "the Law." It is to be *regular,* "day and night." It is to be *personal* meditation and not just an academic exercise. The promise attached to this kind of Bible reading is that Joshua will be "prosperous and successful." The writer of the first psalm echoes this same promise of success to anyone who meditates regularly on the Bible's words (Psalm 1:2,3).

Two words in verse 8 suggest the value of reading the Word out loud. The "Book of the Law" is to be in Joshua's *mouth,* and the Hebrew word translated as "meditate" means literally to "murmur to oneself in a low voice" (as Orthodox Jews commonly do to this day). We miss something if none of our Bible reading is oral.

Just what is this Book of the Law that is so crucial for Joshua's success? In Hebrew it is called the Torah. While *Torah* is usually translated as "law," its root meaning is much broader. It means "instruction" or "teaching." It can refer to all of God's revealed teaching in the Old Testament—his laws, his promises, the prophetic history of his acts among his people of promise. It may be that the "Book of the Law," as God uses the term here, is the same as all five books of Moses. Since Moses wrote Genesis through Deuteronomy and Moses is now dead, those five books exist as God speaks to Joshua. Or it may be that "this Book of the Law" refers to the book of Deuteronomy or a part of it (see Deuteronomy 31:24-26).

If anyone claims that writing skills had not advanced enough to allow Moses to write the Pentateuch by about 1406 B.C., archaeology has proven otherwise. At ancient Ebla in Syria, archaeologists have uncovered thousands of clay tablets written in Sumerian and "Eblaite," a Semitic language closely related to the Hebrew of the Old Testament. The kingdom from which these writings come flourished about 2300 B.C., almost a millennium before Moses. Other discoveries in the Middle East also demonstrate that writing was a well-known art long before Moses' time. While early systems of writing made use of pictures and signs that stood for syllables, alphabetic writing was in use by the time of Moses. Early alphabetic inscriptions that date to a period from 1800 to 1500 B.C. were found in 1905 in the Sinai Peninsula less than fifty miles from Mount Sinai.

Just what physical form the Pentateuch first took is an open question. The history of writing materials shows that by Moses' time writing was done on stone, clay, papyrus, and parchment. (Bound books like ours did not appear until the first century A.D. and were not common until the fourth century.)

Deuteronomy 31:26 tells us that the Book of the Law was kept beside the ark of the covenant. The Lord's command to Joshua in our verses shows that it was enshrined there not as a dust-gathering relic but as a living document to be delved into.

The Lord's strong emphasis on the written word draws our attention. Joshua is just now receiving word directly from the Lord. At times the Lord reveals his will to him by lot (14:2). On one occasion the Lord speaks to him through a special "commander of the army of the LORD" (5:14). Yet the Lord directs Joshua's confidence to his written revelation, the Scriptures. When the Torah is still fresh from the hands of Moses, God directs Joshua to it alone for authority and success.

"Scripture alone" is not just an idea hatched during the Reformation three thousand years after Moses. It is the Lord's principle set in place for the prosperity of his people as soon as the Bible began to appear.

Israel's new leader now responds to the Lord's inspiring words. Confident under the Lord he goes to work and rallies the nation for participation.

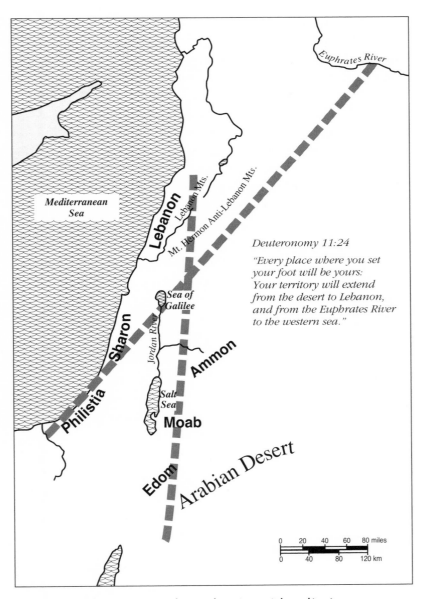

Mediterranean
Sea

Euphrates River

Lebanon

Lebanon Mts.

Mt. Hermon Anti-Lebanon Mts.

Deuteronomy 11:24

*"Every place where you set
your foot will be yours:
Your territory will extend
from the desert to Lebanon,
and from the Euphrates River
to the western sea."*

Sea of
Galilee

Sharon

Jordan River

Ammon

Philistia

Salt
Sea

Moab

Edom

Arabian Desert

| 0 | 20 | 40 | 60 | 80 miles |
| 0 | 40 | 80 | 120 km |

The Promised Land at its widest limits

All Israel will participate

¹⁰**So Joshua ordered the officers of the people:** ¹¹**"Go through the camp and tell the people, 'Get your supplies ready. Three days from now you will cross the Jordan here to go in and take possession of the land the LORD your God is giving you for your own.'"**

Refreshing winds of change have blown through the whole camp of Israel. "But, Lord . . ." is not heard from the new leader. The officers do not balk at Joshua's commands. The people are not grumbling. All Israel wants to share in the work. The Lord deserves all credit for that spirit. He has been working in Israel through his word of encouragement.

Some practical wisdom that Joshua has received from the Lord serves to encourage that cooperative spirit. His "spirit of wisdom" (Deuteronomy 34:9) leads Joshua to employ the art of delegating authority and the art of communication.

Joshua is in charge. But he does not sport such an inflated ego that he refuses to entrust officers with responsibility. When Moses had complained of the burden of carrying the people alone, the Lord showed him how to delegate authority to 70 of Israel's officers (Numbers 11:16,17). The practical lesson is not lost on Joshua. All Israel will benefit. The heat is off just one man. The work will get done. Many people will have the joy of participating in the Lord's work. Wise leaders take advantage of the talents of the whole family of believers for the good of God's church. Leaders who "prepare God's people for works of service" (Ephesians 4:12) and then turn work over to them provide a much greater service than does a one-man show.

Notice also in our verses the good lines of communication. From God to Joshua to officers to all Israel the message will go out. No one is left in the dark about what is happening.

Swift communication is critical. It may already be the seventh of Nisan, the first month of the Jewish calendar. By the tenth of Nisan, all Israel will have to be ready to cross the Jordan (4:19).

Full communication is also crucial for spiritual reasons. If the people know only that they are about to take some land for themselves, the real meaning of the moment will be lost. The full picture is that they are about to receive from God's gracious hand a part of their covenant inheritance. This is a deeply spiritual moment! "Tell the people," Joshua orders the officers. All the people will then have their supplies ready for marching and their hearts ready for receiving the gift.

Down to earth work takes on a spiritual dimension when the full picture is communicated. Even routine tasks become spiritual service when we relate them to life under our God (1 Corinthians 10:31). Gathering supplies for a river crossing will be a rewarding time for Israel when the full story is told.

Many commentators see a problem with Joshua's words "three days from now you will cross the Jordan." The problem is that the Jordan crossing does not seem to take place three days after Joshua's words in verse 11. When we read chapter 2 and the first verses of chapter 3, it seems that nine or ten days elapse before the crossing (2:2,22; 3:1,2). Some critics view this as a contradiction that comes from piecing together documents that disagree. Solutions can be offered that do not accuse the text of opposing itself:

1. "Three days from now" may here be a Hebrew idiom that means simply "very soon now."

2. Joshua may have intended to cross in three days but circumstances prevented it. Note that Joshua speaks the words, not the Lord.

3. "Three days from now" may mean that preparations for crossing were to begin in three
   days but not the crossing itself.
4. The officers may have been instructed to
   delay some days before giving the command.
5. The episode of the spies in chapter 2 may
   take place before or at the same time as
   the events of chapter 1. The crossing may go
   as scheduled in three days. (In Hebrew writing, episodes are sometimes narrated without
   precise connection with what is told before
   and after. At times that style may catch us
   by surprise.)

The officers will rally the whole nation for the Jordan
crossing. But two and a half tribes of Israel already settled
east of the Jordan need a special reminder to participate.
Joshua himself now addresses them.

**¹²But to the Reubenites, the Gadites and the half-tribe of
Manasseh, Joshua said, ¹³"Remember the command that Moses
the servant of the LORD gave you: 'The LORD your God is giving
you rest and has granted you this land.' ¹⁴Your wives, your children and your livestock may stay in the land that Moses gave you
east of the Jordan, but all your fighting men, fully armed, must
cross over ahead of your brothers. You are to help your brothers
¹⁵until the LORD gives them rest, as he has done for you, and until
they too have taken possession of the land that the LORD your
God is giving them. After that, you may go back and occupy your
own land, which Moses the servant of the LORD gave you east of
the Jordan toward the sunrise."**

The background for these verses is given in Numbers
chapter 32, Deuteronomy 3:12-20, and Joshua 13:8-33.
Reuben, Gad, and half of Manasseh were the first tribes to
possess their land. It happened this way: When Israel

rebelled at the report of the spies sent into the land from the south, the nation made a wide detour and approached Canaan from the east. Enroute to this "side door" of Canaan, Israel conquered a large part of Trans-Jordan, the land east of the river (see map, page 25). Trans-Jordan was cattle country with abundant grazing land. Since Reuben, Gad, and Manasseh were "cowboy" tribes with large herds and flocks, the ranges of the Trans-Jordan suited them well and they requested of Moses: "If we have found favor in your eyes, . . . let this land be given to your servants as our possession. Do not make us cross the Jordan" (Numbers 32:5).

Trans-Jordan was not considered the Land of Promise proper, and Moses' first answer was fiery: "Here you are, a brood of sinners" (Numbers 32:14). Those sharp words seem to reflect that the two and a half tribes *did not* originally plan to help their brothers conquer the territory west of the Jordan.

Reuben and Gad then made a promise. If granted the land east of the Jordan, they would first build cities for their families and pens for their livestock; then their fighting men would cross the Jordan with the other tribes and fight with them to subdue Canaan. Only then would they return to their homes east of the river. Moses softened his words, approved their request, and commanded the two and a half tribes to honor the conditions of their land grant.

Not with a harangue but in the tone of a man to his brothers, Joshua now reminds those tribes of Moses' command. He appeals to their sense of brotherhood and unselfishness. Joshua is paraphrasing the words of Moses from Numbers 32:20-22 and Deuteronomy 3:18-20.

A key word that Moses had used in his command was the word *rest* (Deuteronomy 3:20). Joshua picks up on that word: "You are to help your brothers until the LORD gives them rest, as he has done for you." The two and a half tribes are enjoying the "rest" of physical security. Their enemies are defeated, and they are settled after 40 years on the move. They enjoy an obvious advantage over the other tribes. Now if they have a spirit of brotherhood, they will not be satisfied until all Israel shares in that rest.

That emerging rest of physical security that Old Testament Israel was gaining by military might was valuable. But it was not an end in itself and was scarcely worth comparing with the far greater spiritual rest earned by Jesus. The author of Hebrews examines the concept of rest that is sprinkled throughout the book of Joshua and compares it with the more valuable rest found in Jesus. His conclusion: "If Joshua had given them rest, God would not have spoken later about another day" (Hebrews 4:8). "Now we who have believed enter that rest" (Hebrews 4:3). The Old Testament Joshua could give rest to Israel by defeating their physical enemies. But the New Testament Joshua (Jesus is the Greek form of Joshua) has earned endless spiritual rest for the whole guilt-ridden world by conquering sin for us (Isaiah 53:4-6; Matthew 11:28,29).

But first that Old Testament rest had to be gained so that Israel could live in the Land of Promise as God's covenant people and give to the world its Rest-giver. Will Reuben, Gad, and Manasseh honor their promise to help their brothers find that rest? Or, like many today, will they claim that naive promises deserve to be broken in light of life's later realities?

¹⁶Then they answered Joshua, "Whatever you have commanded us we will do, and wherever you send us we will go. ¹⁷Just as we fully obeyed Moses, so we will obey you. Only may the LORD your God be with you as he was with Moses. ¹⁸Whoever rebels against your word and does not obey your

words, whatever you may command them, will be put to death. Only be strong and courageous!"

The eastern tribes will indeed participate in the coming conquest for the sake of their brothers. Israel is one covenant family enjoying the Lord's promise to the whole nation. Each tribe is determined to keep its own promises for the good of all Israel. The eastern tribes will keep their word; that is self-evident and not even directly stated.

Their welcome response goes beyond honoring their promise. They affirm complete loyalty to Joshua and thereby to the Lord whose commands Joshua issues. They call for the Lord's gracious presence with Joshua. They threaten death to anyone who opposes Joshua, since that would be treason in this military context. Then they echo the Lord's own encouragement to Joshua. (Compare with verses 6,7,9.) The children of the grumbling generation have improved on their parents' record. It isn't necessarily always downhill from one generation to the next. The Lord can work amazing changes!

The two and a half tribes show us how to support leaders. We may be tempted to stand on the sidelines and criticize, especially when people in charge reveal some shortcomings. A barrage of loveless words has robbed many faithful servants of their joy in the Lord's work. But here we see Joshua enjoying not only the Lord's encouragement but the strong support of the people he leads. In that God-created atmosphere, success must follow.

Rahab and the spies

2 **Then Joshua son of Nun secretly sent two spies from Shittim. "Go, look over the land," he said, "especially Jericho." So they went and entered the house of a prostitute named Rahab and stayed there.**

²The king of Jericho was told, "Look! Some of the Israelites have come here tonight to spy out the land." ³So the king of Jericho sent this message to Rahab: "Bring out the men who came to you and entered your house, because they have come to spy out the whole land."

⁴But the woman had taken the two men and hidden them. She said, "Yes, the men came to me, but I did not know where they had come from. ⁵At dusk, when it was time to close the city gate, the men left. I don't know which way they went. Go after them quickly. You may catch up with them." ⁶(But she had taken them up to the roof and hidden them under the stalks of flax she had laid out on the roof.) ⁷So the men set out in pursuit of the spies on the road that leads to the fords of the Jordan, and as soon as the pursuers had gone out, the gate was shut.

Joshua is not privy to the Lord's plans for the walls of Jericho, so he draws on his skills as a general and sends two spies into Canaan. About 38 years earlier, Moses dispatched Joshua as a member of a spy team into Canaan (Numbers 13 and 14). Rebellion and 38 wasted years were the outcome of that reconnaissance mission. Joshua's strategy is now different in at least two ways.

First, Joshua sends the agents *secretly*. Not even Israel knows. If the spies return with a bleak report of slim odds for success, Joshua will not have to broadcast the message. The spies will report only to Joshua, as verse 24 will show. A second difference is that the spies will *concentrate on one part of Canaan* ("especially Jericho"). Joshua is calculating a step-by-step conquest, not planning to take the whole land at once, an approach that might be psychologically defeating. His strategy is in harmony with the Lord's plan to give the land "little by little" (Deuteronomy 7:22). It is also in line with the "*daily* bread" approach to life that Jesus directs us to in the Lord's Prayer.

Joshua's bold move in sending out spies does not detract from his trust in the Lord's recent promises. People of faith do not presume miracles. We are to be bold and vigorous while riding the waves of God's promises. The Bible never recommends laziness and presumption. It often calls for confident action under the Lord.

Joshua sends the spies out from Shittim, the last campsite of Israel east of the Jordan River. The full name of the site is Abel Shittim (meadow of the acacia trees). The name describes the pleasant location on a promontory overlooking the plains of Moab. Shittim is about 10 miles from the Jordan and about 15 miles from Jericho.

Good sense leads Joshua to concentrate on Jericho. It is the key city of central Canaan. Jericho controlled the major passes into the heart of the land. It is close to the main fords across the southern Jordan. And it holds control over the fresh spring water critical to the area.

Jericho, named after the Canaanite moon god, is the oldest known city of the world. Deuteronomy 34:3 calls the ancient settlement the City of Palms. Archaeologists say that by the time the spies entered Jericho, the site had been settled for several thousand years. Its abundant supply of water and pleasant year-round climate (because of its location 800 feet below sea level) enticed people to stay. Like other cities of Canaan at Joshua's time (about 1400 B.C.), Jericho was now an independent city-state under a king. If the king and his city fall, Israel will have a first crucial hold on the center of the Land of Promise.

Questions have been raised about why the spies, men of the Lord's covenant and commandments, enter the house of the prostitute Rahab in Jericho. We can offer possible reasons that do not accuse them of deviating from their mission or of fornication. First, a prostitute's house may have offered special cover. Two young male travelers would not attract special notice by entering such a house. Second, a public house of prostitution may have been about the best place in town to get information on Jericho. Third, a prostitute would perhaps not feel a moral obligation to hand spies over to the king. Fourth, Rahab's house on the city wall (verse 15) was ideal for quick escape. The spies would not be trapped in the city center. Fifth, it is clear that the Lord led them to the house of Rahab the prostitute.

Some commentators make it appear that Rahab was not really a prostitute. An NIV footnote on verse 1 suggests that she was possibly an innkeeper. The ancient source of that interpretation is Josephus, a first-century Jewish historian. But while the Hebrew word translated as "prostitute" may be somewhat ambiguous, two New Testament verses clearly call her a prostitute. (See Hebrews 11:31 and James 2:25.) The grace of God toward Rahab is all the more amazing when we know her past.

While at the house of Rahab, the spies' cover is blown; the king learns of their presence and purpose in Jericho. The plans of the spies crumble so that the Lord can work his plans. The two agents hope only to leave Jericho undetected and give a report to Joshua. But the Lord has in mind a greater mission. He will rearrange affairs to bless many— Israel, Rahab and her family, and all people through one of Rahab's descendants.

When plans fail to materialize, we need to remember that the Lord is in charge of our lives. What he finally works out often reveals that our plans were too puny for his purposes. Instead of living in frustration from toppled plans, we can know that "in all things God works for the good of those who love him" (Romans 8:28).

Rahab disobeys the king's order to bring out the spies she has hidden. She acts in the spirit of the Fifth Commandment and wants to protect life. Civil disobedience is the right course when obeying orders means disobeying God's commandments (Acts 5:29).

But what about Rahab's lies that protect the spies? The author of Joshua does not pause to comment on the moral issue of deliberate deception. He neither condemns nor defends her misrepresenting the facts. His purpose is only to report the episode. But questions from readers of this chapter often beg for answers. The following may shed some light on the issue:

1. Rahab's purpose is to protect the lives of the two men. Her motives are in line with God's will. Her heart is "in the right place."

2. All forms of deception are not necessarily immoral. The spies themselves are acting out an obvious deception in Jericho. In 8:2 the Lord orders an ambush, a military stratagem. In Exodus 1:15-21, the midwives deceived Pharaoh to protect the lives of Hebrew baby boys, and God approved of what they did.

3. Rahab had to make a quick decision without batting an eye. She had no benefit of a debate on the ethics of deception. Questions easily answered in the classroom are not always so easily answered on the spot in the real world.

4. Rahab was just emerging from the deep darkness of her old Canaanite beliefs. Her old religion, which practiced prostitution as a part of its liturgy, would probably not question the morality of a useful lie.

5. Ancient ideas about hospitality made it a matter of pride to protect even your greatest enemy if he had once "eaten salt" at your house. Rahab is protecting her guests at all costs, as her culture demanded.

6. Our joy as God's people is not that we have made the right decision in every moral conundrum. Our

overriding joy is this: "If anybody does sin, we have one who speaks to the Father in our defense—Jesus Christ, the Righteous One. He is the atoning sacrifice for our sins" (1 John 2:1,2).

The whole spy episode teems with drama. Rahab hides her two guests, lies to the king's messengers, and sends them on a wild goose chase. Meanwhile the two spies lurk just a few feet out of reach on the roof. If one of them coughs, they are caught. They are covered by stalks of flax laid out to dry for making linen, lamp wicks, or rope. The flax is an ideal hiding cover and in its braided state can be the perfect escape tool.

The quick closing of the city gate at the exit of the pursuers hints at the panicky air hovering over Jericho. Is the gate quickly shut to trap the spies in the city in case Rahab has lied? Or is it slammed shut to put a quick lid on other Israelites who might be lurking outside under the blanket of night? Whatever the reason, the quick closing suggests the deep fears within this ancient city that has chosen man-made gods and superstitions over the living Lord.

Deepest fears arise from a sense of guilt and judgment. Jericho's sin has reached its full measure (Genesis 15:16). God's judgment by Israel's hand approaches. "It is a dreadful thing to fall into the hands of the living God" (Hebrews 10:31). Fears haunt Jericho for good reason. Rahab's rooftop dialogue with the spies continues to reflect Jericho's fears:

[8]Before the spies lay down for the night, she went up on the roof [9]and said to them, "I know that the LORD has given this land to you and that a great fear of you has fallen on us, so that all who live in this country are melting in fear because of you. [10]We have heard how the LORD dried up the water of the Red Sea for you when you came out of Egypt, and what you did to Sihon and Og, the two kings of the Amorites east of the Jordan,

whom you completely destroyed. ¹¹When we heard of it, our hearts melted and everyone's courage failed because of you, for the LORD your God is God in heaven above and on the earth below. ¹²Now then, please swear to me by the LORD that you will show kindness to my family, because I have shown kindness to you. Give me a sure sign ¹³that you will spare the lives of my father and mother, my brothers and sisters, and all who belong to them, and that you will save us from death."

¹⁴"Our lives for your lives!" the men assured her. "If you don't tell what we are doing, we will treat you kindly and faithfully when the LORD gives us the land."

¹⁵So she let them down by a rope through the window, for the house she lived in was part of the city wall. ¹⁶Now she had said to them, "Go to the hills so the pursuers will not find you. Hide yourselves there three days until they return, and then go on your way."

¹⁷The men said to her, "This oath you made us swear will not be binding on us ¹⁸unless, when we enter the land, you have tied this scarlet cord in the window through which you let us down, and unless you have brought your father and mother, your brothers and all your family into your house. ¹⁹If anyone goes outside your house into the street, his blood will be on his own head; we will not be responsible. As for anyone who is in the house with you, his blood will be on our head if a hand is laid on him. ²⁰But if you tell what we are doing, we will be released from the oath you made us swear."

²¹"Agreed," she replied. "Let it be as you say." So she sent them away and they departed. And she tied the scarlet cord in the window.

Not only the fears of Jericho but also the new faith of Rahab are apparent in this section. The two conditions are striking because they are opposites. Phrases like "great fear . . . melting in fear . . . hearts sank . . . courage failed" paint the picture of panic in a nation dead set against God. The Lord is fulfilling the prophecy in Moses' famous victory song after the Red Sea crossing:

> The chiefs of Edom will be terrified,
> the leaders of Moab will be seized with trembling,
> the people of Canaan will melt away;
> terror and dread will fall upon them.
> By the power of your arm
> they will be as still as a stone—
> until your people pass by, O LORD,
> until the people you bought pass by.
> You will bring them in and plant them
> on the mountain of your inheritance.
>
> (Exodus 15:15-17)

Heart-melting signs of impending judgment are all around as Israel closes in on Canaan's border. But while hearts are sinking in fear, Rahab's heart holds the seed of new faith in the Lord. Her expressions show her faith: "I know that the LORD has given this land to you. . . . The LORD your God is God in heaven above and on the earth below. . . . Swear to me by the LORD." Her actions prove her faith: she welcomes the two agents of the Lord's people, gives them lodging, hides them, advises them, helps them escape, and does as they instruct.

Just how did Rahab's trust in the living Lord begin to grow? Since faith is always a gift of God, he is the gracious author of her faith (1 Corinthians 12:3). By his saving message, he turns hearts from fear to confidence in him (Romans 10:17). But how did Rahab hear the message that the Lord of Israel is the Savior-God? We can only venture guesses since the author of Joshua is silent on the question. The Lord's mighty deeds for Israel were known far and wide (verse 10). Perhaps attached to the reports of those deeds was word of his big promise: that he would bless all people through one coming from Israel (Genesis 12:2,3; 26:2-4; 28:13-15). Were travelers unwitting witnesses to Rahab of the Lord's great deeds and saving promises? Or were Israel's two spies the first to tell her clearly about Yahweh, "the LORD," the living Savior-God? We don't know.

But we do know this: Witness about our Savior is never wasted witness. See what the Lord did for a prostitute when someone spoke to her about "the LORD, the compassionate and gracious God, slow to anger, abounding in love and faithfulness" (Exodus 34:6).

Because she proved her faith by her deeds, Rahab is a part of the catalog of the great people of faith listed in Hebrews chapter 11: "By faith the prostitute Rahab, because she welcomed the spies, was not killed with those who were disobedient" (verse 31). James also makes an example of Rahab's deeds that proved her faith: "Was not even Rahab the prostitute considered righteous for what she did when she gave lodging to the spies and sent them off in a different direction?" (James 2:25). These New Testament passages prove that Rahab's faith in the Lord is genuine and that she does not just pretend to have faith to save her skin.

Rahab prepares for her future in light of what she knows will happen under the Lord's promise. She devotes her thoughts and energies toward her new life. In this she is a great example for us. We are to abandon the old and sinful, consider ourselves new people under our God of grace, and act in the light of his promises (2 Corinthians 5:17).

Rahab's concern for her extended family also calls attention to her new faith. She asks the spies to swear by the Lord that they will spare her family in the coming holocaust. Saving herself is not her sole concern. The spies swear the oath Rahab requests. Their oath by the Lord is itself the "sure sign" that guarantees her family's safety

"She let them down by a rope through the window."

(verse 12). This is again evidence of her faith. She accepts an oath "by the LORD" as the sure sign she demands.

In swearing to spare Rahab and her family, are the spies acting against the order of Moses in Deuteronomy 7:2? There Moses commands to "make no treaty" and "show no mercy" to the inhabitants of Canaan. Notice that Moses' command refers to treaties with nations and does not forbid kindness to families. Note also that Moses' words apply after Israel has defeated a nation. The spies do not question whether their oath to Rahab is appropriate. Joshua will approve the oath (6:22) and so will the Lord himself. He has far-reaching plans for Rahab's life. He is always bent on showing grace and forgiveness to the penitent (2 Peter 3:9). Judgment follows only when his grace is trampled on.

Rahab's kindness does not come to an abrupt halt after she gets the oath she wants. Using a rope, she lets the spies down through a window of her house, which is built as part of the city wall. The precise connection between her house and the wall of Jericho is not clear from the Hebrew. The house may have been built on top of the wall or up against it. Or she may have lived within a wide, hollow type of wall known as a casemate wall.

After letting the spies down to the ground, Rahab sends them off in a different direction from the pursuers. The pursuers head for the Jordan to the east, while the spies probably head west where there are hills and a mountain cut with nooks and caves. The mountain Jebel Qarantal is the traditional site of Jesus' temptation. In caves eight miles south, the Dead Sea Scrolls lay hidden in tall clay jars for about 2,000 years. Two clever agents hiding in similar caves could easily escape notice, especially with their pursuers chasing the wrong way.

A note on the author's literary technique may help clear up some confusion over the order of events at this point.

Here and in other chapters, the author uses the literary device known as prolepsis—the placing of an event in a narrative before its logical point in time. The lowering by the rope in verse 15 probably takes place after the conversation in verse 16 and following, but the author mentions it first to fill out the action part of the episode. Again in verse 21 Rahab probably ties the scarlet cord some days later when Israel enters the land (verse 18), but the author mentions it in advance to fill out the story.

Notice how precise the spies are in stating the conditions of their oath. Oaths using the Lord's name call for great care and clarity, as the Second Commandment implies. Military wisdom also demands a clear understanding of the oath's stipulations, lest confusion arise at the critical time of attack. Rahab's family must be inside her house; there must be absolute secrecy about the spy mission; and a scarlet cord must be visible in Rahab's window.

The function of the scarlet cord may be purely practical: to identify the house that Israel will safeguard. The author mentions no other significance of the cord and its color. But to us that scarlet cord may well suggest the new blood-bought condition of the former woman of scarlet. The church from early years pointed out the rich symbolism suggested by the blood-colored cord and associated it with the cleansing blood of Christ.

All through this episode, Rahab's kind help shows that the spies can trust her and that she has no plans to double-cross them. The Lord has shown her mercy and planted faith in her heart. Kind deeds then flow from her. This is the Lord's intended pattern for all who know his grace.

The Lord's grace toward Rahab will not end with her personal rescue. Matthew's genealogy of Jesus shows that Rahab has the high honor of being an ancestress of our Savior (Matthew 1:5). From her line comes King David, forefather of Jesus. The Lord's plans for her included blessing all people through her offspring.

A trusted friend now awaits Israel inside the hostile city of Jericho. Because of the Lord's guiding hand, the spies can leave the city successful beyond their hopes.

²²When they left, they went into the hills and stayed there three days, until the pursuers had searched all along the road and returned without finding them. ²³Then the two men started back. They went down out of the hills, forded the river and came to Joshua son of Nun and told him everything that had happened to them. ²⁴They said to Joshua, "The LORD has surely given the whole land into our hands; all the people are melting in fear because of us."

To hide in the hills, the spies probably went in the opposite direction of Israel's camp at Abel Shittim. After staying three days (see notes on the three days on page 27), they backtrack east to the Jordan, cross the river that is now at flood stage (3:15), and report to Joshua.

The spies' account is refreshing, especially when compared to the negative report of the 10 out of 12 spies 38 years earlier (Numbers 13). Both past and present spies saw the same basic conditions in Canaan. The difference is that these two agents give their analysis from a stance of trust in God's promises.

We can always manipulate bare facts to make them say what we want. If the two men had not accepted God's assurance of success, they could have presented a bleak picture of the chances for taking the land. They could have emphasized the massive city walls, the protective king, the citizens bent on protecting their city, a surging river to cross, and their *luck* to get out alive. But the two agents see the bare facts in the light of God's promises and conclude:

"The LORD has surely given the whole land into our hands." Problems do not blind them from seeing clear evidence that the Lord is keeping his promises.

Faith in God's promises makes all the difference in the way we report on the conditions of our lives. Without trust that the Lord is in control, it is easy to give a negative report. Terrorist attacks, threat of nuclear holocaust, economic uncertainty, moral decay all around, scandals in the church, enemies of the church on the rise—all these may be realities. But with the Lord's promises, we can be both realists and optimists and report that "we are more than conquerors through him who loved us" (Romans 8:37). Taking the Lord at his word makes all the difference in the way we view both our present and our future.

Inspired by the optimistic debriefing report, Joshua now readies Israel for one of the most amazing acts of the Lord in behalf of his Old Testament people.

Crossing the Jordan

3 Early in the morning Joshua and all the Israelites set out from Shittim and went to the Jordan, where they camped before crossing over. ²After three days the officers went throughout the camp, ³giving orders to the people: "When you see the ark of the covenant of the LORD your God, and the priests, who are Levites, carrying it, you are to move out from your positions and follow it. ⁴Then you will know which way to go, since you have never been this way before. But keep a distance of about a thousand yards between you and the ark; do not go near it."

⁵Joshua told the people, "Consecrate yourselves, for tomorrow the LORD will do amazing things among you."

⁶Joshua said to the priests, "Take up the ark of the covenant and pass on ahead of the people." So they took it up and went ahead of them.

In Joshua 1:2, the Lord had commanded Joshua to "get ready to cross the Jordan River." Chapter 3 now picks up where that command left off. Verses 1-13 tell of *preparations for crossing.* The spies' message allows Joshua and Israel to break camp at Shittim with confidence. Israel's enemies are melting in fear and pose no immediate threat.

The people fold their tents, pack their possessions, and collect their flocks and herds. They disassemble the tabernacle and ready the ark of the covenant. Then, early in the morning, they descend from their campsite and travel the few miles to the bank of the Jordan. There they camp for three more days. Why this further delay at the river? The reason will become evident. But first some notes on the Jordan may help us picture more vividly the amazing deeds the Lord is about to perform at this renowned river.

The name Jordan comes from a Hebrew verb that means "to go down." Translated literally, Jordan means something like "The Descender." From the point where this "Descender" exits the Sea of Galilee to where it enters the Dead Sea is about 70 miles as the crow flies. But, as the river flows, the distance is about two hundred miles because of its snakelike path. Archaeologist Nelson Glueck describes the Jordan's run between the Sea of Galilee and the Dead Sea: "Squirming frantically, burrowing madly, seeking wildly to escape its fate, the Jordan's course, from its crystal clear beginning, to its literally dark and bitter end, is a helpless race to a hopeless goal" (quoted in the *Zondervan Bible Dictionary*).

The Jordan system is more than just a river. It has three bold features. The first is *a broad outer valley,* the Ghor, that varies in width from 2 to 14 miles. The Ghor is part of the Great Rift, that colossal crack in the earth's crust that penetrates deep into Africa. The oasis of Jericho sits on the floor of the Ghor and is about five miles from the river proper. Next, within this broad valley is *a narrower and deeper bed,* a flood plain that varies in width from two hundred yards to about a mile. Every year, about the time of the spring flax and barley harvest, the rains and the melting snow of Mount Hermon cause the river to spill over and fill this bed with muddy surging waters. Finally, *the Jordan itself* is about one hundred feet wide and from three to ten feet deep. The current is not only swift but has a zigzag motion that makes crossing treacherous.

In the New Testament, the Jordan is important as the area where John the Baptist preached. In its waters he baptized Jesus. The Jordan theme also flows through a number of Christian hymns. Usually the reference is to the river in its literal sense. Some hymns draw on the Jordan crossing as a picture of the believer passing through death into heaven. A line of "Guide Me, O Thou Great Jehovah" reads, "When I tread the verge of Jordan, bid my anxious fears subside." The hymn "Art Thou Weary, Art Thou Troubled" speaks of "Sorrow vanquished, labor ended, Jordan passed." Chapter 3 of Joshua inspires this rich imagery of the poets.

Why the three-day delay at Jordan's bank? The answer is not found in purely physical concerns. The people already have their supplies in order for crossing (1:11), and the trek of only a few miles does not call for a three-day rest. The reason lies in needing time for spiritual preparation. The Lord is about to perform one of his greatest miracles. The miraculous crossing of the Jordan is an event parallel in power and importance to the Red Sea crossing. The Lord wants his covenant people ready to take in what is about to happen.

It is spring, and the river has swollen to its wider banks. Three days of staring at the surging waters and then turning to see more than two million people walk across without getting their feet wet will lead the Israelites to conclude: we can pass over safely only by the Lord's power. The spiritual training is excellent.

As Israel is forced to stare at the flooding river for three days, so the Lord at times forces us to look at our problems long and hard. His purpose is fatherly discipline (Deuteronomy 8:5). He wants us to conclude: I am totally dependent on my Lord. He is "my strength and my song; he has become my salvation" (Exodus 15:2).

The scene at the river is reminiscent of Jacob at the Jabbok, a tributary of the Jordan about 15 miles north. There Jacob wrestled with the Lord for a blessing before an uncertain reunion with his brother, Esau, whom he had enraged (Genesis 32:22-32). At the Jabbok the Lord gave Jacob the name Israel, "he struggles with God." Now, some five hundred years later, the progeny of Israel also need a special blessing of the Lord at a river.

After three days the officers tell the people that the ark of the covenant, carried by the priests, is to direct their movement. The ark is that chest of acacia wood overlaid inside and out with pure gold. On its golden cover, rest two cherubim, also of gold, their wings spread to overshadow the cover. Inside the ark are the stone tablets from the Sinai covenant, a golden jar with manna, and Aaron's staff that had budded. Priests carried the ark with poles inserted in four golden rings on the sides. (For more details on the ark of the covenant, or ark of the testimony, see Exodus 25:10-22; Numbers 10:33-36; Deuteronomy 10:1-5; and Hebrews 9:4.)

The ark is the symbol of the Lord's covenant and presence with Israel. It is not a magic box that has a mind of its own; nor is it a cultic object that Israel invented and worships. The Lord himself ordered its construction and directed its use as a visible display of his invisible presence. In the wilderness he had used it to direct Israel's movement (Numbers 10:35,36). Now again at the Jordan, the ark carried by the priests is the people's cue to move out. To follow the ark is to follow the Lord's lead. For their safety he goes ahead of his people and clears the way (Deuteronomy 9:3).

The aim of the delay at Jordan's bank is to direct the people to focus on the Lord alone. When Israel's eyes are on the ark of the covenant, their hearts will lean on him who had entered into a solemn contract with them and promised the land just over the river.

The officers' explanation of why the people should follow the ark of the Lord invites application for us. They order: "Follow it. Then you will know which way to go, since you have never been this way before." Those words encourage us to follow the Lord closely at all times and especially when we enter fresh territory. Moving to a new area, graduating, entering a new relationship, starting married life, beginning retirement, standing at the dawn of a new year—whatever the new ground, we follow the Lord. We seek strength and guidance from his Word, request his constant help through prayer, and cast all our cares on him.

Why the command of the officers to "keep a distance of about a thousand yards" between the people and the ark of the covenant? The order is parallel to God's words to Moses at the burning bush: "Do not come any closer," and again to his command at Mount Sinai: "Put limits for the people around the mountain and tell them, 'Be careful that you do not go up the mountain or touch the foot of it'" (Exodus 3:5; 19:12). A healthy respect for the holy Lord of all the universe is the reason for the distance. A thousand yards is close enough for the people to see the ark as their cue for marching, yet far enough to show respect for the Lord.

An awe-filled respect toward our Lord and an intimate love for him are in no way opposing attitudes. They belong side by side as two facets of our relationship with our holy yet gracious God. For that reason, Luther begins his explanation of each of the commandments with the words "We should fear [respect] and love God."

Verse 5 shows directly that the delay at the river is for spiritual preparation. Joshua tells the people, "Consecrate yourselves." At Mount Sinai before the giving of the law, consecration involved washing clothes and abstaining from sex (Exodus 19:10,14,15). Just what the consecration here at the Jordan entails is not spelled out. Perhaps there is no time for outward acts since they have only until the next day to comply. Whether or not symbolic actions are present, consecration means separating from sin and devoting oneself with a whole heart to the Lord.

The purpose of the consecration is to get ready for the "amazing things" the Lord will do the next day. Imagine how the curiosity of the people must have been piqued. What could these "amazing things" be that Joshua promises? There is perhaps more excitement than sleep in the camp of Israel that last night on the east bank of the Jordan.

The three days at the river are well spent. The Lord, through Joshua and the officers, has designed a time of preparation for Israel that would lead to more complete trust, respect, consecration, and anticipation of a special blessing. How much time do Christians spend in spiritual preparation before a worship service? Quiet moments of meditation can lead us to drink in more freely the amazing things the Lord pours out to us by his Word. If experiencing one of the Lord's Old Testament miracles called for three days of getting ready, encountering the amazing message of the cross and empty tomb of Jesus certainly calls for quality preparation. Great spiritual reward follows when we take time to consecrate ourselves and anticipate what the Lord is about to impart through his refreshing Word.

We need to read between the lines of verses 5 and 6 to see that the third day of delay has passed and the exciting events of the new day begin in verse 6. Anticipation mounts as the priests now pick up the ark.

Before we proceed, it is helpful to note that there will be some surprises if we expect a purely chronological account of the crossing. We may feel as if we are on a literary ride through rapids. The author at times rushes forward to complete a subject, then lunges back to fill in some details. The author's style leads some commentators to charge that in chapters 3 and 4, we have an impossible set of contradictions. That claim does not mesh with the reality of inspiration by the Holy Spirit. We can answer many of the negative charges in terms of the author's rich style. Keep in mind the following literary features as we follow Israel across the Jordan:

1. The author establishes a pattern that gives chapters 3 and 4 a structure and unity. Three times he follows this pattern: first the Lord gives Joshua a command; then Joshua passes the command on to the people; finally the people carry out the command. (See 3:7,9,14; 4:1,4,8,15,17,18.) *He does not let strict chronology interfere with this pattern.*

2. The author has arranged his account by topic and not by precise time sequence. His treatment of a subject is logical rather than chronological.

3. The author uses a *dovetailing,* or *overlay,* technique in his narrative. After completing a section,

he goes back and enlarges on some details, then moves on with the story.

Verse 7 begins the first section laid out in pattern form, with the Lord addressing Joshua.

⁷And the LORD said to Joshua, "Today I will begin to exalt you in the eyes of all Israel, so they may know that I am with you as I was with Moses. ⁸Tell the priests who carry the ark of the covenant: 'When you reach the edge of the Jordan's waters, go and stand in the river.'"

⁹Joshua said to the Israelites, "Come here and listen to the words of the LORD your God. ¹⁰This is how you will know that the living God is among you and that he will certainly drive out before you the Canaanites, Hittites, Hivites, Perizzites, Girgashites, Amorites and Jebusites. ¹¹See, the ark of the covenant of the Lord of all the earth will go into the Jordan ahead of you. ¹²Now then, choose twelve men from the tribes of Israel, one from each tribe. ¹³And as soon as the priests who carry the ark of the LORD—the Lord of all the earth—set foot in the Jordan, its waters flowing downstream will be cut off and stand up in a heap."

Why will the Lord perform a miracle for his people at the Jordan? The obvious answer might seem to be to get them into the Promised Land. But he could do that in a non-spectacular way, such as ordering Joshua to make a flotilla of rafts and ferry the people across. The Lord has a miracle in mind for special reasons. Getting them over the Jordan with a renewed confidence in him and with respect for their new leader is his more complete aim.

The Lord states the immediate purpose of his miracle in verse 7. He wants to exalt Joshua in the eyes of all Israel. Joshua is not to exalt himself. The Lord will see to it that he receives the honor due his office. After this special day, no one will be able to accuse Joshua of elevating himself and jumping into the leadership vacuum left by Moses' death. The Lord will perform an amazing act for Israel with Joshua in charge just as he did at the Red Sea when Moses was the leader. Then all Israel will know for certain that the Lord is with Joshua as he was with Moses. It will be clear that Joshua holds credentials from the Lord himself. The Lord wants Israel to hold Joshua in respect and to obey him as his own chosen leader. That attitude will be critical for the coming conquest and will benefit all Israel.

What the Lord wants for Joshua he wants for his kingdom leaders today. The book of Hebrews exhorts: "Obey your leaders and submit to their authority. They keep watch over you as men who must give an account. Obey them so that their work will be a joy, not a burden, for that would be of no advantage to you" (Hebrews 13:17). An attitude of respect for leaders is critical for the success of kingdom work. Joy in his service and advantage to all is the Lord's aim as he works to foster respect for leaders. The leader who scandalizes the church by immoral living or lack of humility, however, has no reason to think that God will exalt him as he is about to do for Joshua, a spirit-filled man of wholehearted obedience to the Lord (Numbers 27:18; 32:12).

God's words "Today I will begin to exalt you" suggest a promise reaching beyond the coming miracle. The great event of this day will be the first of many by which God will exalt him. The verses that lead up to the wonder at Jordan's waters build more and more anticipation. Notice how the author lays out snatches of information that arouse curiosity:

1. "Consecrate yourselves" (verse 5). Why?

2. "Tomorrow the LORD will do amazing things" (verse 5). What kind of amazing things?

3. The priests with the ark are to stand in the river at the water's edge (verse 8). Why this strange arrangement?

4. The people are to come and listen to the words of the Lord spoken by Joshua (verse 9). What is he going to reveal?

5. "This is how you will know that the living God is among you" (verse 10). By what will this be known?

Even after the author tells all this, we still don't know exactly what the Lord is about to do. Suspense builds. Attention is focused. Who can miss the coming miracle now or downplay it by crediting it to mere natural causes?

In verse 10 Joshua reveals a further goal of the imminent miracle. By the mighty wonder that the people will experience, God will verify that he is *living and active right among his people.* There is no real value in merely acknowledging that some higher being exists "somewhere out there." When Joshua says, "This is how you will know that the living God is among you," he uses a Hebrew verb that means "to know from experience." The entire nation will encounter the living God through a dynamic action right in their midst. The Lord is not some vague and distant being but an intimately active God. His action will prove beyond doubt that he is a living God, unlike the gods of the other nations who have only idols, so much "air," as the Hebrew calls them.

The miracle will also serve to plant Israel's feet on the ground of the Promised Land. While this is the most obvious aim of the miracle, neither the Lord nor Joshua mentions it directly. Even before his people touch the turf of Canaan, the Lord aims to work in them a more complete faith in him by the miracle. Then Israel will be more ready to accept the land as God's gift, live in it under his promises, and wait for the Messiah promised by covenant to Abraham. Faith in him and his covenant promises is the big aim. Only after faith is firmly in place will his people put the gift of the land in the right perspective.

Still another purpose of the coming miracle is to exhibit before Israel the *Lord's complete determination to drive out the nations pitted against them.* The power displayed at the miracle will be a preview of the Lord's power against the Canaanites. In moments of doubt during the conquest, Israel can remember what the Lord did for them at the Jordan. Once again, deeper trust in him is what the Lord will cultivate by an amazing action.

Joshua names seven nations, ripe for judgment, that the Lord is resolved to drive out of his Promised Land. The number 7 often carries the idea of fullness in the Bible. The seven nations named may symbolize the *full number of Israel's enemies.*

The fullness idea in the number 7 may also show that these nations are now *fully ripe for God's judgment.* In Genesis 15:16, God had told Abraham that the sin of the people of Canaan had "not yet reached its full measure." In great patience he gave those nations more than half a millennium of grace to repent of their rejection of him, their witchcraft, cultic prostitution, and child sacrifices. They answered his grace with more detestable practices. The time of judgment has come. God's agent will be the army of Israel. Read Deuteronomy 18:9-12 to see why the Lord is about to judge the people of Canaan.

Other Old Testament lists of the nations to be driven out range from 2 to 12 names. It is obvious that the authors do not intend to name every single people of the land but only to give names that represent them. (See

Genesis 10:15-18; 13:7; 15:19-21; Numbers 13:29.) The significant number 7 caught the apostle Paul's attention. In a sermon he specifically mentions the "seven nations in Canaan" (Acts 13:19).

These are seven nations ripe for God's wrath:

1. *Canaanites.* The name comes from Canaan, son of Ham. The term *Canaanites* is often used in a collective sense for all the people in the land promised to Israel. Here it is used in a narrow sense for the people living along the coast of the Mediterranean and along the Jordan River. (See Numbers 13:29; Joshua 5:1; 11:3.)

2. *Hittites.* In Joshua 1:4 the Lord had promised Israel "all the Hittite country." We commented there that this term may be a summary expression for all of the Promised Land or may refer only to the northern part of it. A great Hittite empire was founded about 1800 B.C. in Asia Minor (present-day Turkey). The Hittites may have been the third most powerful force in the ancient Middle East after the Egyptians and the Mesopotamians.

3. *Hivites.* These people seem to have lived primarily in the north. In Joshua 9:7,17, the Hivites occupy four confederate cities, one of which was Gibeon. The Bible accounts do not present the Hivites as a warlike people.

4. *Perizzites.* We know very little about the Perizzites. Joshua 17:15 indicates that they lived in forested land. Their name may mean "dwellers in unwalled villages."

5. *Girgashites.* All we can say of these people is that Genesis 10:16 names them as descendants

of Canaan and that Joshua 24:11 locates them west of the Jordan.

6. *Amorites*. Like the Hittites, Girgashites, and Jebusites, the Amorites descended from Canaan, son of Ham (Genesis 10:15,16). In Hebrew their name always appears in the singular as "the Amorite" (Amos 2:9). The name literally means "the high one." Because of their prominence, their name is used at times for all the Canaanites, as in Genesis 15:16 and Joshua 24:15. In a narrow sense "the Amorites" refers to inhabitants of the mountain regions of Canaan, as in Numbers 13:29 and Deuteronomy 1:7. Sihon and Og, mentioned in Joshua 2:10, were "two kings of the Amorites east of the Jordan," whom Israel had already defeated.

7. *Jebusites*. These people seem to inhabit the hill country (Numbers 13:29; Joshua 11:3). Jerusalem was their city (Joshua 15:63). Jerusalem is sometimes referred to as Jebus (Judges 19:10). The Jebusites, a warring people, held on to their royal city of Jerusalem until the time of David (Joshua 15:63; 2 Samuel 5:6,7).

The approaching miracle at the Jordan will show that the Lord will "certainly" drive out all these nations. Their numbers and strength are as nothing to him.

In verse 11 the ark of the covenant is again the focus for Israel's eyes. By his close association with the ark, the Lord shows that he is the one about to perform the amazing things and that *he* is the one who will lead Israel into the Jordan. By following the ark into the Jordan, Israel will be following the Lord.

In calling God "the Lord of all the earth," Joshua emphasizes that God is the absolute owner of all things. He has the perfect *right* and *power* to dethrone the seven nations just listed and to turn their land over to Israel. The land is his to take and give as he sees fit. Who can dispute this prerogative of "the Lord of all the earth"? The same phrase is repeated in verse 13 for emphasis. God's people have nothing to fear when they follow the mighty owner of the universe.

The Lord has told Joshua what will occur the instant the feet of the ark-bearing priests touch the Jordan. At last in verse 13, Joshua tells Israel, and through his words we finally learn what the miracle will be. The Lord will cut off the Jordan's flow, and its waters will stand up in a heap!

Since Joshua is speaking in verses 9-13, it is clear that God has shared with him what will happen. This fact stresses that Joshua's leadership role is God-given, like that of Moses. Notice also that the miracle will be similar to the Red Sea event under Moses. The Lord will show by this second watery wonder that he is with Joshua as he was with Moses. He is beginning to exalt Joshua as he exalted his predecessor. The new leader deserves Israel's honor.

Now, will the miracle unroll as Joshua predicts? Since the people know what to look for, they will be all the more attentive. If the waters are cut off as Joshua has announced, he will be publicly exalted, God will prove he is living and active among his people, and his determination to drive out the nations will be on display. All eyes are poised to compare the reality with the advance billing.

¹⁴So when the people broke camp to cross the Jordan, the priests carrying the ark of the covenant went ahead of them. ¹⁵Now the Jordan is at flood stage all during harvest. Yet as soon as the priests who carried the ark reached the Jordan and their feet touched the water's edge, ¹⁶the water from upstream stopped flowing. It piled up in a heap a great distance away, at a town called Adam in the vicinity of Zarethan, while the water

flowing down to the Sea of the Arabah (the Salt Sea) was completely cut off. So the people crossed over opposite Jericho. [17]The priests who carried the ark of the covenant of the LORD stood firm on dry ground in the middle of the Jordan, while all Israel passed by until the whole nation had completed the crossing on dry ground.

Verse 14 picks up the line of action left off in verse 6. Ark, priests, and people move out to the water. The river is not a gently flowing stream but is now "at flood stage." It is the first month of the Jewish calendar, Nisan, our March/April, and Mount Hermon's melting snows and the spring rains have deluged the Jordan Valley. The timing could not be worse for safe crossing or better for an exhibition of the Lord's power and protection.

At the very moment the priests' feet touch the surging Jordan, the water from upstream stops flowing! The water "piled up." The same word is used in the Hebrew of Exodus 15:8, hinting that this miracle is similar to the Red Sea miracle under Moses. What Joshua forecast is happening! The Lord is with Joshua as he was with Moses.

The location of Adam is not known for certain. There is no other reference to it in the Bible. But the explanation that it is "a great distance away" stresses the magnitude of the miracle. The suggested sites for Adam, where the Jordan waters pile up, fall within a range of 12 to 20 miles from the crossing point. It would not take long even for more than two million people to cross through such a wide and dry corridor.

The Arabah is the Hebrew name for the portion of the Great Rift Valley between the Dead Sea and the Gulf of 'Aqaba on the Red Sea. The Dead Sea was known in ancient times as the Sea of the Arabah or Salt Sea. From the point of crossing opposite Jericho down to the Dead Sea is about five

An Israelite family crosses the dry Jordan River

miles. The waters south of the crossing evidently kept on flowing into the Dead Sea but had no way of replenishing themselves until the miracle was completed.

A variant reading of a Hebrew preposition in verse 16 gives a different picture of what happened to the water. If we read "it piled up in a heap . . . *from* a town called Adam" instead of "*at* a town called Adam," then the waters piled up over the whole distance between Adam and the crossing point. This leaves the portion from the crossing to the Dead Sea as dry ground. No matter which reading we choose, the Lord provided a very wide stretch of dry land for crossing.

Verse 17 emphasizes the safe crossing of everyone. "All Israel," "the whole nation," crosses on dry land. No one is drowned. No one is left behind. The slowest, the lamest, the oldest, the youngest—every single Israelite passes over. The Lord's attention to detail reaches to each individual.

Many commentators note that landslides into the Jordan have at times stopped the flow of water. "The collapse of very soft limestone banks temporarily damming this meandering stream is recorded for 7 December, 1267, and again in 1906. Preceded by an earthquake, it was observed again on 11 July, 1927."[1] The Lord used the east wind at the Red Sea miracle and could have used a landslide to work his wonders at the Jordan. But it is impossible to explain away by mere natural phenomena or coincidence what takes place in Joshua chapters 3 and 4. The following facts all attest to a miracle of the Lord:

1. The miracle is predicted by the Lord and Joshua.
2. There is split-second timing linking the stopping of the water and the feet of the priests at the water's edge.
3. The river is at flood stage at the time of crossing.

4. A mere landslide would not exalt Joshua any more than the east wind by itself could exalt Moses at the Red Sea. The whole context points to an amazing act of the Lord to exalt Joshua.

Like all of God's miracles, the amazing act at the Jordan is not designed merely to dazzle. It inspires trust in the Lord and authenticates his chosen leader.

Ours is the powerful Lord of all the earth, who made the waters of a river pile up in a heap to let his people pass. More than that, our God is the Savior, Jesus, "accredited by God to you by miracles, wonders and signs" (Acts 2:22). By his greatest miracle, his own resurrection from the dead, we own "an inheritance that can never perish, spoil or fade— kept in heaven for [us]" (1 Peter 1:4). "When [we] tread the verge of Jordan," our fears can sink and our faith can soar. He will "land [us] safe on Canaan's side" (*Christian Worship* [CW] 331:3).

Chapters 3 and 4 of Joshua are a unit. They tell of the same miracle and fulfill the same immediate purpose of God's exalting Joshua (3:7 and 4:14). The division into two chapters is somewhat artificial. Chapter 4 now serves to flesh out some details of the crossing. The focus is on stones that commemorate the miracle.

Two memorials

4 When the whole nation had finished crossing the Jordan, the LORD said to Joshua, ²"Choose twelve men from among the people, one from each tribe, ³and tell them to take up twelve stones from the middle of the Jordan from right where the priests stood and to carry them over with you and put them down at the place where you stay tonight."

⁴So Joshua called together the twelve men he had appointed from the Israelites, one from each tribe, ⁵and said to them, "Go over before the ark of the LORD your God into the middle of the Jordan. Each of you is to take up a stone on his shoulder, according to the number of the tribes of the Israelites, ⁶to serve as a sign among you. In the future, when your children ask you, "What do these stones mean?" ⁷tell them that the flow of the Jordan was cut off before the ark of the covenant of the LORD. When it crossed the Jordan, the waters of the Jordan were cut off. These stones are to be a memorial to the people of Israel forever."

In verses 1-3, the Lord gives Joshua a command; in 4-7, Joshua relays the order to the people; and in 8-14, we see the people carry it out. This is the second time we have seen this three-part design. (See 3:7,9,14.) The pattern impresses that the Lord initiates all that is happening, that Joshua is his chosen leader, and that the Lord blesses the Israelites as they obey. The Lord's command to Joshua that sets the action in motion centers on building a 12-stone memorial to commemorate the miracle.

Chapter 4 of Joshua has drawn more fire from critics than any other. Some see an editor hopelessly trying to tie together two irreconcilable stories about two memorials. Others see a bungling editor botching a simple story into a confused account. But while some are spilling gallons of ink on "difficulties," a child can read these same verses and describe the basic events with little trouble. In fact, chapter 4 is recorded with teaching children in mind (verses 6,21). The chapter is not overly complicated if we accept the inspired report on its own terms without presuming to tell the author how he should have told it. See the three points on the author's literary technique on page 50 to help appreciate his style.

As verse 1 begins, all Israel has crossed the river safely. But the ark and priests are still standing in the middle of the dry riverbed. At this point the Lord's command, evidently given earlier, is repeated. Joshua is to choose a man from each of the 12 tribes. Joshua spoke that command in 3:12 without revealing the task of the 12 men. That preview piqued our curiosity. Now the Lord spells out their function. Each man is to carry a stone from where the priests stand in the middle of the Jordan and lay it at the place where Israel will camp that night. Notice that the Lord involves each tribe through its representative. Note also that the 12 men selected are laymen, not from the priestly tribe of Levi. The Lord wants not just a few professional "church people" involved but the whole nation.

It is fascinating to see in the Hebrew of verse 3 that the Lord gives his command right from the middle of the river. The Hebrew says, "Tell them to take up twelve stones *from here,* from the middle of the Jordan." By his association with the ark, the Lord is in the thick of things, holding back the waters, protecting his people at the very point of danger. He is no distant being. He is the living God among his people as he said he would be in 3:10.

Since Joshua listens as the Lord speaks "from here," Joshua too must be standing in the middle of the riverbed.

The new leader does not relax in his tent while the people he leads face dangers.

When Joshua relays the Lord's command to the people in verses 4-7, the repetition serves for emphasis. Again we hear that men from *each tribe* are to take part in this special activity. It is not the clergy alone who are to broadcast the wonderful works of God. Repeated also is the command that the stones are to come from the middle of the Jordan, the place of the ark. The stones from that special spot will punctuate the presence of the Lord in association with his ark. They will stress that *he alone* was the cause of the miracle.

New details surrounding the 12 stones emerge from Joshua's order. The stones will "serve as a sign," a token representing the marvelous event. Just as the rainbow served as a sign (Genesis 9:13) of the Lord's covenant with Noah, so these 12 stones will be a continuing sign among Israel that the hand of the Lord is powerful for his people.

The rocks are to serve especially as a "stone springboard" for parents to teach their children about the Lord's amazing deeds at the Jordan. Even those too young to read will learn the meaning, as parents take time to satisfy their children's natural curiosity about this special pile of stones. Notice that children are not to come away with just a fascination for the miracle. They are to gain a deeper appreciation of their covenant Lord who marvelously cut off the waters of the surging Jordan to let his chosen people pass. Far beyond mere infatuation with wonders, they are to grow in their relationship with their Lord.

Joshua calls the stones a memorial. The whole nation is to use these stones as a lasting reminder of the Lord's grace and power displayed at the Jordan on that great day of first entry into the land. The Hebrew word translated as "memorial" implies not just an object that leads to a bare recalling of events. But, like the English word, it suggests something that brings one to meditate on the deeper meaning. The sight of the stones should call to mind that the Lord keeps his promises, has exalted Joshua, is determined to drive out the Canaanites, and is the giver of the land.

⁸So the Israelites did as Joshua commanded them. They took twelve stones from the middle of the Jordan, according to the number of the tribes of the Israelites, as the LORD** had told Joshua; and they carried them over with them to their camp, where they put them down. ⁹Joshua set up the twelve stones that had been in the middle of the Jordan at the spot where the priests who carried the ark of the covenant had stood. And they are there to this day.**

Israel does precisely what the Lord ordered and Joshua relayed. A man from each of the 12 tribes takes up a stone from a point in the middle of the river where the ark rested and deposits the stones at the place they would camp that night.

The author has not prepared us for what happens in verse 9. Our reaction may be surprise or even perplexity. Either on his own or from a command of the Lord not recorded for us, Joshua sets up a *second memorial* of 12 stones, probably at the spot where the priests stood with the ark. It seems likely that this spot is the one in the middle of the Jordan and not the point on the east edge of the river where the priests' feet first touched the water. Though these stones might be under water during the flood stage weeks, they would probably be high, dry, and visible for most of the year.

Both in the Hebrew and in the NIV translation, verse 9 is somewhat ambiguous. We can take the words to mean that he set up the stones where the priests stood, that he got them from that place, or both. No matter how we read the verse, the point is clear. Joshua built a second memorial to God's miracle. The Septuagint, the third century B.C. translation of the Old Testament into Greek, says "*other* stones" to make obvious that the memorial of verse 9 is different from the one in verse 8.

Is Joshua acting on his own to build this second memorial? Does his gratitude to the Lord spill over so that he cannot stand idle as the 12 men carry their stones? Does he want to say a special thanks by this memorial since the Lord is exalting him personally through this miracle? The picture that Scripture paints of this Spirit-filled man of God certainly allows for yes answers. His faith, dedication, and zeal for honoring God are inspiring examples for Israel and for us. Like him, we need to take time to contemplate and celebrate the wonderful works of God and then to lead others to remember them too.

Joshua's memorial is there "to this day." That is, it is still in place as the author writes the book of Joshua. The phrase "to this day" appears a dozen times in Joshua. It shows that the writing of the book is somewhat removed from the events themselves. It also impresses that the author is presenting historical *facts,* not mere myths. The first readers of the book of Joshua had a tangible link to the actual events. By the phrase the author also says to us that "these words are trustworthy and true" (Revelation 21:5).

Israel's stones from the Jordan remind us that it is a good practice for us to memorialize special times of God's grace in our lives. Above our certificates of achievement belong the cross and a memento of our baptisms. The apostle Peter reminds us that we ourselves are "like living stones" (1 Peter 2:5). Our grateful lives should shout God's praises for his saving acts. The way we live should invite the question

"Why live such a life dedicated to God?" just as Israel's children asked, "What do these stones mean?"

In verses 10-14, the author goes back to reemphasize aspects of the crossing, to bring out new details, and to show that the Lord's immediate purpose in the miracle is fulfilled.

> ¹⁰**Now the priests who carried the ark remained standing in the middle of the Jordan until everything the LORD had commanded Joshua was done by the people, just as Moses had directed Joshua. The people hurried over, ¹¹and as soon as all of them had crossed, the ark of the LORD and the priests came to the other side while the people watched. ¹²The men of Reuben, Gad and the half-tribe of Manasseh crossed over, armed, in front of the Israelites, as Moses had directed them. ¹³About forty thousand armed for battle crossed over before the LORD to the plains of Jericho for war.**
>
> ¹⁴**That day the LORD exalted Joshua in the sight of all Israel; and they revered him all the days of his life, just as they had revered Moses.**

The location of the priests with the ark is repeated in verse 10. Because of the repetition, no reader can forget that the Lord by his ark is in the middle of the miracle, making it happen and carefully orchestrating every part of it. While reading 3:17, we may have gotten the impression that the ark-bearing priests by now have completed the crossing. But we see in 4:10 that they have not moved from their mid-river ground. They hold position until everything the Lord directs is complete.

A new detail brought out in verse 10 is that the people "hurried over." There is nothing in this expression to suggest a frantic rush for fear that disaster might soon strike. The Lord is in perfect control as he holds back the surging waters for his people. That the people "hurried over" suggests that the whole crossing went quickly and smoothly. It also implies that there was no dallying. The priests holding the ark should not be forced to hold their position for longer than necessary. And the crossing had to be completed in less than a day so camp could be set up by that night (4:3).

Another new detail that emerges from these verses is the position of the fighting men of the two and a half eastern tribes of Reuben, Gad, and half of Manasseh. In chapter 1 we heard that these tribes promised to cross the Jordan with the other nine and one-half. Although they already possessed their land and had no personal stake in crossing over, the participation of this army of the eastern tribes emphasizes that they are keeping their promise. The Lord is performing his miracle for *all* of Israel, even the eastern tribes. Moreover, the land will be received through the battles of an army. The figure of "about forty thousand" armed men is considerably less than the total figures for the armed men from these two and a half tribes given in the Numbers chapter 26 census. The 40 thousand is evidently a special "crack force" representing the tribes while their other troops defend the families in Trans-Jordan.

Striking in these verses are the three references to Moses. "As Moses had directed" is stated in verses 10 and 12 to stress the continuity with the past. What is unfolding for Israel is not some chance event. What is happening is tied to past promises of the Lord and commands of the Lord's servant Moses. It is always reassuring to know that the Lord is fulfilling carefully laid plans for his people and that mere chance does not govern our lives.

In verse 14 the author connects Joshua with Moses in a very direct way. After the miracle the Israelites revere Joshua "just as they had revered Moses." The man who had once been "Moses' aide" (1:1) by the Lord's design now enjoys the same honor as the great Moses. The Lord's immediate purpose for the mighty Jordan miracle announced in 3:7

now stands fulfilled: The Lord exalted Joshua in the sight of all Israel. Notice the lengths to which God has gone so that Israel would revere its leader. God must be sincere about wanting respect for those he places in charge of his people!

In the whole miracle account, Joshua is pictured as a faithful servant carrying out the Lord's commands. He is unassuming, unquestioning in obedience, confident in the Lord, not demanding honor or posturing for position. The Lord honors such people (1 Samuel 2:30). First came God's gift of faith to Joshua (Numbers 27:18); then his whole-hearted obedience followed (Numbers 32:12). His faith reflected through obedience is the key to Joshua's successful leading of God's people.

¹⁵Then the LORD said to Joshua, ¹⁶"Command the priests carrying the ark of the Testimony to come up out of the Jordan."

¹⁷So Joshua commanded the priests, "Come up out of the Jordan."

¹⁸And the priests came up out of the river carrying the ark of the covenant of the LORD. No sooner had they set their feet on the dry ground than the waters of the Jordan returned to their place and ran at flood stage as before.

Once again the author shows that the ark of the covenant, signifying God's presence, is at the very center of events. This time it is called "the ark of the Testimony." The law tablets inside the ark testify to the Lord's covenant with Israel. The two names for the ark are virtually identical in meaning since *covenant* and *testament* are often interchangeable expressions. Compare the two parallel terms *new covenant* and *new testament.*

Verses 16-18 may sound strangely repetitious to our ears. The repetition results from the author following his pattern:

God commands Joshua; Joshua commands Israel; Israel does as commanded.

The conclusion of the miracle is introduced by the words "no sooner had [the priests] set their feet on the dry ground than . . ." "No sooner" shows that without question this was a miracle. The timing between the priests' last step out of the riverbed and the return of the surging waters is too perfect for blind chance. The Lord has performed the miracle; his ark held the waters back.

Now that the details of the crossing have been brought out, the text moves forward with the basic story line.

¹⁹On the tenth day of the first month the people went up from the Jordan and camped at Gilgal on the eastern border of Jericho. ²⁰And Joshua set up at Gilgal the twelve stones they had taken out of the Jordan. ²¹He said to the Israelites, "In the future when your descendants ask their fathers, 'What do these stones mean?' ²²tell them, 'Israel crossed the Jordan on dry ground.' ²³For the LORD your God dried up the Jordan before you until you had crossed over. The LORD your God did to the Jordan just what he had done to the Red Sea when he dried it up before us until we had crossed over. ²⁴He did this so that all the peoples of the earth might know that the hand of the LORD is powerful and so that you might always fear the LORD your God."

The crossing took place on a single day. The day is noted precisely as "the tenth day of the first month" of the Jewish calendar. The old name for the first month was Abib, literally "young head of grain," since the grain harvest came at that time. The later name for the first month is Nisan. The month corresponds to our March/April.

The mention of the tenth of Nisan is significant for several reasons. It is a reminder that God stopped Jordan's waters in the springtime when they surged their strongest at flood stage. It prepares us for the first celebration of Passover in the Promised Land on the 14th of Nisan, an event coming up in chapter 5. It ties together Jordan's miracle with the Red Sea crossing, also in Nisan, and thus links Joshua with Moses. Since the Passover lamb was chosen on the tenth of Nisan (Exodus 12:3), each year when Israel selected the lamb, they would also remember the Jordan miracle.

We cannot pinpoint the exact location of Gilgal, Israel's first campsite in Canaan. The best we can say is that it lies between the Jordan and Jericho. Many identify it with Khirbat el-Mafjer, about two miles from Jericho. The mention of Jericho in locating Israel's campsite anticipates what is about to happen at that famous city. The author is arousing our interest for the next episode.

Notice the repetition of Joshua's command about teaching children the meaning of the 12-stone memorial at Gilgal. We saw it before in verses 6 and 7. By saying it again, Joshua and the author are stressing the need for careful instruction of children about the Lord's saving acts. The generation that fails to teach its children about the Lord's salvation is the last to know!

Are verses 23 and 24 part of answers to children's questions about the stones? Or are they comments by Joshua to the people gathered at Gilgal? The context does not determine an answer. But whether for children or for people of all ages, they are powerful words of encouragement to remember what the Lord has done for his people this day.

In verse 24 the Jordan miracle meets us head on. Its application is not just for ancient Israel. It's for us. One of God's stated purposes in drying up the Jordan is "so that all the peoples of the earth might know that the hand of the LORD is powerful." He uses his power to provide safety for his people and to make good on his promises. Though at times it may appear otherwise, he is always in control. He deserves our confidence.

In chapters 3 and 4, we have seen the Lord shepherding his covenant people from the acacias at Abel Shittim to the palms on the plains of Jericho. In between, the obstacle of the Jordan at flood stage is like nothing under his powerful hand. The Lord has fully accomplished his aims: Joshua is exalted; Israel has reason to trust in the Lord; God has shown his resolve to drive out the enemy nations; the Jordan miracle is memorialized for future generations; his people walk on the promised ground; and the whole earth can know of his power.

A down payment has been made on God's promise to bless all people by the Offspring of Israel. Fourteen centuries after the miracle, Jesus will walk in the Promised Land. Near the point of crossing, he will be baptized in the Jordan's waters and show that he, the sinless Lamb of God, is willing to be counted a sinner so that we can be washed clean. The Lord's words through Isaiah find fulfillment at the Jordan and each time the Lord accompanies his people through dangers:

> Fear not, for I have redeemed you;
> I have summoned you by name; you are mine.
> When you pass through the waters,
> I will be with you;
> and when you pass through the rivers,
> they will not sweep over you.
>
> (Isaiah 43:1,2)

Circumcision and Passover renewed

5 Now when all the Amorite kings west of the Jordan and all the Canaanite kings along the coast heard how the LORD had dried up the Jordan before the Israelites until we had crossed over, their hearts melted and they no longer had the courage to face the Israelites.

²At that time the LORD said to Joshua, "Make flint knives and circumcise the Israelites again." ³So Joshua made flint knives and circumcised the Israelites at Gibeath Haaraloth.

⁴Now this is why he did so: All those who came out of Egypt—all the men of military age—died in the desert on the way after leaving Egypt. ⁵All the people that came out had been circumcised, but all the people born in the desert during the journey from Egypt had not. ⁶The Israelites had moved about in the desert forty years until all the men who were of military age when they left Egypt had died, since they had not obeyed the LORD. For the LORD had sworn to them that they would not see the land that he had solemnly promised their fathers to give us, a land flowing with milk and honey. ⁷So he raised up their sons in their place, and these were the ones Joshua circumcised. They were still uncircumcised because they had not been circumcised on the way. ⁸And after the whole nation had been circumcised, they remained where they were in camp until they were healed.

⁹Then the LORD said to Joshua, "Today I have rolled away the reproach of Egypt from you." So the place has been called Gilgal to this day.

One of the Lord's aims in the Jordan miracle was "that all the peoples of the earth might know that the hand of the LORD is powerful" (4:24). The Lord quickly starts fulfilling this purpose. The drying up of the Jordan by the Lord soon drained the courage out of Israel's enemies all the way to the Mediterranean coast.

At times, fear of the Israelites leads their enemies to wage war (9:2). But now the enemies do nothing but melt in fear. The Lord is carefully controlling how the hostile nations will react to his people's success. At this point he wants Israel to have a quiet time for important spiritual matters. So the Amorite and Canaanite kings shrink from any thought of a face-off with Israel. The Lord even determines how the enemies of his people can react! He is completely in charge.

The word *covenant* does not appear in verses 1-12, but it is certainly implied. This section deals with the two main ceremonies associated with the Lord's covenants with Israel: circumcision and Passover. The Lord has provided a time of peace for their renewal.

Reflect on how appropriate the renewing of circumcision is at this point for Israel. Circumcision was the pledge and seal of God's covenant with Abraham. By solemn contract he had promised Abraham a great name, a special land, numerous children, and a particular offspring through whom all the earth would be blessed (Genesis 12:1-3; Galatians 3:16). Now, five centuries later, the children of Abraham, two million strong, stand on the promised soil with their enemies so afraid that they don't dare make a move. And the promise of the Savior is still firmly in place. It is obvious that God is keeping all his promises to Abraham. Israel would now delight in the rite that was "the sign of the covenant" (Genesis 17:11), just as a bride delights in wearing a ring that is a sign of love and a promise of faithfulness.

It is the Lord himself who gives the command to "circumcise the Israelites again." There is no hint of reprimand in his words. He is not scolding Israel for not doing this earlier. The atmosphere surrounding his words is one of celebration in light of Israel's God-given successes.

The word translated as "again" literally means "a second time." The idea is not to recircumcise individuals but to start for a second time the practice of circumcision. At Mount Sinai Moses had commanded a spiritual circumcision of hearts (Deuteronomy 10:16). But while Israel was on the march through the desert, there had been no physical circumcision.

The Lord even specifies the instrument to be used: "flint knives." Why the use of the more ancient flint knives when metal had been in use for centuries? There are at least two possible reasons. First, the use of the old tool is a reminder that circumcision is an old, long-standing sign of God's covenant, stretching back about five hundred years to the time of Abraham, when flint was in more common use. The Lord is leading his people to reflect on the ancient covenant and compare the old promises with the present reality. Second, flint knives may have been the better surgical tool.

Circumcision was not unique to Israel. It was a common Near Eastern practice many centuries before Abraham's time, as is shown by Egyptian drawings and an ancient stone model found near Nineveh. Why did the ancients circumcise? Among the theories are these: as a *tribal mark* to distinguish one group of people from another, as a *rite of passage* from boyhood to manhood (still common today among some African tribes), as a *substitute for human sacrifice,* and as a *way of promoting personal hygiene.*

While circumcision was not unique to Israel, the new meaning God gave it certainly was. He made it an act of grace from him to his people. He made it a sign and seal of his covenant promises to Abraham. Keep this in mind when reflecting on the meaning of Joshua chapter 5. God himself is reaffirming his solemn contract to bless Israel.

In a secondary way, circumcision is a sign of man's consecration to God. The idea is not "See the pains to which I go to dedicate myself to God, even cutting away part of my body." Rather, it is "My gracious Lord has made his covenant with me and has given me a sign of his promises in my very body by circumcision. I am honored to wear this sign of his promises and affirm his covenant relationship."

Remember that normally eight-day-old babies were circumcised. It is evident that those babies were not choosing the Lord; he was choosing them by grace to be a part of his covenant family.

What is the significance of the cutting away of flesh in circumcision? Genesis 17:14 suggests the answer when the Lord says, "Any uncircumcised male, who has not been circumcised in the flesh, *will be cut off from his people;* he has broken my covenant." The cutting off of the skin is a very serious form of oath by which the participant implies, "May I be cut off from the covenant people as my skin has been cut off if I break the Lord's covenant." The sign in the flesh of that implied oath would be a lifelong reminder of God's solemn contract and the individual's confirmation of it.

The circumcision ceremony takes place at Gibeath Haaraloth, literally, "hill of the foreskins." The NIV prints the place name in capital letters, but the Hebrew does not need to be understood as a proper noun. If Gibeath Haaraloth is a proper noun, Israel must have begun to call the hill by that name after this event, although at least one commentator suggests that the Canaanites had circumcised there earlier.

Verses 4-7 are a short but powerful sermon by the author of Joshua to all readers of his inspired book. In his explanation of why the mass circumcision was necessary, he presents to us strong warning as well as God's overwhelming love and faithfulness.

The Lord does what he says. He keeps his threats as well as his gracious promises. He swore that not one from the generation that rebelled against him and refused his promises would taste the milk and honey of the land he pledged to their forefathers. And sure enough, every one of them died in the desert! But the Lord's promises could not be destroyed by the disobedience of one generation. His grace and faithfulness are striking in the words "So *he* raised up their sons in their place" (verse 7). He could not, would not, let his promise to Abraham go unfulfilled. Both the land gift and the obedience of the generation receiving the land are the results of God's own gracious work. Throughout Israel's Old Testament history, he would raise up a remnant of faithful believers. Through them he would make good on his vow to give the world its Savior (Jeremiah 23:3-6).

The author explains that there was no circumcision during the desert-wandering years and that is why a mass circumcision is now necessary. What he does not reveal is *why* there was no circumcision in the desert or in Moab. We can only speculate.

After the rebellion of Numbers chapter 14, God himself may have suspended this sign of his covenant. According to this view, circumcision was suspended only 38 years, since the rebellion did not take place until about two years after the exodus from Egypt. A second suggestion is that hardships connected with desert travel put a stop to circumcising during the entire 40-year period. A third theory is that Israel, not the Lord, stopped the practice after the Numbers chapter 14 rebellion because, in light of God's anger, circumcision would have been out of place until his judgment on the rebels was complete. A fourth idea stresses God's grace in the reinstatement.

Before renewal of circumcision, the Lord may have wanted first to display his faithfulness in spectacular fashion. He takes pains to gain his people's hearts by defeating the kings Sihon and Og, by the marvelous miracle at the Jordan, and by planting Israel's feet in Canaan. One commentary notes that it is the rule of divine grace first to give and then to ask. In God's eyes, it was now the right time for renewal of circumcision. By demonstrating his faithfulness first, he had won his people's hearts. The act of circumcision would now be anything but a dead ceremony.

By projecting the census figures of Numbers chapter 26, we can estimate that the entire population of Israel was at least two million people at this time, about a million of them males. Assuming that circumcision ended 38 years earlier, all males age 38 and younger now needed to be circumcised. The men between 39 and 60 had already been circumcised in Egypt. (Only Joshua and Caleb were over 60.) About one-third, then, were already circumcised and about two-thirds (perhaps about 650,000) are now circumcised at Gilgal. When verse 8 tells of "the whole nation" being circumcised, it is referring to males from every tribe of Israel, not each male in Israel.

With two-thirds of Israel's males recovering from surgery, we would expect the nation to be vulnerable to attack. In Genesis chapter 34, the men of Shechem were still in pain and unable to fight three days after their circumcision. But here the men of Israel have time to recuperate in safety. The Lord is protecting them by melting the hearts of the Canaanites through the Jordan miracle. No one dares to think about attacking the Lord's people at this time. The Lord also seems to give quicker healing to the men of Israel than the Shechemites experienced. His care is total.

The settlement at the hill where the ceremony takes place receives the meaningful name Gilgal. The name comes from a Hebrew verb that means "to roll." The name is fitting because, as the Lord explains, "Today I have rolled away the reproach of Egypt from you." We heard of the place earlier in 4:19, where the author calls it by the name Gilgal, though its actual naming comes a bit later. We mentioned at that point that Gilgal's exact location is not certain. Joshua 15:7 mentions that it is at the northern boundary of Judah. Josephus says that it is about two miles from Jericho and about ten miles from the Jordan. There seem to be five different places in the Old Testament with the name Gilgal.

What is the reproach of Egypt that the Lord "gilgals," or rolls away, at this place of circumcision? The reproach is evidently not the slavery and bondage in Egypt. That bondage ended at the exodus 40 years earlier. "The reproach of Egypt" must refer to the sarcasm the Egyptians could have leveled against Israel and God if all Israel had died in the desert after release from bondage. Exodus 32:12, Numbers 14:13-16, and Deuteronomy 9:28 lead us to this interpretation. In these passages Moses expresses what the Egyptians would be able to conclude if Israel does not make it into Canaan. In Deuteronomy 9:28, Moses says, "Otherwise, the country from which you brought us will say, 'Because the LORD was not able to take them into the land he had promised them, and because he hated them, he brought them out to put them to death in the desert.'"

Now slander can never be mouthed by any Egyptian because the Lord himself has rolled it away. He has seen to it that his people enter the land of milk and honey and renew their covenant with their Lord, who obviously loves them.

It is striking that the words *Gilgal* and *Golgotha* are related. If the Lord rolled away reproach at Gilgal, think of the slander that Jesus rolled away by his sacrifice for our sins at Golgotha! Ever since the crucifixion, no one can sneer that God does not love us, that we are not his dear redeemed people, and that we will not live in the eternal promised land. Not even the devil, "the slanderer," can make reproach stick to God's people. Knowing that, the apostle Paul asks boldly, "Who will bring any charge against those whom God has chosen?" (Romans 8:33).

No uncircumcised male could eat the Passover meal according to God's command in Exodus 12:48. Now his people could also enjoy this second great celebration of the Lord's covenant faithfulness.

¹⁰On the evening of the fourteenth day of the month, while camped at Gilgal on the plains of Jericho, the Israelites celebrated the Passover. ¹¹The day after the Passover, that very day, they ate some of the produce of the land: unleavened bread and roasted grain. ¹²The manna stopped the day after they ate this food from the land; there was no longer any manna for the Israelites, but that year they ate of the produce of Canaan.

The Passover meal was more than food for the body. It was also a time of food for thought and spiritual nourishment. The Passover celebration recalled the great release from Egypt exactly 40 years earlier. Passover for the Israelites meant deliverance. It was a proof and seal of the Lord's resolve to rescue them from any trouble that might get in the way of his covenant promises. A murdering pharaoh and the waters of the Red Sea had been pushed aside by the Lord so that he could keep his word.

The last time Israel had celebrated Passover was one year after the exodus while in the Desert of Sinai (Numbers 9:1-5). The nation had observed only two Passovers so far, the original and the one of Numbers chapter 9. That means that Passover was a new experience for the vast majority. Those younger than 39 had never celebrated it, not even as infants. Even some of those over 39 would have been too young to remember.

This year not just children but grown men and women would be asking the Passover question: "What does this ceremony mean?" (Exodus 12:26). This must have been one of the most joyous Passovers of all time as the answers come from Israelites who had personally experienced the bondage, the rescue, the desert years, and now were walking in the land their Lord had promised. Those in their 40s and 50s must have delighted in sharing the story of how the destroyer angel "passed over" their houses in Egypt after they had sacrificed the Passover lamb and painted its blood on their door frames.

The author emphasizes that Israel is celebrating this third Passover "while camped at Gilgal on the plains of Jericho." The mention of Jericho reminds us that enemies are waiting nearby. Yet Israel eats this covenant meal in peace and rejoices in its reconciliation with the Lord. There is no hint of fear, no need to cut short the festivities before the enemy strikes. A verse of a later psalm fits well here on the plains of Jericho: "You prepare a table before me in the presence of my enemies" (Psalm 23:5).

The location and Passover lambs suggest another Scripture sentence. In this same general area 15 centuries later, John the Baptizer pointed to Jesus, the Passover Lamb, and said: "Look, the Lamb of God, who takes away the sin of the world!" (John 1:29).

The Passover and the Feast of Unleavened Bread form a double festival, as we see in Leviticus 23:4-8. The eating of unleavened bread in verse 11 relates to this second part of the double festival. The text does not make the direct connection, since Jewish readers would need no explanation. By the Lord's command, unleavened bread was eaten during the seven days that follow Passover, days 15 to 21 of Nisan. The special detail about this particular unleavened bread is that it is made from the grain of the Promised Land.

A second historical note says that the Lord now stopped providing manna, the unique white food that he had rained down from heaven for 40 years, and whose name means "What is it?"

There is no touch of sadness implied with mention of the end of the manna years in verse 12. Quite the opposite. The manna itself tasted good, "like wafers made with honey" (Exodus 16:31). But, for the most part, the manna era left a bad taste in the mouths of the Israelites. It was an epoch of wandering through the "vast and dreadful desert, that thirsty and waterless land, with its venomous snakes and scorpions" (Deuteronomy 8:15). It was a season of punishment, of death, of long waiting for the years to pass. Even God's gracious giving of manna during those years carried with it a hard purpose, "to humble and to test you" (Deuteronomy 8:16).

Now a new age has dawned. The nation stands in that "good land—a land with streams and pools of water, . . . a land with wheat and barley, vines and fig trees, pomegranates, olive oil and honey; a land where bread will not be scarce" (Deuteronomy 8:7-9). By God's grace Israel is beginning to eat from fields they neither planted nor tended. (See Deuteronomy 6:10-12.) It is a day of covenant confirmation in which the Lord shows that judgment is over and he is reconciled with his people. The manna years were only a minor-key prelude to a far happier song. The end of manna is an occasion for joy in God's fulfilled promises.

Great military campaigns are about to start for Israel. We might expect that the camp at Gilgal would be a beehive of activity with assault planning, troop training, and sword sharpening. Instead abundant time, a whole week or more, is devoted to the Lord for spiritual purposes. The soldier's sword rests while the ceremonial flint knife renews the covenant of circumcision; the father's knife carves the roasted lamb of Passover for his family, and unleavened bread is broken and eaten with thanks to the Lord.

We see here an excellent illustration of taking time for *first things first*. Israel seeks first the covenant relationship the Lord has established. According to his promise, he will see to it that military success follows and all physical needs are satisfied. Jesus makes the same promise to us: "*Seek first* his kingdom and his righteousness, and all these things will be given to you as well" (Matthew 6:33).

Not only great military challenges face Israel, but powerful temptations are waiting also. The people will be tempted to live like the people of the land, to go after their gods, to satisfy their sexual urges like the Canaanites, to live for material things, and to covet the booty from battles that is to be devoted only to the Lord. But a tempted Israelite who has worshiped at Gilgal can say: "I belong to my gracious Lord through his solemn covenant. My circumcision and the Passover meal I have just eaten prove it. How can I sin against him who has made me his own?"

Circumcision and Passover naturally remind us of their superior New Testament counterparts: Baptism and the Lord's Supper. Through the Word and water of Baptism, we are covenanted into the family of the triune God (Matthew 28:19), washed clean of our sins (Acts 22:16), clothed with Christ's perfection (Galatians 3:27), and given the gift of salvation (1 Peter 3:20,21). At the Lord's Supper, we receive Jesus' body with the bread (Matthew 26:26) and his "blood of the covenant" with the wine "for the forgiveness of sins" (Matthew 26:28). What comfort is ours as we enjoy these blessings from our covenant Lord, who makes us his very own through Christ! What power against temptation is ours in Baptism and in Jesus' Supper, as we delight in his covenant promises and, in thanks, dedicate our lives to him!

While we cannot determine a chronology of events in the first five chapters of Joshua with certainty, we propose the following:

- At the beginning of the month of Nisan, perhaps in the year 1406 B.C., the Lord encourages Joshua in his new role as leader.

- About the same time, Joshua sends spies to Jericho.
- On the fifth of Nisan, Israel travels to the east bank of the Jordan and camps for four more days.
- On the tenth of the month, the nation crosses the river, sets up two memorials, and camps at Gilgal that night.
- The ceremony of circumcision is renewed on the 11th.
- The first Passover in 39 years is celebrated at twilight of the 14th of Nisan.
- The people eat the first produce of Canaan on the 16th.
- On the 17th manna stops falling from heaven.

This two-week period of Israel's history is one of the most significant portions of the Old Testament era.

Though we have not completed chapter 5, we have arrived at the end of the first part of Joshua. So far we have witnessed preparations for taking the land. The next part, which deals with capturing the land, is introduced by a fascinating meeting between Joshua and an unnamed "commander."

PART TWO

The Land Is Captured
(5:13–12:24)

The fall of Jericho

¹³Now when Joshua was near Jericho, he looked up and saw a man standing in front of him with a drawn sword in his hand. Joshua went up to him and asked, "Are you for us or for our enemies?"

¹⁴"Neither," he replied, "but as commander of the army of the LORD I have now come." Then Joshua fell facedown to the ground in reverence, and asked him, "What message does my Lord have for his servant?"

¹⁵The commander of the LORD's army replied, "Take off your sandals, for the place where you are standing is holy." And Joshua did so.

Just where do these three verses fit? Stephen Langton, the 13th-century archbishop of Canterbury who gave us the chapter divisions in our English Bibles, thought they fit best connected to the events of chapter 5. Some say these verses stand all by themselves as an unattached episode. Others think they are linked directly to the first five verses of chapter 6, an idea that provides a clear answer as to who the "commander of the LORD's army" is. We prefer the last interpretation, as our section heading shows. But whatever our ideas of where these verses fit, as we read them, we sense a certain mystery, surprise, and awe through them that is in keeping with the one Joshua meets here.

Joshua is evidently away from the Gilgal camp by himself, analyzing Jericho, Israel's first target. The Hebrew says literally that Joshua was "in Jericho," probably meaning "in the immediate vicinity of Jericho." Joshua's utter *surprise* as he meets the sword-carrying man comes out clearly in the Hebrew: "He raised his eyes, looked, and *lo and behold!*"

Why the drawn sword in the man's hand? Does he want to fight Joshua? or Israel? or Israel's enemies? While Joshua is startled, he is not afraid to walk up to the mysterious stranger to ask whose side he's on. Isn't this evidence of Joshua's bravery, strengthened by the Lord's encouragement and recent miracle!

The stranger's answer is as surprising as his sudden appearance. In the Hebrew he answers first with an abrupt "No." In phrasing his question, Joshua implies that the stranger is a mere human taking sides in human combat. The sharp "no" or "neither" rejects that idea and leads to the surprising revelation that he is "commander of the army of the LORD."

Since Joshua himself is the only general of the Lord's *earthly* army, the "man's" answer implies that he is a *heavenly* commander. His words "I have now come" suggest that he has arrived for just this time when battles are about to begin. Joshua's skills and the strength of Israel's army cannot ensure victory. The "commander" and "the LORD's army" must always be behind the scenes to give success. Beyond that, Joshua would have the wrong perspective if he were to think that the Lord always takes sides in human combat and that the Lord must always be on his side. Rather, Joshua is to make sure that he is *on the Lord's side,* follows the *Lord's* commands, and fights the *Lord's* battles.

Notice how these verses successively zoom in to sharpen the focus on the mysterious visitor. In verse 13 he is simply "a man" with a sword. In verse 14 he is "commander of the army of the LORD," whom Joshua bows before and calls "my Lord." In verse 15 he speaks exactly the same words the

Joshua and the angel

Lord spoke to Moses from the burning bush (Exodus 3:5) and his presence causes the place to be holy.

Who is he? An angel, perhaps the archangel Michael, commanding the heavenly hosts? Or is this the Lord himself in visible form? Some say that he cannot be the Lord since he calls himself the "commander of the army of the LORD." But note that when the Lord appeared to Moses in the burning bush, he is first called "the angel of the LORD" (Exodus 3:2), and in the next verses, it is "the LORD" who speaks. Add to that the striking fact that the commander in verse 15 speaks the words the Lord spoke to Moses. Is our author revealing, without spelling it out, that this is the Lord himself appearing to Joshua, just as he had appeared to Moses?

Early Jewish interpreters had two differing ideas on the commander. One is that Joshua was experiencing a vision here and therefore there is *no real appearance* of anyone. The other is that the commander is the angel Michael. Early Christians believed him to be the Son of God in visible form. Origen, one of the early Christian church fathers (ca. A.D. 185–254), wrote, "Who else is the prince of the host of the virtues of the Lord, save our Lord Jesus Christ?"[2] Other early Christian interpreters thought the commander was an angel through whom the Lord revealed himself.

No matter how we answer the question "Who is he?" Joshua receives in this awesome encounter another strong message of encouragement from the Lord just before battles begin. In verse 14 Joshua had asked for a message. Now he gets it. The holy, powerful Lord is with him just as he was with Moses. If Israel sheds all worldly pollution, just as Joshua removed his dusty sandals, and fights the Lord's battles in reverent obedience, heavenly armies will ensure victory.

Who can stand up against the Lord with his heavenly and earthly forces? Can the Canaanites, Hittites, Amorites, or any of the nations? Can Jericho, Ai, Hazor, and the other cities? "If God is for us, who can be against us? . . . We are more than conquerors through him who loved us" (Romans 8:31,37).

6 Now Jericho was tightly shut up because of the Israelites. No one went out and no one came in.

²Then the LORD said to Joshua, "See, I have delivered Jericho into your hands, along with its king and its fighting men. ³March around the city once with all the armed men. Do this for six days. ⁴Have seven priests carry trumpets of rams' horns in front of the ark. On the seventh day, march around the city seven times, with the priests blowing the trumpets. ⁵When you hear them sound a long blast on the trumpets, have all the people give a loud shout; then the wall of the city will collapse and the people will go up, every man straight in."

This section may continue the episode of Joshua meeting the commander. If so, verse 1 is a parenthetical comment in the middle of the account, verses 2-5 are part of the message Joshua requested in 5:14, and the commander is the Lord himself.

These verses open the most significant and best known chapter in Joshua. Chapter 6 makes it especially plain that the land and its cities are an outright gift of God. Israel will not take Jericho because of a superior army. The city will collapse into their hands as a gift from the Lord.

The first two verses hold a striking contrast. There is the "tightly shut up" impregnable city with "its king and its fighting men." And then there is the Lord's calm assurance that Jericho's fall is as good as done. The picture is like that of the boy David before the champion Goliath (1 Samuel 17). Jericho stands there with its wall, swords, spears, javelins, and a reputation accumulated over hundreds of years. But in spite of the odds, God's people can expect certain victory. Like David, when they act "in the name of the LORD

Almighty, the God of the armies of Israel" (1 Samuel 17:45), the odds become meaningless.

Why has the Lord planned a seven-day ritual before he causes the city to fall? Part of the answer lies in exercising Israel's faith. Yes, the walls will collapse by the work of the Lord. But he wants Israel completely resting its faith on him before he hands over the gift. Just as the days at the river forced the people to place all confidence in the Lord before the miracle, so now during seven days of marching around mighty Jericho, the Lord will direct all faith toward himself.

The author of Hebrews stresses the faith aspect of the coming victory. He says, "By faith the walls of Jericho fell, after the people had marched around them for seven days" (Hebrews 11:30). Their obedience to the Lord's commands will show their faith, a faith the Lord will build up during the seven days of spiritual and physical exercise. Their faith will lead them to accept God's promised victory.

The Lord always wants much more than that his people receive his material gifts. He wants an ever-growing trust in him as the giver of those gifts. To that end he directs and rules our lives. Our faith relationship with him is far more important than the individual gifts, just as Israel's faith in him was much more valuable than Jericho.

Verses 2-5 do not intend to give all the details that God commanded to Joshua. Their chief intent is to show that the orders come from God. He is directing the assault. The victory will be his. In keeping with the author's interesting style, further details of God's orders will emerge as Joshua commands the people and the people carry out the orders. Our interest might lapse if the author presented all of God's words to Joshua and then repeated them in his relay to the people and in their actions that follow. By now we are well acquainted with this pattern: the Lord addresses Joshua, Joshua passes on the message, and Israel acts on it. This is the sixth time we are seeing it.

The symbolic number 7 is striking in its repetition in the Lord's command: seven priests, seven trumpets, seven days of marching, seven times around the city on the seventh day. We saw the significance of 7 as a symbol for completeness in connection with the seven nations to be conquered. The number 7 also symbolizes holiness by association with God, who established the concept of 7 in his seven-day creation week. At creation it is natural to think of 7 as God's special number and to see its twofold meaning of *completeness* and *holiness*.

The repeated 7 emphasizes that what is about to happen at Jericho is God's doing. The orders are his orders. It will be *his* judgment on the city, *his* victory, and *his* gift to Israel. Nothing will happen because of some magical hocus-pocus on the part of Israel. The author of Joshua lays to rest any charges that Israel is merely acting out some superstitious ritual.

The sight and sound of the seven trumpets will be a reminder that the Lord himself is present. At Mount Sinai very loud trumpet blasts signaled his presence (Exodus 19:16,19). The Hebrew shows that the trumpets are made of rams' horns. Their military function was to muster troops, stop fighting, or announce victory.

The ark of the covenant especially symbolizes the Lord's presence, as it did at the Jordan. Once again, the Lord is at the center of what's happening.

All the people will become involved on the seventh day when they raise a mighty shout that announces the Lord's victory. The same Hebrew word for shout is used in Psalm 33:3, where believers in the Lord are encouraged to "shout for joy." Why shouldn't God's people shout for joy? "He is our help and our shield" (Psalm 33:20), and "He gives us the victory through our Lord Jesus Christ" (1 Corinthians 15:57).

After the people deliver their loud shout, the Lord will deliver the city over to them. The walls of Jericho will collapse so completely that anyone will be able to walk "straight in." No natural cause, such as an earthquake, can accomplish what the Lord has in store for Jericho. The area is susceptible to tremors and quakes. But this will be a unique happening, directly from the powerful hand of God.

The Lord announced the Jordan miracle in advance and the people watched it unfold precisely as told. Now they have every reason to follow his orders confidently and accept his victory by faith.

⁶So Joshua son of Nun called the priests and said to them, "Take up the ark of the covenant of the LORD and have seven priests carry trumpets in front of it." ⁷And he ordered the people, "Advance! March around the city, with the armed guard going ahead of the ark of the LORD."

⁸When Joshua had spoken to the people, the seven priests carrying the seven trumpets before the LORD went forward, blowing their trumpets, and the ark of the LORD's covenant followed them. ⁹The armed guard marched ahead of the priests who blew the trumpets, and the rear guard followed the ark. All this time the trumpets were sounding. ¹⁰But Joshua had commanded the people, "Do not give a war cry, do not raise your voices, do not say a word until the day I tell you to shout. Then shout!" ¹¹So he had the ark of the LORD carried around the city, circling it once. Then the people returned to camp and spent the night there.

¹²Joshua got up early the next morning and the priests took up the ark of the LORD. ¹³The seven priests carrying the seven trumpets went forward, marching before the ark of the LORD and blowing the trumpets. The armed men went ahead of them and the rear guard followed the ark of the LORD, while the

trumpets kept sounding. ¹⁴So on the second day they marched around the city once and returned to the camp. They did this for six days.

The order of the march comes out clearly now, as Joshua gives God's commands, and the people carry them out. First in line is the *armed guard.* The city will not fall by the force of soldiers. But this armed guard will have a role later in the city's destruction. Joshua 24:11 mentions that at least some of the people of Jericho resisted Israel. Joshua reminds the people in that verse, "The citizens of Jericho fought against you." So the soldiers in the march had a purpose.

Next in line are the *seven priests* with their seven trumpets sounding during the march.

Then comes *"the ark of the LORD's covenant,"* the focus of the whole assembly. Joshua names the ark first in his orders in verse 6. It alone is mentioned in the first day of circling the city in verse 11. It is the central feature because it shows the Lord's presence.

The *rear guard,* mentioned for the first time in verse 9, closes out the line of march.

Are all the people involved in the march? The verses do not say so explicitly. But verse 11 may imply that they are. After the first day's march, "the people returned to camp."

A detail not mentioned in the Lord's orders comes out in Joshua's command in verse 10. Everyone is to be silent during the seven days until Joshua gives the command for the loud shout. Complete silence, except for the sound of the trumpets, as the city is circled 13 times! Think of the tension that must have created within Jericho, and the sense of awe among the Israelites. This atmosphere is in keeping with the Lord's judgment marching ever closer toward the unrepentant city.

St. Paul Lutheran Church
301 North Church Avenue
Ogilvie, MN 56358

The repetition that comes from relating the same procession on the second day is dramatic. We not only review the facts through this repetition. A feeling for what is happening also builds up. We gain a solemn sense of God's judgment on those who despise his grace. And we feel the security that God alone can give, as we march in our minds with Israel around the city again and again.

We don't know exactly how big Jericho was, but the average size of an ancient city was from 5 to 25 acres. The small area that ancient cities covered would make it easy for marchers to go around Jericho in a short time and seven times on the seventh day. We are not told how wide the line of march is or how many people are involved. But if hundreds of thousands make the march, it is likely that many are still waiting to start when the first marchers finish circling.

Old Testament Jericho is commonly identified with Tell es-Sultan, a "tell," or mound of ruins, about a mile northwest of present-day Jericho and four and a half miles west of the Jordan River by road. The present site covers about eight and a half acres, evidence that even larger ancient cities were small by present-day standards. The bulk of the population probably lived outside the city walls and gathered inside during times of danger. Digging straight down from the top of Tell es-Sultan, 65 feet to its base, takes you through thousands of years and at least 25 phases of habitation. Its defensive walls are the earliest discovered so far in human history. According to archaeologists, when Joshua arrived at Jericho, buried on the site was a circular stone tower that was as far removed from Joshua in time as twice the time from Joshua to us. The excavated tower still stands, visible to all who visit the tell today.

If Tell es-Sultan is ancient Jericho, which level is from Joshua's time? The question has long intrigued scholars.

John Garstang, who excavated the site from 1930 to 1936, thought he had solid evidence of Joshua's Jericho. He found a city surrounded by a double wall that had been violently destroyed. He placed a 15-century B.C. date on the city. But Kathleen Kenyon, as a result of her excavations from 1952 to 1961, found that almost nothing now present at the site is from 1500 to 1200 B.C. Garstang's city, she concluded, is actually from the third millennium B.C.

A new look at the evidence from Tell es-Sultan brings many of Kenyon's interpretations into question. Bryant G. Wood, an authority on Canaanite pottery, presents strong evidence for a 1400 B.C. destruction of a level of the tell. He notes the abundance of pottery found from that period and the existence of Egyptian scarabs (beetle-shaped amulets) from that same time. Carbon-14 testing of debris points to a 1400 B.C. date for devastation. There is clear evidence of leveled walls and destruction by burning. Fascinating is the discovery of large stores of grain in the houses destroyed at the same time. This abundant grain correlates with two facts from the Joshua account: (1) Jericho was taken during Nisan, the month of the spring barley harvest; (2) the city did not fall after a long starvation siege, common at the time, but after just seven days while plenty of food was still in the houses (*Biblical Archaeology Review,* March/April 1990).

Because of intense interest in Jericho, we can be sure the last spade has not pierced Tell es-Sultan and the last interpretation of evidence has not been written. Not all scholars are absolutely convinced that Tell es-Sultan is Old Testament Jericho. But a suitable alternative in the area has not been found.

Back to the Joshua account. Israel has circled the ancient city once a day for six days. The solid walls still stand. But the sun is rising on day seven.

¹⁵**On the seventh day, they got up at daybreak and marched around the city seven times in the same manner, except that on that day they circled the city seven times.** ¹⁶**The seventh time around, when the priests sounded the trumpet blast, Joshua commanded the people, "Shout! For the LORD has given you the city!** ¹⁷**The city and all that is in it are to be devoted to the LORD. Only Rahab the prostitute and all who are with her in her house shall be spared, because she hid the spies we sent.** ¹⁸**But keep away from the devoted things, so that you will not bring about your own destruction by taking any of them. Otherwise you will make the camp of Israel liable to destruction and bring trouble on it.** ¹⁹**All the silver and gold and the articles of bronze and iron are sacred to the LORD and must go into his treasury."**

The moment of truth has come. But just before the climactic collapse, Joshua impresses on the people some critical instructions. The "shout" command is mentioned first. But, in actual time, it must have come last, or the din of the shouting would have drowned out the rest of Joshua's words. We've seen a number of times that precise chronological order is not the author's chief concern.

The crucial command is that the whole city is to be "devoted" to the Lord. An NIV footnote explains, "The Hebrew term refers to the irrevocable giving over of things or persons to the Lord, often by totally destroying them." The Hebrew word is *cherem*. Its basic meaning is "to prohibit" or "to cut off from ordinary use." Our word *harem,* taken from Arabic, is from the same Semitic root.

Israel is absolutely prohibited from making private use of anything within Jericho. Everything is to be completely destroyed and thereby devoted (cheremed) to the Lord. And if an Israelite takes some cherem (devoted things), then the camp of Israel itself will become cherem (a thing

Seven priests blow seven trumpets

"liable to destruction"). The author is preparing us for the next chapter.

Cities "at a distance" that did "not belong to the nations nearby" did not have to be completely destroyed (Deuteronomy 20:10-15). But Jericho, a key Canaanite city within the Land of Promise, falls under the full cherem. Moses had spelled out the reason for the complete destruction of the cities of the land: "Otherwise, they will teach you to follow all the detestable things they do in worshiping their gods, and you will sin against the LORD your God" (Deuteronomy 20:18). Jericho, which probably means "moon city," may have been an ancient center of moon worship. We know Canaanite worship included detestable practices such as ritual prostitution. "Children were even sacrificed in funerary jars, buried at the foundations of temples and other buildings."[3] The full grown sin of Canaan and the spiritual protection of Israel called for radical action.

Jericho's destruction "must be seen as a prelude and foreshadowing of a more final judgment that God will mete out to those whose unrighteousness will be full in the end of days."[4]

This is the second time in Joshua we have seen the term *cherem*. In its verb and noun forms it appears 79 times in the Old Testament. The first time in Joshua, the word came from the mouth of Rahab (2:10) when she spoke of the complete destruction of the Amorite kings. By her use of this somewhat technical term, Rahab showed the depth of her understanding of the Lord of Israel, whose judgment levels wickedness but whose mercy covers all who look to him.

Joshua's last minute orders about Rahab recall the spies' oath (2:17-20), an oath honored by Joshua and the Lord. Joshua's instructions also serve to highlight God's grace. She and her family are to be spared while destruction engulfs the rest of Jericho. The contrast between her house as an oasis of safety and the holocaust everywhere else will be vivid. Her faith in the Lord and her actions have changed her fate (Hebrews 11:31; James 2:25).

Rahab and her family serve as a picture of the invisible church. The Greek word for church, *ecclesia,* means literally "those called out." God has called all believers, like Rahab, "out of darkness into his wonderful light"; no matter what their background or nationality, he has caused them to be called "the people of God" (1 Peter 2:9,10). Like Rahab, the church of all believers has been "called out" of the destruction which awaits those who refuse his love and safety.

Joshua's instructions are complete. Everyone knows precisely what to do and what God will do.

²⁰**When the trumpets sounded, the people shouted, and at the sound of the trumpet, when the people gave a loud shout, the wall collapsed; so every man charged straight in, and they took the city. ²¹They devoted the city to the LORD and destroyed with the sword every living thing in it—men and women, young and old, cattle, sheep and donkeys.**

²²**Joshua said to the two men who had spied out the land, "Go into the prostitute's house and bring her out and all who belong to her, in accordance with your oath to her." ²³So the young men who had done the spying went in and brought out Rahab, her father and mother and brothers and all who belonged to her. They brought out her entire family and put them in a place outside the camp of Israel.**

²⁴**Then they burned the whole city and everything in it, but they put the silver and gold and the articles of bronze and iron into the treasury of the LORD's house. ²⁵But Joshua spared Rahab the prostitute, with her family and all who belonged to her, because she hid the men Joshua had sent as spies to Jericho—and she lives among the Israelites to this day.**

Everything unfolds exactly as the Lord promised. The old spiritual "Joshua Fought the Battle of Jericho" doesn't place the emphasis where it belongs. *The Lord* fought the battle of Jericho while Joshua and Israel took the gift.

Who can doubt the Lord's promises now! The waters of the surging Jordan and now the walls of Jericho are no obstacle when God needs to make good on his word. The flattened walls invite all future generations of Israel to say: "Come and see the works of the LORD, the desolations he has brought on the earth. The LORD Almighty is with us; the God of Jacob is our fortress" (Psalm 46:8,11).

The destruction of the city is total. All living things are killed. Readers of Joshua sometimes grieve or even cringe at the thought. That is natural. Jesus wept over unrepentant Jerusalem and the impending destruction of the children within its walls (Luke 19:41-44). God says: "As surely as I live . . . I take no pleasure in the death of the wicked, but rather that they turn from their ways and live" (Ezekiel 33:11). There is no hint that Israel enjoyed its role in the taking of life at Jericho. They were acting under God's orders as the agents of his judgment. As "the Lord of all the earth" he has the perfect right to end the time of grace of those who have mocked his love and chosen their sin. We cringe not so much at the physical death of Jericho's citizens as at their eternal loss.

The religion for which God judged Jericho sounds tragically similar to attitudes around us. Canaanite religion "was more than nature worship and more than humanism; it was a candid profession of faith in sex as that alone which saves and satisfies."[5]

Notice again the wonderful contrast as the rescue of Rahab comes into view in the middle of judgment and destruction. By referring to her as "the prostitute," Joshua accents God's grace toward her. In her past life, she was as debased as the rest of Jericho. But with the two young spies as God's agents, he brings her to safety. Through faith in the God of Israel, the former prostitute receives not only physical rescue but eternal deliverance.

Why Rahab and her family are first placed "*outside* the camp of Israel" is not stated. The arrangement must have been temporary since the author goes on to say that "she lives *among* the Israelites to this day."

The phrase "to this day" serves a number of purposes here:

1. It indicates that some years elapsed between the Jericho episode and the time of writing.
2. It shows that what the author writes about Jericho's destruction and Rahab's rescue is historical reality. Rahab's presence among Israel—as well as her descendants—verifies the account.
3. It emphasizes God's grace in snatching a former prostitute from the flames of destruction and bringing her into his chosen nation.
4. The phrase also shows that God's choice of Israel as his covenant people does not absolutely exclude people of other nations. Israel has no reason to feel smug about its selection. Rahab the Canaanite and later Ruth the Moabite become part of Israel and are even in the direct line leading to the Savior.

Matthew 1:5 tells that Rahab and a man named Salmon were the parents of Boaz, great-grandfather of David (see also Ruth 4:18-22). Jewish tradition says that Rahab became the ancestress of eight prophets and priests and that Jeremiah was from her line. One tradition claims that Joshua himself married her. There is no mention of Joshua's wife in the

Bible. Joshua's words "as for me and my household" in Joshua 24:15 are the closest reference to his family.

After burning the destroyed city and putting the gold, silver, and articles of bronze and iron into the Lord's treasury, Joshua performs a final act against Jericho.

²⁶At that time Joshua pronounced this solemn oath: "Cursed before the LORD is the man who undertakes to rebuild this city, Jericho:

> **"At the cost of his firstborn son**
> **will he lay its foundations;**
> **at the cost of his youngest**
> **will he set up its gates."**

²⁷So the LORD was with Joshua, and his fame spread throughout the land.

The Hebrew word for "to pronounce a solemn oath" is a verb made from the noun for the number 7. To make an oath is "to seven." The "sevenings" of Israel against Jericho are not complete with the seven days of marching around the city. The last holy act comes by Joshua's oath.

The oath is in the form of Hebrew poetry with its characteristic rhythm and two parallel parts. The poetic form leads some to think that Joshua is using a curse formula. Even if it is a formula, Joshua is not "witching" the site through a string of words used as a magic phrase. The Lord is pleased with the oath, evidently commanded it himself, and worked through it. A mere recitation of words does not bring about the result.

The curse of the oath was fulfilled by the Lord some five hundred years later during the reign of King Ahab (874–853 B.C.). First Kings 16:34 says: "In Ahab's time, Hiel of Bethel rebuilt Jericho. He laid its foundations at the cost of his firstborn son Abiram, and he set up its gates at the cost of his youngest son Segub, in accordance with the word of the LORD spoken by Joshua son of Nun."

The Lord wanted to preserve the collapsed site as a continuing reminder of his gift to Israel. People could live in Jericho without the curse affecting them (Joshua 18:21; Judges 3:13; 2 Samuel 10:5). But when its foundations and gates were rebuilt, the Lord's curse took hold. Later in Joshua we will read that the site of Jericho came under the allotment of the tribe of Benjamin (18:21).

Our book's most famous chapter ends by telling us that its central character has quickly become famous— and why. The Lord is with him! Joshua did not push back Jordan's waters or push over Jericho's walls. The Lord is the hero. Yet in his gracious way, the Lord shares his fame with his obedient servant. Joshua trusts and obeys. The Lord gives success and exalts him according to his promises (1:8; 3:7). Great leaders, in God's view, are people of humble faith, obedience, and service (1 Samuel 15:22; 16:7; Matthew 20:26). We can learn much about God-pleasing leadership by watching Joshua.

Joshua's obedience and fame come into sharp contrast with the disobedience and infamy of Achan in chapter 7.

Achan's sin

7 **But the Israelites acted unfaithfully in regard to the devoted things; Achan son of Carmi, the son of Zimri, the son of Zerah, of the tribe of Judah, took some of them. So the LORD's anger burned against Israel.**

²Now Joshua sent men from Jericho to Ai, which is near Beth Aven to the east of Bethel, and told them, "Go up and spy out the region." So the men went up and spied out Ai.

³When they returned to Joshua, they said, "Not all the people will have to go up against Ai. Send two or three thousand

men to take it and do not weary all the people, for only a few men are there." ⁴So about three thousand men went up; but they were routed by the men of Ai, ⁵who killed about thirty-six of them. They chased the Israelites from the city gate as far as the stone quarries and struck them down on the slopes. At this the hearts of the people melted and became like water.

The account opens with the ominous word *but,* alerting us to trouble. Then the inspired author reveals to us the cause of the disaster at Ai. Joshua and Israel will not learn until later. The defeat results from one man taking some of the forbidden things (the "cherem") that belonged to the Lord alone.

The whole nation is held responsible for the unfaithfulness of one of its members. The Lord is obviously dealing with his covenant people as a unit. While we might be impressed that only one of hundreds of thousands disobeyed the commands at Jericho, the holy Lord is not only angry at the action of one. His wrath burns against all Israel. His covenant with its clear stipulations about the devoted things has been violated. Achan's act removed a condition of the sacred contract and sent covenant blessings spilling to the ground. His radical disobedience was like kicking a leg out from under a table heaped with delectable food and destroying the whole dinner for everyone. God's fierce anger that acts "like a devouring fire" (Deuteronomy 9:3) against Israel's enemies now flares at his own people. It will not be cooled until the offense against his covenant is removed.

Achan's sin that poisons the whole nation reminds us "to watch over one another for the preventing of sin, because others' sins may redound to our damage."⁶ His act is also a reminder that we do not commit "victimless sins." No one is an island. What we do affects or infects others. And even if my sins don't seem to touch another, I am my own victim.

The meaning of the name Achan is unknown. The author of 1 Chronicles calls him Achar, which has the fitting meaning of "troubler" (1 Chronicles 2:7).

The sin of "the troubler" is hidden from Joshua as he prepares for the next conquest by sending spies to Ai as he had earlier for Jericho.

Journals of archaeology have carried many articles on the so-called problem of Ai. What is the problem? Ai, which means "ruin," has long been identified with et-Tell, Arabic for "the ruin." But there is no archaeological evidence of settlement there in the Late Bronze Age (1500–1250 B.C.), the time of Joshua's conquest. There is evidence of a flourishing community in the third millennium B.C. But that material is from a thousand years before Joshua. The choice of et-Tell as ancient Ai seems to fit with the description in verse 2, which says that Ai is "near Beth Aven to the east of Bethel." Bethel is commonly identified with Beitin, an Arab village about 12 miles north of Jerusalem. The location of Beth Aven is unknown.

Why is there no evidence of occupation at et-Tell during Joshua's time? Many reasons have been offered. Among them are these:

1. Et-Tell is not biblical Ai, which must be somewhere else in the area.
2. Ai at the time of Joshua was already a ruin since its name means just that. The site of the ruin may have been used only as a temporary military outpost that left no remains.
3. Chapters 7 and 8 of Joshua are a folk story invented to explain the ruins at Ai, ruins that really predated Joshua by a thousand years.
4. The writer of Joshua mistakenly transferred the events of chapters 7 and 8 from Bethel to Ai.

While the last two explanations are popular, they obviously fly in the face of the Bible's inerrancy. It is best to leave the problem of Ai unanswered for the time being without presuming to give foolproof solutions. It is interesting when archaeology can present material evidence of Bible accounts, but our faith in the Bible's reliability does not hang in the balance until a spade digs up the proof. Interpretations of archaeologists change due to the inexact nature of the science. The Bible stands changeless and reliable on its own, due to its inspiration by the Holy Spirit. The findings from a dig in Israel this summer may change what was an irrefutable interpretation five years ago. Interpretations wither and fall, "but the word of our God stands forever" (Isaiah 40:8; 1 Peter 1:25). "When seeming discrepancies occur between the Bible and archaeology, a judicious response would be to withhold judgment. Historically, many have leaped to pronounce sentence while the jury was still out, only to find that later archaeological discoveries resolved the conflict."[7]

If Ai is et-Tell, the spies traveled 15 miles uphill, west and slightly north from Jericho. The location is a strategic one on the central ridge of mountains that is the backbone of Canaan. The spies find only a few men at Ai and recommend to Joshua a minimal force to take the city. Some commentators imply that the spies are showing a cocky, presumptuous attitude after the great Jericho victory. That seems to be reading something into the text.

Joshua sends the higher figure of recommended troops to Ai. Yet the defeat of Israel is overwhelming. A hundred thousand marines could not have changed the outcome since Achan robbed Israel of the Lord's blessings. When God is opposed to human plans, they fail.

Israel's body count is "about thirty-six." That does not sound like a round figure to us who are used to a number system based on 10. But ancient numbering, taken from the Sumerian system, was based on multiples of 6. We hold a vestige of the old system in our 60-minute hours and 360-degree circles. To say "about 36" is comparable to us saying "about 50."

The figure of about 36 killed may not strike us as reflecting an utter rout. But remember that Joshua was expecting quick and complete victory. Any kind of repulse would be shocking after God's promise of total success (1:3), the recent collapse of Jericho, and the spies' report.

The exact locations of the disaster are engraved on Israel's memory. That is clear from the author's vivid description: "They chased the Israelites from the *city gate* as far as the *stone quarries* and struck them down *on the slopes.*" The NIV translates *shebarim* as "stone quarries." It can also stand as a proper noun, *Shebarim.* The root of the word means "to break to pieces," suggesting a quarry. The people themselves are emotionally broken to pieces in defeat and react just as their conquered enemies had in the past. Their hearts melt and become like water. The enemies' sandal is now on the foot of God's special nation. How could this be? The leaders vent their perplexity and grief in the customary way of the Mideast.

⁶Then Joshua tore his clothes and fell facedown to the ground before the ark of the LORD, remaining there till evening. The elders of Israel did the same, and sprinkled dust on their heads. ⁷And Joshua said, "Ah, Sovereign LORD, why did you ever bring this people across the Jordan to deliver us into the hands of the Amorites to destroy us? If only we had been content to stay on the other side of the Jordan! ⁸O Lord, what can I say, now that Israel has been routed by its enemies? ⁹The Canaanites and the other people of the country will hear about this and they will surround us and wipe out our name

from the earth. What then will you do for your own great name?"

The defeat not only routs Israel but disarms Joshua before the Lord. His place of prayer before the ark may show that he senses that something related to the Lord's covenant is radically wrong.

It would not be wise to use all of Joshua's prayer as a model. *Searching faith* may be a term that describes his expressions. While grasping for answers from the Lord, weaknesses surface. It is a slap in God's face to suggest that Israel should have stayed on the other side of the Jordan when God himself had commanded the crossing, blessed it with a miracle, and promised conquest. Joshua's words come dangerously close to those of the grumblers in the desert (Exodus 14:11,12; 16:3; 17:3; Numbers 14:2,3).

Joshua's bold appeal at the close of his prayer is much like Moses' prayer arguments (Exodus 32:11-13; Numbers 14:15,16; Deuteronomy 9:28,29). Since the Lord has tied his own name to the success of his people, Joshua reasons that the Lord must work things out for his own reputation. Bold faith mixed with glaring weakness characterizes the prayer.

Paul gives comforting commentary on the imperfect prayers of all believers: "We do not know what we ought to pray for, but the Spirit himself intercedes for us. . . . The Spirit intercedes for the saints in accordance with God's will" (Romans 8:26,27).

It is the Bible's pattern to reveal flaws in giants of faith like Joshua. One reason for this is to warn us that faith in our leaders, even great spiritual leaders, dare never be absolute. Christians are not to be blind hero worshipers. Only Jesus deserves our absolute trust. Another purpose is to show us that all who are saved, including the Bible's greatest heroes, are saved by God's grace, through faith, and not by their works. We need not despair when we have a profound sense of guilt and weakness. The "greats" sinned too but were pardoned by grace through faith in their Savior-God.

Joshua's weaknesses are rarely revealed in the Bible. On one occasion Moses had reprimanded him for wanting to silence two prophets (Numbers 11:24-30). Joshua 9:14,15 will hint at another shortcoming. Now the Lord himself admonishes him.

¹⁰The LORD said to Joshua, "Stand up! What are you doing down on your face? ¹¹Israel has sinned; they have violated my covenant, which I commanded them to keep. They have taken some of the devoted things; they have stolen, they have lied, they have put them with their own possessions. ¹²That is why the Israelites cannot stand against their enemies; they turn their backs and run because they have been made liable to destruction. I will not be with you anymore unless you destroy whatever among you is devoted to destruction.

¹³"Go, consecrate the people. Tell them, 'Consecrate yourselves in preparation for tomorrow; for this is what the LORD, the God of Israel, says: That which is devoted is among you, O Israel. You cannot stand against your enemies until you remove it.

¹⁴"'In the morning, present yourselves tribe by tribe. The tribe that the LORD takes shall come forward clan by clan; the clan that the LORD takes shall come forward family by family; and the family that the LORD takes shall come forward man by man. ¹⁵He who is caught with the devoted things shall be destroyed by fire, along with all that belongs to him. He has violated the covenant of the LORD and has done a disgraceful thing in Israel!'"

The Lord's rebuke of Joshua is sharp and cutting. God does not allow a monologue to continue for long when he is almost accused of evil. The Lord implies that Joshua should know that the covenant has been violated. Had he not promised that success would follow when his covenant was honored and that disaster would result when its stipulations were broken? Instead of lying with his face in the dust nursing a defeatist attitude, Joshua should be busy resolving the problem.

Without revealing the name of the culprit, the Lord spells out the reason behind the Ai disaster. "They have violated my covenant. . . . They have taken some of the devoted things." The plural pronoun *they* again shows that the Lord holds all Israel guilty. He is not satisfied that almost all have honored the covenant conditions. Who dares suggest that God is not concerned about the sins of individuals as long as corruption is not widespread?

The Lord says he will no longer be with Israel unless the "devoted things" are destroyed. His words sting, just as did his announcement at the time of the prophet Hosea: "You are not my people, and I am not your God" (Hosea 1:9). Think of the impact of these crushing words on the Israelites! They will have no claim on the Promised Land, no right to divine protection or success in battles. They are on their own with Canaanites lusting for revenge, smarting from Jericho's defeat, and inspired by the rout at Ai. The surging Jordan blocks retreat to the east with no hope of another miracle. Israel is no longer the Lord's "treasured possession" and "a kingdom of priests and a holy nation" (Exodus 19:5,6). The covenant violation must be removed.

The Lord does not leave Israel groping for a plan to solve the problem. His grace is evident even in the middle of his burning anger. He instructs Joshua on how to discover the person who dared to break his sacred pact with Israel. First the people must consecrate themselves in preparation for appearing before the Lord the next day. As at Mount Sinai, the consecration perhaps includes washing clothes and abstaining from sexual relations, outward symbols of inner consecration (Exodus 19:10,14,15). Then as tribes, clans, families, and individuals appear before the Lord, he himself will catch the culprit. The exact manner by which the Lord will "take" or "catch" the guilty one is not stated. Perhaps it is by lot, with names written on shards of pottery that are then selected from a container.

Besides convicting the criminal, the painstaking procedure clears all the innocent. It also gives Achan time to step forward and repent before the steady hand of the Lord points the accusing finger at him. For us readers, the procedure emphasizes that the Lord, whose anger burns at sin, has eyes like blazing fire to cut through any attempted cover-up. What is the point of hiding guilt when everything is laid bare before God's penetrating gaze?

¹⁶Early the next morning Joshua had Israel come forward by tribes, and Judah was taken. ¹⁷The clans of Judah came forward, and he took the Zerahites. He had the clan of the Zerahites come forward by families, and Zimri was taken. ¹⁸Joshua had his family come forward man by man, and Achan son of Carmi, the son of Zimri, the son of Zerah, of the tribe of Judah, was taken.

The 12 tribes before the Lord may remind us of the disciples before Jesus at the Last Supper, seeking the identity of the betrayer and saying, "Surely not I, Lord?" (Matthew 26:22). That night Judas was taken. This day the tribe that Judas is named after is taken.

It is a low moment for the tribe of Judah. Soon Judah will receive the first and largest share of land. Later it will give Israel its famous kings. The whole nation will be called *the Jews* after the name of this single tribe. Finally, from

Judah will come the world's Savior, "a light for revelation to the Gentiles and for glory to [God's] people Israel" (Luke 2:32). But this infamous day serves as a check on the pride of the tribe whose name means "praised."

During the long ordeal, Achan never steps forward. What is going on in his mind? Does he think he can escape God's detection? Can anyone?

The chapter started with Achan's genealogy, which is now repeated in verse 18. What we readers have known, Israel now learns. The repetition of Achan's family line stresses that the Lord's hand has no trouble reaching through tribes, clans, families, and individuals to make this pointed judgment: "You are the man!" Before the Lord, cover-up is in vain. Repentance is the only safe course of action.

> [19]Then Joshua said to Achan, "My son, give glory to the LORD, the God of Israel, and give him the praise. Tell me what you have done; do not hide it from me."
>
> [20]Achan replied, "It is true! I have sinned against the LORD, the God of Israel. This is what I have done: [21]When I saw in the plunder a beautiful robe from Babylonia, two hundred shekels of silver and a wedge of gold weighing fifty shekels, I coveted them and took them. They are hidden in the ground inside my tent, with the silver underneath."

Joshua is a layman from the tribe of Ephraim, but his approach is thoroughly "pastoral." Achan has caused disaster for Israel by fracturing the covenant and then added to his sin by failing to step forward. We might expect Joshua to grab him by the throat and rant about the humiliation he had caused his army. But Joshua's concern is not revenge for personal injury. He yearns for repentance from this son of Israel and for God's glory in the resolution of the matter.

The words *my son* set the tender tone of Joshua. "He might have justly called him 'thief,' and 'rebel,' 'Raca,' and 'thou fool,' but he calls him 'son.' . . . This is an example to treat even offenders with the spirit of meekness, not knowing what we ourselves should have been and done if God had put us into the hands of our own counsels."[8] Joshua's fatherly manner comes from the spirit the Lord has given him (Numbers 27:18).

"Give glory to the LORD" is an expression that means the same as "tell the whole truth, so help you God." New Testament Jews used the same solemn charge to get the blind man to tell the truth in John 9:24. God is always glorified through the truth, because the truth shows his ways to be right and causing good for his people.

Achan's confession is late. But it is complete and may even serve as a model. He makes no attempt to shift the blame or minimize his guilt. He bares all before Joshua and the Lord. His sin, he admits, was not just a matter of momentary weakness. It was calculated: "I saw . . . coveted . . . took." The hiding made it a continuing act of evil. The completeness of his confession is seen in the details he offers: the robe is from Babylonia, *Shinar* in the Hebrew; the silver weighs two hundred shekels, or about five pounds; the gold weighs fifty shekels, or about one and a quarter pounds. He even offers the precise detail of the hiding arrangement in his tent, "with the silver underneath."

We who have rationalized our sins can guess what went through Achan's mind when temptation leaped out at him. "No one will know. What a waste if I don't take some of this! I'm not being greedy; I just want to take care of my family. What I'm taking is a pittance compared to all the wealth here. There must be thousands of other Israelites doing the same thing."

But now Achan "comes clean" and confesses his personal, specific guilt. Confessions can become deliberately vague. "Yes, I'm a sinner just like everyone else here." Those may be the words of one trying to take refuge in broad terms and hide in everyone's guilt. It is good at times to catalog specific sins to ensure that we are not just mouthing vague confessions while denying personal guilt.

Joshua does not want the breach of covenant to last a second longer. To feel the Lord's fierce anger is unbearable.

²²**So Joshua sent messengers, and they ran to the tent, and there it was, hidden in his tent, with the silver underneath. ²³They took the things from the tent, brought them to Joshua and all the Israelites and spread them out before the LORD.**

²⁴**Then Joshua, together with all Israel, took Achan son of Zerah, the silver, the robe, the gold wedge, his sons and daughters, his cattle, donkeys and sheep, his tent and all that he had, to the Valley of Achor. ²⁵Joshua said, "Why have you brought this trouble on us? The LORD will bring trouble on you today."**

Then all Israel stoned him, and after they had stoned the rest, they burned them. ²⁶Over Achan they heaped up a large pile of rocks, which remains to this day. Then the LORD turned from his fierce anger. Therefore that place has been called the Valley of Achor ever since.

The very ground that is God's gift is used by Achan as the hiding place for the forbidden items beneath his tent. It is a tragic twisting of God's blessings to use his gifts for evil instead of his glory.

What the messengers find in Achan's tent shows that his confession was genuine in all its details. That is impressed by the repetition of the exact spot where the silver is hidden.

All the devoted things are spread out "before the LORD," perhaps meaning before the ark of the covenant.

The items belonged to God, his covenant was violated by the theft, and he must be glorified in the resolution of the sin.

The Lord himself had already commanded what to do with the covenant violator and all that belonged to him (see verse 15). Israel does not act on its own in the punishment. The Law of Moses stated that children were not to be put to death for the sins of their father (Deuteronomy 24:16). The stoning of Achan's children may show that they were involved in the crime. The Lord who reads hearts is never unjust. Many commentators point out that burial of the forbidden things in the family tent implies their knowledge and approval of the sin.

Israel's camp at Gilgal is evidently the place where the stolen items are spread out before the Lord. But the stoning takes place in a valley away from camp. The plain around Gilgal is said to be nearly void of stones. The Wadi el-Kelt, a stone-filled dry riverbed that leads to the Jordan Valley, is identified by some as the site of stoning. After the execution of the Lord's orders, the site is known as the Valley of Achor, or "trouble."

The name is obviously similar in sound to the name of the one who *troubled* all Israel and met his final *trouble* in this stony valley.

The name stuck. The prophet Hosea wrote of the Valley of Achor some seven hundred years later. Hosea mentions Achor in the context of an inspiring prophecy of the Savior's time. Quoting the Lord, Hosea writes: "I . . . will make the Valley of Achor a door of hope" (Hosea 2:15). The Messiah's saving acts would fill the earth's most dismal low points with uplifting hope. By his blood he would set in place the unconditional new covenant in which the Lord declares, "I will forgive their wickedness and will remember their sins no more" (Jeremiah 31:34).

Stoning Achan's family

The stoned victims are at last burned, as the Lord ordered in verse 15. Their fate is the same as the city of Jericho (6:24). The Lord had made no idle threat when he warned Achan and all Israel, "Keep away from the devoted things, so that you will not bring about your own destruction" (6:18).

Over Achan's grave the people heap up the third stone memorial to appear in the land since Israel's entry. The first two shouted the Lord's praises for a miracle. This one voices stern warning. The familiar phrase "to this day" points to the historical reality of the Achan episode. The first readers of the book of Joshua could walk to the Valley of Achor, contemplate the grim heap of stones still there, and take solemn warning.

The author makes no comment about Achan's eternal fate. Some writers stress the word *today* in Joshua's sentence, "The LORD will bring trouble on you today." They suggest that after today, Achan will enjoy the trouble-free eternity of heaven. His execution, even by God's orders, does not in itself imply eternal death. Faith in the Savior-Lord may well have been present in Achan at the time of his honest confession before Joshua. "Physical death as punishment for sin was given prominence in Old Testament times. This shows God's displeasure with sin. Conclusions as to the eternal destiny of individuals so punished had better not be made rashly."[9]

The interlude of chapter 7 ends. The covenant with its promise of success is in place. Harmony between the Lord and his people is restored. Once again the positive tone heard throughout Joshua will ring out.

Ai destroyed

8 Then the Lord said to Joshua, "Do not be afraid; do not be discouraged. Take the whole army with you, and go up and attack Ai. For I have delivered into your hands the king of Ai, his people, his city and his land. ²You shall do to Ai and its king as you did to Jericho and its king, except that you may carry off their plunder and livestock for yourselves. Set an ambush behind the city."

Joshua had been undone when the men of Ai routed Israel. Now, in light of Joshua's former despair, the Lord heaps up encouragement. It is a new day. The Achan scandal is over, and the Lord has turned from his anger. It is time for the Israelites to get on with the conquest.

The Lord's favor that follows his wrath reminds us that shocking scandals do not mean lasting doom. The Lord's mercy shines again on all who look to him. "His anger lasts only a moment, but his favor lasts a lifetime" (Psalm 30:5). "'In a surge of anger I hid my face from you for a moment, but with everlasting kindness I will have compassion on you,' says the Lord your Redeemer" (Isaiah 54:8). He had separated himself from Israel for a time. He had not divorced her.

Notice that it is the Lord himself who is giving the orders and directing the battle plans. Joshua and Israel will be victors when they simply carry out his commands.

"The whole army" is to go up against Ai. That may not mean every Israelite soldier. The total army numbered about 600,000 while the population of Ai was just 12,000 (8:25). "The whole army" may refer to an entire division, a larger force than the one sent out on the disastrous campaign.

The conquest of the king of Ai and all that belongs to him is as good as accomplished before a sword is drawn.

The Lord does not need anyone's help. He chooses to employ the army of his people as the agent of his victory.

The army will "go up" to Ai from Israel's camp. The Hebrew expression generally refers to an army's advance regardless of a climb in elevation. But here, the advance from Gilgal to Ai involves a 15-mile ascent into the central mountains. Some of the soldiers know the trip well from the recent assault and rout. The march would take five or six hours.

The Lord tells Joshua to "do to Ai and its king as you did to Jericho and its king." We did not hear in chapter 6 what Joshua did to the king of Jericho. But we can infer that he was killed, hanged, or impaled on a tree, after which his body was placed at the city gate.

Ai, like Jericho, is to be totally destroyed, but with an exception: Israel can take Ai's "plunder and livestock." The Lord's orders to "totally destroy" Canaan's cities (the "cherem" orders) are carried out in various degrees of strictness as the Lord directs. Jericho, as the first city taken, held special significance; therefore God gave the strictest orders concerning its destruction. Jericho was evidently like the "first offspring" and belonged completely to the Lord (Exodus 13:2,12,13). Ai, the second city, is treated somewhat differently. The people can have some of its booty.

It is the Lord himself who orders an "ambush" as the special tactic that will topple Ai. Some commentators seem to do a double take at the Lord devising this trick or stratagem. Is there a moral problem here with the Lord plotting a deceptive military maneuver? Obviously not, if he commands it. There is a difference between clever military strategy and a boldfaced lie.

The area around Ai is cut with gorges and ravines ideal for hiding an ambush force. The ambush is to be "behind the city," that is, to the west of Ai since the force will be approaching from the east.

³So Joshua and the whole army moved out to attack Ai. He chose thirty thousand of his best fighting men and sent them out at night ⁴with these orders: "Listen carefully. You are to set an ambush behind the city. Don't go very far from it. All of you be on the alert. ⁵I and all those with me will advance on the city, and when the men come out against us, as they did before, we will flee from them. ⁶They will pursue us until we have lured them away from the city, for they will say, 'They are running away from us as they did before.' So when we flee from them, ⁷you are to rise up from ambush and take the city. The LORD your God will give it into your hand. ⁸When you have taken the city, set it on fire. Do what the LORD has commanded. See to it; you have my orders."

⁹Then Joshua sent them off, and they went to the place of ambush and lay in wait between Bethel and Ai, to the west of Ai—but Joshua spent that night with the people.

¹⁰Early the next morning Joshua mustered his men, and he and the leaders of Israel marched before them to Ai. ¹¹The entire force that was with him marched up and approached the city and arrived in front of it. They set up camp north of Ai, with the valley between them and the city. ¹²Joshua had taken about five thousand men and set them in ambush between Bethel and Ai, to the west of the city. ¹³They had the soldiers take up their positions—all those in the camp to the north of the city and the ambush to the west of it. That night Joshua went into the valley.

The battle of Ai with its preparations and fighting is reported in detail. Other battles in the book of Joshua are skimmed over quickly. This shows that the book's aim is not to serve us the "whole pie" of Joshua's conquests. Its purpose is to teach spiritual truths by offering select "slices" of conquest history chosen by the Spirit of truth. He has chosen for our menu episodes that serve his teaching purposes. The aim of chapter 8 is to show that victory is certain and complete when the Lord's people follow him in covenant faith. Chapter 7 showed us the result of disobedience and the withdrawal of God's blessing.

In keeping with the Spirit's aim, verse 3 reports that Joshua and Israel obediently begin to carry out God's battle plan. Success is now in the making.

The carefully worked out plan should not escape our notice. Christians sometimes balk at following a mission strategy, a stewardship program, or a planned evangelism outreach. Less calculated approaches and spontaneity, it is implied, are more in harmony with God's way of operating. Our chapter shows that there are times when God's people will want to follow a definite strategy. There is nothing intrinsically holy about a haphazard approach to God's work.

Joshua sends out an ambush force west from Gilgal toward Ai. They march about 15 miles under the cover of night and lie in wait west of Ai toward Bethel. The next day Joshua and the main army march toward Ai and set up camp north of the city, in plain view of the enemy. That night Joshua and the army enter the valley separating their camp and Ai. They will serve as decoys. When the army of Ai attacks, Joshua's men will flee in feigned defeat. As the men of Ai pursue, the ambush force lurking west of Ai can charge in and take the unguarded city.

The general strategy and preparations are clear from the account. But a problem arises from the two different numbers given for the ambush force: "thirty thousand" in verse 3 and "about five thousand" in verse 12. There are several solutions to the apparent problem:

1. There may be a scribal error in one of the two verses. The commentator Keil says that five thousand is the correct figure. In ancient Hebrew, numbers were designated by letters of the alphabet. If Keil is correct, a copyist here substituted a *lamed* (el, *l*) for a *he*

(atch, *b*). Even our computer age has not eliminated problems in the transmission of numbers in publications. Remember that it is the Bible's original manuscripts (the so-called autographs) that are inerrant. A copyist, in a momentary lapse, could have caused a discrepancy.

2. Joshua may have appointed two ambush forces. Some Jewish commentators suggest that 5,000 troops camped close to the city and 30,000 farther away.

3. A single ambush force of 25,000 soldiers may have had the task of blocking a retreat while the remaining 5,000 attacked Ai.

While there may be some questions in our minds about the precise arrangements, there is no confusion in Israel's army under the directions of the Lord's general. The trap is set. Now Joshua, in the dark of night, triggers the action by entering the valley toward Ai with his main army.

¹⁴When the king of Ai saw this, he and all the men of the city hurried out early in the morning to meet Israel in battle at a certain place overlooking the Arabah. But he did not know that an ambush had been set against him behind the city. ¹⁵Joshua and all Israel let themselves be driven back before them, and they fled toward the desert. ¹⁶All the men of Ai were called to pursue them, and they pursued Joshua and were lured away from the city. ¹⁷Not a man remained in Ai or Bethel who did not go after Israel. They left the city open and went in pursuit of Israel.

¹⁸Then the Lord said to Joshua, "Hold out toward Ai the javelin that is in your hand, for into your hand I will deliver the city." So Joshua held out his javelin toward Ai. ¹⁹As soon as he did this, the men in the ambush rose quickly from their position

and rushed forward. They entered the city and captured it and quickly set it on fire.

²⁰The men of Ai looked back and saw the smoke of the city rising against the sky, but they had no chance to escape in any direction, for the Israelites who had been fleeing toward the desert had turned back against their pursuers. ²¹For when Joshua and all Israel saw that the ambush had taken the city and that smoke was going up from the city, they turned around and attacked the men of Ai. ²²The men of the ambush also came out of the city against them, so that they were caught in the middle, with Israelites on both sides. Israel cut them down, leaving them neither survivors nor fugitives. ²³But they took the king of Ai alive and brought him to Joshua.

The ploy works without a flaw but not because Joshua is so clever and Israel so powerful. Success comes because it is the Lord's plan and his blessing rests on his obedient people.

The author mentions some precise details of the battle site. That may indicate that he is an eyewitness or that he is using a report of an eyewitness in his inspired account. The army of Ai enters battle at a point "overlooking the Arabah." The term *Arabah* usually refers to the part of the Great Rift Valley where the Dead Sea rests. Here it may mean the part of the valley near Ai that broadens out into a wilderness plain. Israel makes a mock retreat "toward the desert." The Hebrew literally says "toward the *road* of the desert." This may be a reference to an ancient desert highway running eastward toward the Jordan.

Verse 17 reveals that the army of Bethel unites with Ai to repulse Israel. Bethel (house of God) is usually identified with the Arab village of Beitin. It lies about two miles northwest of Ai.

Bethel and Ai are also named side by side in Genesis 12:8. There we hear that Abraham pitched his tent "with

Bethel on the west and Ai on the east." That note comes soon after the Lord first promised Abraham the land and blessings for all nations through his special offspring (Genesis 12:1-7). Later, Bethel is where Abraham's grandson Jacob dreamed his famous ladder dream (Genesis 28:10-22) in which the Lord renewed the covenant promises first given to Abraham. The mention of Bethel in verse 17 is thus significant. Israelites reading the name Bethel could recall the Lord's land promise there and see its fulfillment unfolding *at the very same site!* The reference to Bethel implies that the Lord is faithful in keeping his promises, the land is now being given, and the Promised One will come and bless all peoples on earth.

In Joshua 12:16, the king of Bethel is listed as one of the conquered kings of the land. Since Bethel's defeat is not related anywhere else in Joshua, its king is perhaps captured together with the king of Ai in the battle before us.

At the critical moment in the battle, when Ai and Bethel are unguarded, it is time for a special symbol and signal. The Lord himself commands Joshua to hold his javelin out toward Ai. Once more it is clear that the Lord is in charge. He is orchestrating the battle. It will be his victory. The javelin in Joshua's hand is a picture of the city now in Israel's grasp. It also symbolizes the impending destruction of that city.

But the javelin is more than a symbol. It is the trigger that sends the ambush force into action. The distance involved makes it difficult to think that the leader of the ambush could actually see the raised javelin. Perhaps the javelin touched off a series of prearranged signals that reached the leader. Or perhaps the author is hinting at a miracle of timing when he says, "As soon as he did this, the men in the ambush rose quickly."

Joshua holds out his javelin toward Ai

Notice the parallel between Joshua holding out the javelin and the scene of Moses holding up his hands for victory over the Amalekites (Exodus 17:10-13). Joshua holds the position that the great Moses once held. He deserves the respect and obedience once given to Moses. The Lord is continuing to exalt Joshua in the people's eyes.

The ambush force captures the unguarded city and sets it ablaze. The smoke against the sky signals Joshua's main force to turn from its mock retreat. The armies of Ai and Bethel are caught in the middle. The author's language emphasizes that victory is total. The enemy is cut down without survivors or fugitives. Only Ai's king is taken alive.

²⁴When Israel had finished killing all the men of Ai in the fields and in the desert where they had chased them, and when every one of them had been put to the sword, all the Israelites returned to Ai and killed those who were in it. ²⁵Twelve thousand men and women fell that day—all the people of Ai. ²⁶For Joshua did not draw back the hand that held out his javelin until he had destroyed all who lived in Ai. ²⁷But Israel did carry off for themselves the livestock and plunder of this city, as the LORD had instructed Joshua. ²⁸So Joshua burned Ai and made it a permanent heap of ruins, a desolate place to this day. ²⁹He hung the king of Ai on a tree and left him there until evening. At sunset, Joshua ordered them to take his body from the tree and throw it down at the entrance of the city gate. And they raised a large pile of rocks over it, which remains to this day.

The "cherem" orders are carried out at Ai as they were at Jericho. The city and its people are given over to the Lord by total destruction. We may shudder at the carnage of 12,000 men and women that day. But the lesson must not be lost. We see at Ai, as we saw at Jericho, a stark scene of how utter rejection of the Lord's grace ends. The population of the city is destroyed but, as the Lord had instructed earlier, Israel carries off Ai's livestock and plunder.

The raised javelin is critical for the victory. That symbol, ordered by God, stresses that the victory is by his powerful hand and is his gift to Israel as they obey in covenant faith.

We hear for a second time that Ai is burned (verse 28). At Ai's first capture it was burned by the ambush force (verse 19), signaling Joshua's troops to turn and attack. Now Joshua himself burns the city as part of the orders to give it over totally to the Lord by destruction. In the Hebrew, two different expressions are used for the burning to show the different purposes. Burning of the conquered cities is mentioned only in regard to Jericho, Ai, and Hazor (11:11).

Ai means "the ruin." Even before Joshua's destruction of the city, ancient ruins may have rested on the site to give its name. Now he makes Ai "a *permanent* heap of ruins." The Hebrew word translated as "heap of ruins" is *tel*. That word is used today for the rounded mounds on Israel's landscape that hide ancient debris. The Arabic spelling for such a mound is t-e-l-l. It is easy to see why et-Tell is the site commonly identified as Ai. Both the name and the location near Bethel suggest the connection.

The author accents the desolation of the site even more when he says that "the ruin" (Ai) is not only a tel but "a desolate place to this day." The first readers of the book of Joshua could walk to the site and see the desolate mound of sand over the debris. The familiar phrase "to this day" once again expresses the historical reality of the Lord's total victory at Ai. The author of Joshua writes of real events, not folk legends.

Verse 23 records that the king of Ai was taken alive. The author does not reveal how he was killed. The hanging of the king in verse 29 does not refer to his execution but to the public display of his lifeless body. (See Deuteronomy

21:22.) His body was perhaps impaled on a wooden pole or "tree." The law demanded that a body could not be left hanging overnight (Deuteronomy 21:23). Joshua removes it at sunset. He applies Israel's law even in the case of this heathen king, testimony to his respect for the dignity of a human being who was created in God's image.

A fifth stone memorial appears in Canaan when the king's body is placed at the city gate and a large pile of rocks is raised over it. Like the mound over the city, the rocks over the king's body remain "to this day," to the day of the writing of Joshua. The memorial broadcasts a warning to all who think they can defy the Lord of the universe. At the same time, it speaks of the success of the Lord's people, who cherish his covenant and find in him their victory.

Joshua knows the source of success. In a spirit of joy, he and the entire nation trek 20 miles north for a special three-part ceremony at Mounts Ebal and Gerizim.

The covenant renewed at the two mountains

The background for this passage is Deuteronomy chapters 11, 27, and 28. There Moses commanded that when God would bring the nation across the Jordan, Israel should (1) copy the words of the law, the covenant stipulations, on large stones and set them on Mount Ebal; (2) build an altar on Ebal and offer sacrifices to the Lord; and (3) proclaim covenant blessings from Mount Gerizim and curses from Mount Ebal.

[30]Then Joshua built on Mount Ebal an altar to the LORD, the God of Israel, [31]as Moses the servant of the LORD had commanded the Israelites. He built it according to what is written in the Book of the Law of Moses—an altar of uncut stones, on which no iron tool had been used. On it they offered to the LORD burnt offerings and sacrificed fellowship offerings.

After the victories at Jericho and Ai, we might expect Israel to keep on striking enemies "while the iron is hot." But success will not vanish if time is taken for devotion. The people are still unsettled—without houses and fields. But first things first!

The idea that we should wait to put our spiritual life in order until we are established in our new community, school, or employment finds no support in the Bible. "Seek first his kingdom" (Matthew 6:33) is illustrated in these verses.

The utter defeat of Ai makes Israel's hold on the center of the land secure for the moment. The whole nation, including women, children, and aliens, can make the 20-mile walk due north up the backbone of the land without fear.

Some interpreters see a problem here. They think this episode is out of chronological order and belongs at the end of the book. They assume Israel could not have assembled peacefully in the heart of the land without more extensive conquests. But the adverb *then* at the beginning of this section connects this episode with what has just been told. The mental state of the enemies after the Ai massacre is probably the same as after the Jordan crossing: "Their hearts melted and they no longer had the courage to face the Israelites" (5:1). The Lord takes care of security problems so his people can have time for spiritual renewal.

The site in these verses is striking not only for its security; it is also historically significant. It was here that the Lord first promised Abraham, "To your offspring I will give this land" (Genesis 12:7). Shechem, the place of that promise, sits between Mounts Gerizim and Ebal in the hill country soon to be allotted to Ephraim, Joshua's tribe. Abraham had built an altar to the Lord there immediately after the promise.

Now Joshua, with God's land-promise being fulfilled, builds an altar to the Lord on Mount Ebal near Abraham's historical site, as Moses had commanded.

The act links Israel with the *Abrahamitic covenant,* which promised Israel its land and the world its Savior. The act also ties Israel to the *Mosaic covenant,* which guaranteed the nation a prosperous life in the Land of Promise if its stipulations were kept.

Joshua builds his altar exactly as Moses had commanded. It is made with uncut fieldstones "on which no iron tool had been used." (Compare verse 31 with Deuteronomy 27:5,6.) Why no iron tools? Perhaps to eliminate any hint that this altar is an idol. Or perhaps because iron was associated with swords and war, and this is a time of covenant peace between God and his people. Joshua is still in the Bronze Age, but iron tools and weapons are already in common use.

In 1980 an archaeological survey found an altar on the northeastern side of Mount Ebal. It is made of large uncut fieldstones. The fill within the altar structure held bones of young male bulls, sheep, goats and fallow deer—sacrificial animals. This prompted the immediate question "Could this be the altar Joshua built?" The altar has been dated to the early Iron Age, 1220–1000 B.C. That would seem to make it at least two centuries too late for the early date of Joshua.

On the newly made altar, Israel "offered to the LORD burnt offerings and sacrificed fellowship offerings." Again, the author is showing how the people are following Moses' commands in every detail (Deuteronomy 27:6,7).

Burnt offerings are described in Leviticus chapter 1. The sacrificed animal was a perfect bull, ram, or male bird. The animal was completely burned up. The Hebrew word for this kind of sacrifice means "going up." A burnt offering made *atonement* for unintentional sins and also expressed *total devotion* to the Lord. After the Achan episode, we can appreciate the rich meaning of Israel's atonement at this time.

Fellowship offerings (or peace offerings) are described in Leviticus chapters 3 and 7. Any perfect animal from the flock or herd could be offered. All the fat was offered to the Lord by burning it, but the meat was eaten in a communal meal. Fellowship offerings expressed *thanksgiving* and *peace* between God and man. The Hebrew name for this offering is related to the Hebrew greeting *shalom,* which means "peace" or "wholeness."

Moses directed the first Israelites in the Land of Promise to eat the fellowship offerings "*rejoicing* in the presence of the LORD your God" (Deuteronomy 27:7). If we think of Old Testament offerings only as solemn ceremonies, we will fail to appreciate the joy that radiates from Mount Ebal this thank-filled day.

The offerings from Joshua's altar on Mount Ebal point to the altar of the cross on Calvary. There, about 25 miles south of Ebal, "God was reconciling the world to himself in Christ" (2 Corinthians 5:19). Old Testament sacrifices served as pictures of the atonement earned by Jesus on the cross (Hebrews 10).

In Deuteronomy chapter 27, Moses' order to copy the law on stones comes first. Joshua now carries out that command after the sacrifices.

³²There, in the presence of the Israelites, Joshua copied on stones the law of Moses, which he had written. ³³All Israel, aliens and citizens alike, with their elders, officials and judges, were standing on both sides of the ark of the covenant of the LORD, facing those who carried it—the priests, who were Levites. Half of the people stood in front of Mount Gerizim and half of them in front of Mount Ebal, as Moses the servant of the

LORD had formerly commanded when he gave instructions to bless the people of Israel.

From Moses' orders we learn more details about the copying of the law. The author assumes we know the commands of Deuteronomy 27:1-4. The stones are large, big enough to serve as monuments, since they are to be set up on Mount Ebal. The stones are first coated with plaster. The number of stones is not revealed.

Joshua copies the Law of Moses on the wet plaster covering the stones. Notice that the law is not in oral form. Joshua already has it in written form from the hand of Moses. It is kept beside the ark of the covenant (Deuteronomy 31:26). Joshua does not need to add or interpret a syllable, only to copy.

What portion of the Law of Moses does Joshua copy? Various ideas have been offered: (1) perhaps the whole Torah, the first five books of the Bible; (2) maybe just parts of the law such as the Ten Commandments, the book of Deuteronomy, or the blessings and curses from Deuteronomy; (3) perhaps all the purely law sections of Moses' five books, excluding the historical narratives and the genealogies.

According to a Jewish tradition in the Talmud, Joshua copied the Law of Moses in 70 languages so that all the people of the world could read it. Even if Joshua made just one copy, it must have been a long but meaningful ceremony observed by all Israel. This was no 50-minute service. The writing of the sacred law emphasizes that the covenant law of the Lord is now the law of the new land he is giving.

The prominence of God's ark of the covenant during this ceremony shows that this is a covenant renewal ceremony. All Israel, every level of its own people together with aliens now associating with them, is formally surrendering itself to the covenant rule of the Lord in the new land.

The arrangement is like this: the priests with the ark stand in the middle of the valley between Mount Ebal to the north and Mount Gerizim to the south; six tribes stand before Mount Ebal and six before Gerizim (Deuteronomy 27:12,13). Two million or more pairs of eyes fix on the ark of the covenant and contemplate their chosen status as people with whom God has made a sacred contract.

The view from 2,849-foot Gerizim and 3,077-foot Ebal is panoramic and magnificent. From both mountains one can see most of the frame the Lord placed around the Land of Promise in Joshua 1:4: the snows on Mount Hermon in Lebanon to the north; the Mediterranean to the west; the hills around Jerusalem to the south; the green Jordan valley and the mountains of Gilead to the east. On a clear day, all are in plain view. What a fitting place to renew the holy pledge between Israel and the Lord!

In this land, Jesus, the land's heir (Galatians 3:16), will establish a new covenant with all people by his blood. Near where the ark of the covenant stands between the mountains, he will speak with a Samaritan woman at Jacob's well and say: "Whoever drinks the water I give him will never thirst. Indeed, the water I give him will become in him a spring of water welling up to eternal life" (John 4:14). Everything that Joshua and Israel are doing—the taking of the land, the sacrificing, the copying of the law—is a prelude. It leads to the day the Savior will live in that land, keep the law in our place, and offer himself as the sacrifice of atonement for our eternal life.

The altar has been built and sacrifices made. The law has been copied and the people are in place for the third part of the special confirmation service:

³⁴Afterward, Joshua read all the words of the law—the blessings and the curses—just as it is written in the Book of

133

the Law. ³⁵There was not a word of all that Moses had commanded that Joshua did not read to the whole assembly of Israel,
including the women and children, and the aliens who lived
among them.

Moses commanded this part of the ceremony twice
(Deuteronomy 11:29,30; 27; 28). Again, we learn additional
details from Moses' orders.

The valley between Gerizim and Ebal provides a natural
amphitheater with excellent acoustics. Everyone must be
able to hear the reading of the law. Verse 34 says that
Joshua is the reader of the law, while Moses had ordered
the Levites to read. It could be that both were involved. Or
perhaps Joshua commanded the Levites to recite and as
leader he is credited with being the reader.

Just a few weeks earlier, Moses had preached the law to
the nation. Now they hear it all again. We are reminded that
being disciples means *continuing* to delve into God's Word.
The Lord may have said some things just once. But by giving his Word in written form, he shows that we are to hear
again and again what he has spoken for our blessing.

The blessings are read and the six tribes on Mount
Gerizim thunder their amens. Gerizim is the mountain of
blessing perhaps because it stands at the right when facing east, the ancient direction of orientation (*to orient* literally means to "face east"). The right side is considered
the fortunate or blessing side. Some of the words of
blessing read like this:

> The LORD will establish you as his holy
> people, as he promised you on oath, if you
> keep the commands of the LORD your God
> and walk in his ways. Then all the peoples on
> earth will see that you are called by the name
> of the LORD, and they will fear you. The LORD

will grant you abundant prosperity—in the fruit of your womb, the young of your livestock and the crops of your ground—in the land he swore to your forefathers to give you.

The LORD will open the heavens, the store-house of his bounty, to send rain on your land in season and to bless all the work of your hands. You will lend to many nations but will borrow from none. (Deuteronomy 28:9-12)

From Numbers 6:27, we see what it means to bless. It means to put the name of the Lord on his people and to apply his gracious promises to those people as they find themselves in their helpless condition.

After the reading of the blessings, the curses are read and the six tribes on Mount Ebal thunder their amens. Some of the curses read like this:

Cursed is the man who carves an image or casts an idol—a thing detestable to the LORD, the work of the craftsman's hands—and sets it up in secret. . . . Cursed is the man who dis-honors his father or his mother. . . . Cursed is the man who moves his neighbor's boundary stone. . . . Cursed is the man who withholds justice from the alien, the fatherless or the widow. (Deuteronomy 27:15-19)

If blessing means *applying* God's gracious name and promises, then cursing is the *withdrawing* of that name and those promises. We have a graphic picture of God's curse in the utter disaster at Ai.

Everyone deserves God's curse. But "Christ redeemed us from the curse of the law by becoming a curse for us" (Galatians 3:13). Matthew Henry suggests that if it had not been for Israel's sacrifices that pointed to Jesus' sacrifice, the curses pronounced on Mount Ebal would have been put into force immediately.

These blessings and curses from the mountains are not magic formulas that produce results by the mere sound of the words. Rather, God's people were to "take them to heart" to receive God's intended results (Deuteronomy 30:1-5). In the same way, mere Bible reading does not bless. Thoughtful meditation, treasuring and pondering, does.

Notice that the scope of the blessings and curses is Israel's life in the Promised Land. Through them the Lord is regulating the lives of his covenant people for their 1,400 years in the land, until the time came for him to make a new and permanent covenant in Jesus Christ. The preservation of his chosen nation with its promise of a Savior is the Lord's specific aim here.

The law is read to all who are part of Israel—women, men, children, and the aliens now among them. The Lord's covenant is with the whole nation, and everyone must know his will. No individual in Israel can say, "I had no way of knowing the Word of the Lord." This is no exclusive little clique. There are no thoughts of racism, sexism, or that God's Word is too difficult for children.

The presence of aliens is mentioned for a second time in verse 35 (see also verse 33). The true faith is for all nations, even during the years before the Lord gave the Savior of the nations. Racial purity is not the Lord's aim, even among his special nation. People such as Rahab the Canaanite and her extended family are part of Israel. Rahab gave up her gods for the living Lord and his covenant. She will become the ancestress of Israel's kings and even of the King of kings. Other aliens among Israel are the "many other people" who went up with them from Egypt (Exodus 12:38). The years the Israelites spent as aliens in Egypt were to give them tender hearts toward the aliens now among them (Deuteronomy 10:19).

The event at the two mountains in Israel's heartland must have been one of the most impressive confirmation services of all time. The world's largest football stadium could contain only a fraction of Israel's over two million worshipers. Think of the sound dynamics from over a million people on each mountain, responding to the reading with their booming, "Amen!" The spirit of this massive assembly is refreshing, as the Lord's people renew his covenant and shout approval to his rule.

Whether our own congregations are large or small, part of each worship service involves confirming God's new covenant with us. Confirmation is not a onetime event but a continuing amen to what God has given us through Christ. Jesus reminds us that the value of our inheritance is far greater than the land Israel received. He says: "Your Father has been pleased to give you the kingdom" (Luke 12:32). In great and small assemblies, "Let the Amen sound from his people again" . . . and again!

Besides covenant renewal, the ceremony at Ebal and Gerizim served to (1) express Israel's thankfulness; (2) witness to the living God in the heart of Canaan; (3) display God's protection with enemies still all around; (4) point to the sacrifice of the world's Redeemer through Israel's offerings; (5) show by what terms blessings in the land will come; (6) demonstrate consecration to the Lord during these fleeting golden years of Israel's spiritual life; and (7) give courage for the continuing conquest.

The Gibeonite deception

9 Now when all the kings west of the Jordan heard about these things—those in the hill country, in the western foothills, and along the entire coast of the Great Sea as far as Lebanon (the kings of the Hittites, Amorites, Canaanites, Periz-**

zites, Hivites and Jebusites)—²they came together to make war against Joshua and Israel.

These two verses serve as an introduction to chapters 9 through 11. The kings west of the Jordan are determined to stand up against Israel after hearing about Jericho, Ai, and the covenant renewal at the two mountains. But even as they plot to make war, the yet unpenned words of Psalm 2 hang over their heads:

> Why do the nations conspire
> and the peoples plot in vain?
> The One enthroned in heaven laughs;
> the Lord scoffs at them.
>
> (Psalm 2:1,4)

The political power in Canaan is in the hands of kings ruling independent city-kingdoms. The picture we see in these verses is reflected also in the Amarna Letters, written about this same time from Canaan (see introduction, page 9). To resist an invading nation, independent kings would have to swallow their individual pride and amass their combined might.

The author pinpoints the area ruled by these kings. At the same time, he gives us a short course in Canaan's geography. East to west, the western kings hold sway:

- in "the hill country"—the central mountain area; Jerusalem rests on this "backbone" of the land.
- in "the western foothills"—the lower hills between the Mediterranean coast and the hill country.
- along "the coast"—the long stretch of plain along the Mediterranean.

By listing the six nations, the author gives us a feeling for the strong opposition against Israel. We can also appreciate the security the Lord provided for the gathering at Ebal and Gerizim when we see what was lurking at the fringes of that peaceful place. All six nations, plus the Girgishites, were listed before. See the comments on page 55 for descriptions. The phrase "they came together" describes the *combined determination* of the kings. They never will muster their joint armies and actually come together physically.

³However, when the people of Gibeon heard what Joshua had done to Jericho and Ai, ⁴they resorted to a ruse: They went as a delegation whose donkeys were loaded with worn-out sacks and old wineskins, cracked and mended. ⁵The men put worn and patched sandals on their feet and wore old clothes. All the bread of their food supply was dry and moldy. ⁶Then they went to Joshua in the camp at Gilgal and said to him and the men of Israel, "We have come from a distant country; make a treaty with us."

The first word, *however,* contrasts the people of Gibeon with the six nations named previously. The Gibeonites are different in the way they face the Israelite threat. Israel's enemies have three options: flee, fight, or seek a treaty. Though the men of Gibeon are all good fighters and their city is bigger than Ai, they choose the last plan. They apparently have no king but base their government on a council of elders (see verse 11). Perhaps this explains why their plans are different from the king-led cities.

Gibeon (hill city) is eight miles northwest of Jerusalem and about the same distance southwest of Ai. The short distance between Gibeon and Ai indicates that the Gibeonites know well what has just happened there. Gibeon is identified with el-Jib, where handles from wine jars stamped with the name Gibeon were found. Items found from Joshua's time include flasks, lamps, and jugs. The pool of Gibeon, with its 79-step spiral staircase, hints that the city was famous for its water supply. The pool is mentioned in 2 Samuel 2:13.

The scheme of the Gibeonites might provoke a chuckle. They pretend to be a delegation from some distant land. Yet they are Hivites (verse 7) from a city just 20 miles down the road to the west of Israel's camp at Gilgal. Did a Gibeonite strategist in a panicky sweat lie awake late at night to plan this scheme? An elaborate ruse, convincing props, and a well-rehearsed troupe of ragtag actors! The scene before Joshua would be laughable if serious issues affecting Israel's future in the land were not at stake.

For the Gibeonites, it is a matter of life and death that their trick holds together. If the inspired author intends humor here, it is *serious* humor. The Gibeonites must have been aware of the regulations of Deuteronomy 20:10-18. Those words stipulate that cities at a distance from the Promised Land can be offered a peace treaty and their citizens allowed to live as forced laborers; but cities of the land itself must be destroyed. Hivites are specifically mentioned as people to "completely destroy" (Deuteronomy 20:17). And the Gibeonites are Hivites.

Joshua and all Israel know these regulations well. They have just reviewed them at the great confirmation service. So now they proceed with suspicion as the dusty delegation with moldy bread asks for a treaty.

⁷The men of Israel said to the Hivites, "But perhaps you live near us. How then can we make a treaty with you?"

⁸"We are your servants," they said to Joshua.

But Joshua asked, "Who are you and where do you come from?"

⁹They answered: "Your servants have come from a very distant country because of the fame of the LORD your God. For we have heard reports of him: all that he did in Egypt, ¹⁰and all that he did to the two kings of the Amorites east of the Jordan—Sihon king of Heshbon, and Og king of Bashan, who reigned in Ashtaroth. ¹¹And our elders and all those living in our country said to us, 'Take provisions for your journey; go and meet them and say to them, "We are your servants; make a treaty with us."' ¹²This bread of ours was warm when we packed it at home on the day we left to come to you. But now see how dry and moldy it is. ¹³And these wineskins that we filled were new, but see how cracked they are. And our clothes and sandals are worn out by the very long journey."

¹⁴The men of Israel sampled their provisions but did not inquire of the LORD. ¹⁵Then Joshua made a treaty of peace with them to let them live, and the leaders of the assembly ratified it by oath.

The author reveals that the Gibeonites are Hivites, people clearly listed among the nations to be destroyed. He wants us to appreciate the dilemma Israel will soon face.

At this point in the account, some critics see a difficulty in the text. They note that the Gibeonites first address Joshua; then the men of Israel speak to the delegation that are now called Hivites; then their dialogue is with Joshua again. The conclusion drawn is that two separate accounts, one with Joshua and the other with the men of Israel as spokesmen, have been spliced together. Finding the strains of a text thought to be woven together from opposing sources fills many pages of some commentaries on Joshua. But are there really problems here caused by conflicting sources? Can't the Gibeonites talk to Joshua as well as to the other men of Israel? Can't the author call them both Gibeonites and Hivites for variety and special emphasis? We need to let the text speak for itself and let ancient Hebrew writing move along in the style chosen by the Spirit.

It is natural for the Israelites to be suspicious, for they know all about deceit from their own ancestors. The very name Israelite suggests the elaborate scheme of Jacob (Israel) to get the blessing of his father Isaac (Genesis 27). There are also curious questions about the Gibeonite claims. If they come from a distant country, why are they afraid of Israel? And why are they so vague about their origin?

First the men of Israel quiz them. Then Joshua interrogates. The Gibeonites' answers again bring to our attention the well-rehearsed trick. Some new details emerge from their responses. Their homeland is now said to be "*very* distant." They present themselves now not as equals but as "servants" content to live under Israel if only a treaty will be ratified. It is "the fame of the LORD" that has led them to approach Joshua. There is no deception in this last detail except that they are careful not to mention that they know of the Lord's power displayed at nearby Jericho and Ai. If they do, they will show themselves to be people of the vicinity.

Every detail of their story suggests a long trip from far away. Their appearance also backs up the story. The men of Israel can even "taste" the distance by biting into the moldy bread that was warm from the oven the day they left their faraway land.

The ruse works. Israel's suspicions are laid aside after the men of Israel "sampled their provisions." That expression may mean that the Israelites inspected the Gibeonites' items to see if they backed up their story, or it may refer to eating the customary meal that sealed a treaty.

A sharp comment from the author says that Israel "did not inquire of the LORD." This is a serious matter. The author's inspired comment indicates that what Israel has done is naive and hasty—and wrong. The Lord's will has not been sought! The Lord's direction could have been received through the Urim and Thummim, the objects in the breastplate of the high priest. (See Exodus 28:30.) In Numbers 27:18-21, the Lord says directly that Joshua is to "obtain decisions" through Eleazar the priest "inquiring of the Urim before the LORD." Joshua and Israel may have acted *rationally* in the Gibeonite matter but not *spiritually*. This is the second time a weakness of Joshua is brought out (see 7:10).

We are reminded here that decisions may be wise and rational by human standards; yet, at the same time, they may be hasty and ill-advised unless the Lord's will is sought. Even after careful judgment, we are to say, "If it is the Lord's will, we will live and do this or that" (James 4:15). Not only good sense but God's will determines whether a decision is wise. We seek his will while making important decisions when we proceed humbly, determine whether our decision in any way opposes God's clear Word, let love for God and people motivate us, and pray for God's guidance and blessing. Like all good things the Lord has created, the decision-making process is also "consecrated by the word of God and prayer" (1 Timothy 4:5).

Joshua, as leader, makes the treaty. The Hebrew for "made a treaty" says literally "cut a covenant." The literal expression brings out the custom of sealing a treaty by cutting a sacrificed animal in half (Genesis 15:10,17,18). The practice may imply an oath such as, "May I also be cut if I break this pact." The agreement of Israel is called "a treaty of peace" (shalom) and a treaty "to let them live." It will be clear from the next chapter that these treaty terms imply more than nonaggression on Israel's part. Joshua is guaranteeing the safety of the Gibeonites and obligating himself to military support if they are threatened.

Joshua is not alone in the treaty-making process. Israel's leaders swear a solemn oath by the Lord to ratify the pact. That oath is critical for seeing the dilemma the nation must now grapple with.

¹⁶Three days after they made the treaty with the Gibeonites, the Israelites heard that they were neighbors, living near them. ¹⁷So the Israelites set out and on the third day came to their cities: Gibeon, Kephirah, Beeroth and Kiriath Jearim. ¹⁸But the Israelites did not attack them, because the leaders of the assembly had sworn an oath to them by the Lord, the God of Israel.

The whole assembly grumbled against the leaders, ¹⁹but all the leaders answered, "We have given them our oath by the Lord, the God of Israel, and we cannot touch them now. ²⁰This is what we will do to them: We will let them live, so that wrath will not fall on us for breaking the oath we swore to them." ²¹They continued, "Let them live, but let them be woodcutters and water carriers for the entire community." So the leaders' promise to them was kept.

We are not told precisely how Israel discovered the trickery. We learn only that three days after the treaty Israel "heard" the truth. The author emphasizes that the Gibeonites are nearby people who should have been destroyed; they are "neighbors" and "living near."

The matter is serious. Israel's action is prompt. They make the 20-mile march to Gibeon to confront the tricksters. For the first time, we learn that Gibeon is part of a larger federation of four cities. The predicament now looms larger. The leaders of Israel feel the quandary hanging heavy on them. It is they who swore the oath. The grumbling of the whole assembly, apparently concerned about the Lord's commands in Deuteronomy 20:10-18, makes the dilemma all the more unpleasant.

What is the dilemma? Israel did not carry out the Lord's order to completely destroy these people of the land. Israel's leaders made an oath "by the LORD, the God of Israel" to spare the Gibeonites and establish a treaty. Such an oath dare not be broken. The oath resulted from the Gibeonites' ruse.

Israel should have inquired of the Lord before taking the oath and making the treaty. Not only the trick but also Israel's failure has led to the predicament. Now, what to do? God's command says to *destroy* the Hivites, but the oath in God's name requires that the Israelites spare them.

Our verses do not claim to be laying down a general principle. They do not tell what to do when an oath has been taken after one party has not acted in good faith. The text does reveal how Israel chose to resolve the problem, a choice that God himself honored.

By standards of strict justice, the Israelites could make a strong case for not honoring the treaty once they learned of the deception. But strict justice is not their only concern. God's name is at the center of their decision.

They will let the Gibeonites live because they promised by God's name to do so. To break that oath would bring contempt upon God and his wrath on Israel. Their course of action does not ignore God's command to destroy the Hivites. In light of the oath, the Hivites cannot be conquered. But they *can* be put into a position that will not let them tempt Israel with idolatry. They will be Israel's servants at the Lord's tabernacle and later in the temple. This would be no small assignment, since the daily sacrifices and ceremonial washings there required a constant supply of wood and water. "Woodcutters and water carriers" will be the Gibeonites' lowly title. Two of the four Hivite cities have names which relate to the work they will do: Beeroth (wells) and Kiriath Jearim (woodsville).

> **²²Then Joshua summoned the Gibeonites and said, "Why did you deceive us by saying, 'We live a long way from you,' while actually you live near us? ²³You are now under a curse: You will never cease to serve as woodcutters and water carriers for the house of my God."**
> **²⁴They answered Joshua, "Your servants were clearly told how the Lord your God had commanded his servant Moses to give you the whole land and to wipe out all its inhabitants from before you. So we feared for our lives because of you, and that is why we did this. ²⁵We are now in your hands. Do to us whatever seems good and right to you."**
> **²⁶So Joshua saved them from the Israelites, and they did not kill them. ²⁷That day he made the Gibeonites woodcutters and water carriers for the community and for the altar of the Lord at the place the Lord would choose. And that is what they are to this day.**

There is a penalty for the Gibeonites' deception. The penalty is the "curse" of being servants. Yet the curse is not without blessings. They will be protected, and their service will be in God's house. Like Cain in Genesis 4:10-16, they will feel the curse, but they will also enjoy safety. It is interesting that the curse Noah had issued against Canaan centuries before is partially fulfilled in the lowly service of these Canaanites from Gibeon. Noah's curse had said:

> Cursed be Canaan!
> The lowest of slaves
> will he be to his brothers. (Genesis 9:25)

Fear, the Gibeonites tell Joshua, motivated their deception. After their explanation they place themselves into

Joshua's hands with no fight and no protest. Gibeon is an "important city" and "all its men were good fighters" (Joshua 10:2). Yet here they say to Joshua, "Do to us whatever seems good and right to you." All this is evidence of the Lord's work. He is keeping his promise. No one is able to stand up against Joshua (1:5). This time Joshua doesn't even have to swing a sword to see that promise fulfilled.

The author states that the Gibeonites are still woodcutters and water carriers "to this day." That often-used expression suggests some distance between the events of chapter 9 and the time of writing. The book is evidently written before the temple was built, as the words "the place the LORD *would* choose" imply. The tabernacle and its altar moved from Gilgal to Shiloh to Nob and finally to the hometown of the servants of the altar, Gibeon. When Solomon built the temple in Jerusalem, about 950 B.C., the Gibeonites' service must have continued there. The comments of verse 27 give clues to the time of the writing of the book of Joshua.

The Lord honored Israel's treaty with the Gibeonites. That is clear from 2 Samuel chapter 21. There we learn that Saul ignored the treaty and tried to annihilate the Gibeonites. The Lord answered Saul's sin with three years of famine during David's reign.

In Psalm 15, David asks the Lord, "Who may live on your holy hill?" (verse 1). Part of the answer is "He . . . who keeps his oath *even when it hurts*" (verse 4). Joshua's ninth chapter reminds us not only to be careful about what we promise but also to do what we say we will, *even when it is hard*. Keeping promises for the Lord's sake is part of being *light* in the world, which Jesus says Christians are. People often rationalize promise breaking and claim, "I didn't really know what I was getting myself into." A powerful witness radiates from the child of God who follows through on a hard-to-keep oath. Promises kept by a Christian are small reflections of God's promises kept for the world's salvation at the high cost of Christ's death.

Israel soon has the opportunity to show that it will keep its oath to the Gibeonites even when it hurts.

The sun stands still

10 Now Adoni-Zedek king of Jerusalem heard that Joshua had taken Ai and totally destroyed it, doing to Ai and its king as he had done to Jericho and its king, and that the people of Gibeon had made a treaty of peace with Israel and were living near them. ²He and his people were very much alarmed at this, because Gibeon was an important city, like one of the royal cities; it was larger than Ai, and all its men were good fighters. ³So Adoni-Zedek king of Jerusalem appealed to Hoham king of Hebron, Piram king of Jarmuth, Japhia king of Lachish and Debir king of Eglon. ⁴"Come up and help me attack Gibeon," he said, "because it has made peace with Joshua and the Israelites."

⁵Then the five kings of the Amorites—the kings of Jerusalem, Hebron, Jarmuth, Lachish and Eglon—joined forces. They moved up with all their troops and took up positions against Gibeon and attacked it.

The kings of the land now have a new reason to dread Israel. Not only have the Lord's people destroyed Jericho and Ai. But now a formidable city, Gibeon, has made a treaty with Israel. Together they present a mighty problem.

This fear of the Israelites is amazing. Just recently they had wandered in the desert as a band of people without a homeland. The Lord, in keeping his promises, has forced a dramatic change.

The name Jerusalem occurs for the first time in the Bible in verse 1. The city was mentioned earlier in Genesis 14:18

under the name Salem. Apart from the Bible, early references to Jerusalem are found in the Ebla Tablets of about a thousand years before Joshua and in the Amarna Letters of about his time. The meaning of *Jerusalem* is not certain. The last part of the name, *salem,* refers to "peace," as in shalom. *Jeru* is disputed. It perhaps means "foundation" or "dwelling." "Dwelling of peace" may be the meaning of the name. The site may have been considered a place of peaceful dwelling because of its high position on the mountain range that runs up the center of the land. In Judges 19:10,11, Jerusalem is called Jebus after its inhabitants, the Jebusites.

The king of Jerusalem, unlike what the name of his city suggests, no longer thinks of himself as dwelling in a safe place. Both he and his people are alarmed at the sudden changes in Canaan brought about by Israel. The king's name, Adoni-Zedek, means "my lord is righteous" or "lord of righteousness." His name is similar to that of an earlier king and priest of Jerusalem, Melchizedek (Genesis 14:18). His name meant "my king is righteous" or "king of righteousness." Both names are perhaps official titles.

Adoni-Zedek's fear makes sense. Gibeon is just eight miles northwest of Jerusalem, and Israel's camp at Gilgal, only 20 miles down the road to the northeast. Israel and the Gibeonites, "living near" one another, could team up in a hurry against Jerusalem. The thought of the kings of Jericho and Ai impaled on trees would not bring peace of mind either. Add to that the knowledge that all of Gibeon's men are "good fighters." The fact that Gibeon apparently has no king does not detract from its military potential.

Some interpreters suggest that Gibeon, without a king, may be under the jurisdiction of the king of Jerusalem. That would further explain his alarm and quick reaction to the Gibeon-Israel treaty.

Adoni-Zedek appeals for help to the kings of cities southwest of Jerusalem. He gathers a league of five to negate the five that make up the Israel-Gibeon pact. The newly formed league of five are called Amorite kings. The name means "the high one" and may be a reference to their living in the mountain areas. "Amorite" is used in a broad and a narrow sense. In its broader sense, it means all the early inhabitants of Canaan. In its narrower sense, it refers to the people of the hills as opposed to the people along the coast.

By listing the Amorite kings and cities twice, the author accents the amassed military force facing Gibeon. Teaming up with the king of Jerusalem are the kings of these cities:

Hebron—The name means "alliance," befitting the context; later it is also called Kiriath Arba (20:7). It is 20 miles southwest of Jerusalem. Abraham had once settled there (Genesis 13:18). It was the first city of Canaan entered by Joshua and the other 11 spies sent out by Moses (Numbers 13:22).

Jarmuth—It is 16 miles west and slightly south of Jerusalem. The name means "height," in keeping with its commanding position that overlooks the coastal plain.

Lachish—Its site is 25 miles southwest of Jerusalem. At Joshua's time Lachish is a provincial capital of the Egyptian empire; it guards the southernmost invasion corridor to Jerusalem.

Eglon—Located seven miles southwest of Lachish, it is positioned to overlook a valley near the place where the hill country and coastal plain meet.

The tension mounts as the armies of the five Amorite cities move into position against Gibeon and begin their assault. The Amorites apparently are afraid to confront Israel head-on. They first go after her weaker ally.

⁶**The Gibeonites then sent word to Joshua in the camp at Gilgal: "Do not abandon your servants. Come up to us quickly and save us! Help us, because all the Amorite kings from the hill country have joined forces against us."**

⁷**So Joshua marched up from Gilgal with his entire army, including all the best fighting men. ⁸The LORD said to Joshua, "Do not be afraid of them; I have given them into your hand. Not one of them will be able to withstand you."**

Joshua has the perfect opportunity to avenge the Gibeonites' trickery that led to the treaty. He could let the five kings slaughter them. But he has sworn by the Lord's name and will keep the oath even when it hurts.

In begging "Save us!" the Gibeonites use the same Hebrew word that is a part of Joshua's name. His name means "the Lord saves." In Hebrew the cry "Save us, Joshua!" would be "Hoshea, Yehoshua!" They have asked the right man for help, a man associated with the living Lord who can save, and a man who keeps his word. Similar cries for help would be raised to the one who is both Lord and Savior, the one whose name is the Greek form of Joshua: "Jesus, Son of David, have mercy on me!" (Luke 18:38); "Lord, save us!" (Matthew 8:25); "Jesus, remember me when you come into your kingdom" (Luke 23:42).

Joshua's response shows that the treaty involves defense and is more than an agreement not to attack Gibeon. He never hesitates but gathers his best forces and makes the 20-mile, all-night march from Gilgal to Gibeon.

Joshua shows himself to be the kind of friend everyone would like to have. And the kind of friend we should be! He also serves to picture his namesake, Jesus—the friend of sinners who laid down his life for friends and enemies alike.

The Lord's encouragement shows that he has approved of Joshua's treaty with the Gibeonites and wants him to honor it. The encouragement is similar to other words of the Lord spoken to inspire Joshua: "Do not be terrified" (1:9); "I have delivered Jericho into your hands" (6:2); "No one will be able to stand up against you" (1:5).

We also need to hear God's encouragement regularly for the specific challenges we face. The person who turns away and says, "I've heard all that before," may find him- or herself without strength at a time of crisis.

⁹**After an all-night march from Gilgal, Joshua took them by surprise. ¹⁰The LORD threw them into confusion before Israel, who defeated them in a great victory at Gibeon. Israel pursued them along the road going up to Beth Horon and cut them down all the way to Azekah and Makkedah. ¹¹As they fled before Israel on the road down from Beth Horon to Azekah, the LORD hurled large hailstones down on them from the sky, and more of them died from the hailstones than were killed by the swords of the Israelites.**

¹²**On the day the LORD gave the Amorites over to Israel, Joshua said to the LORD in the presence of Israel:**

> **"O sun, stand still over Gibeon,**
> **O moon, over the Valley of Aijalon."**
> ¹³ **So the sun stood still,**
> **and the moon stopped,**
> **till the nation avenged itself on its enemies,**

as it is written in the Book of Jashar.

The sun stopped in the middle of the sky and delayed going down about a full day. ¹⁴There has never been a day like it before or since, a day when the LORD listened to a man. Surely the LORD was fighting for Israel!

¹⁵**Then Joshua returned with all Israel to the camp at Gilgal.**

The 20-mile night march from Gilgal would take perhaps eight to ten hours. It may have been aided by moonlight, as hinted by the reference to the moon in verse 12. It was a difficult march up and over Canaan's central mountain ridge, a rise of 3,000 feet from Gilgal. Even after the hard, fast march and without a night's sleep, Joshua catches the Amorites by surprise and conquers them in a great victory at Gibeon.

The author shows clearly that *the Lord* is the cause of the total victory: "The LORD threw them into confusion before Israel." "The LORD hurled large hailstones down on them from the sky." "The LORD gave the Amorites over to Israel." "Surely the LORD was fighting for Israel!"

When the routed enemy tries to flee downhill to the northwest, Israel follows along the sharply descending Beth Horon road. Then, when the fleeing Amorites head south toward the lower hills, Israel continues to cut them down all the way to Azekah and Makkedah southwest of Jarmuth. What Israel's swords cannot do, the Lord's hand accomplishes fully.

The author saves the most striking detail of the battle for his summary of the victory: the sun stood still for about a day! That information is introduced in the quotation from Joshua's prayer. The first readers of the book of Joshua already know that prayer since it was included in the Book of Jashar, or "book of the righteous." That book was a collection of poems singing the praises of Israel's heroes. The collection was evidently added to as time went by. David's lament over Saul and Jonathan was later included in the same book according to 2 Samuel 1:18. The Book of the Wars of the LORD was another similar collection (Numbers 21:14). Both of these books are long lost.

Joshua's words are a prayer to the Lord, but within that prayer he addresses the sun and moon directly. He perhaps speaks his prayer in the early morning after the all-night march with the sun and moon both visible. His place of

The Lord hurled large hailstones down on them

prayer seems to be west of the city from where he sees the sun to the east "over Gibeon" and the moon to the west "over the Valley of Aijalon," a wide basin west of Gibeon. "Pointing like a pistol at the heart of Judea,"[10] the Valley of Aijalon provides the easiest approach to the mountains and to Jerusalem, 14 miles southeast.

The battle may have begun about dawn with Israel's surprise attack. Then, some time into the battle, Joshua may have been concerned whether there would be enough daylight to complete the victory. Made bold by the Lord's promises, he prays. The Lord "listened," and in response to his prayer, "the sun stopped in the middle of the sky and delayed going down about a full day." When the Bible speaks of the sun standing still, it is not making a scientific statement, as if to say that the sun circles the earth instead of the other way around. Rather, it is using everyday language as we do when we speak of the sun rising and setting.

Much discussion centers on precisely what did happen that day. Many commentators flatly deny the supernatural event. Some point to the poetic language of the account and say that the writer is expressing in figurative terms that Israel was able to pack about two days of fighting into one. Some speak of an electrical storm that flashed its lightning all night so that it almost seemed like two straight days. Some point to the volcanic eruption of the Island of Santorini of about 1400 B.C. and relate its fallout to the hailstones that killed the fleeing Amorites.

Among interpreters who fully acknowledge God's supernatural act, there are various ideas about the nature of the miracle. Many questions can be raised. Did the earth suddenly stop rotating on its axis? Did the rotation slow down to about half its normal rate? Did God cause a special refraction of the sun's rays so that even after sunset its light remained bright? Did he tilt the earth so that the Middle East became "the land of the midnight sun"? Was the miracle just local or universal? Is it possible that God prolonged the darkness for Israel's surprise attack so that we should speak of "the long night" instead of "the long day?" (The Hebrew word for "stand still" in verse 12 means literally "to be silent" or "to cease." Could the sun's light have ceased, as a few suggest?)

Questions about the details may abound. But this we know: God intervened in a spectacular fashion to give his people a mighty victory. "Surely the LORD was fighting for Israel!"

This day is unique not only because the Lord made the sun stand still. It is unique also because the Lord performed this amazing act *in response to Joshua.* "The LORD listened to a man." We need not think of Joshua presuming to make demands of almighty God in his prayer. Rather, we see him as a man who knew God's promises of victory, a man who trusted God's grace and power, a man who was not afraid to ask for God's help.

Joshua's bold prayer should encourage us to approach God's throne of grace with confidence. The same God who once made the sun stand still at a man's request listens to our prayers! He has complete authority over the universe to do as he pleases for the good of his people. We are not trapped in a system that came about by accident and is run only by laws of nature. We are under the care of him who made and rules the sun and everything else. And he is pleased to listen and answer!

We can be especially bold in prayer when we know that the eternal Joshua, Jesus, is the one listening to our requests and that he is the head over everything for the good of his church (Hebrews 4:14-16; Ephesians 1:22).

> You are coming to a king—
> Large petitions with you bring,

> For his grace and power are such,
> None can ever ask too much. (CW 409:2)

The fact that the Lord responded to Joshua's bold prayer brings honor to Joshua. Just as at the Jordan miracle, the Lord lets his leader share in his glory this day. He is continuing to exalt Joshua so that all Israel will revere and obey him throughout the conquest. Respect for leaders works for the advantage of all.

Verse 15 says that Joshua and all Israel went back to their camp at Gilgal. From what follows, it seems that could not have happened quite yet. The problem is solved if verse 15 continues the quote from the Book of Jashar or if it is a statement that anticipates what actually comes later.

Five Amorite kings killed

¹⁶Now the five kings had fled and hidden in the cave at Makkedah. ¹⁷When Joshua was told that the five kings had been found hiding in the cave at Makkedah, ¹⁸he said, "Roll large rocks up to the mouth of the cave, and post some men there to guard it. ¹⁹But don't stop! Pursue your enemies, attack them from the rear and don't let them reach their cities, for the LORD your God has given them into your hand."

²⁰So Joshua and the Israelites destroyed them completely—almost to a man—but the few who were left reached their fortified cities. ²¹The whole army then returned safely to Joshua in the camp at Makkedah, and no one uttered a word against the Israelites.

²²Joshua said, "Open the mouth of the cave and bring those five kings out to me." ²³So they brought the five kings out of the cave—the kings of Jerusalem, Hebron, Jarmuth, Lachish and Eglon. ²⁴When they had brought these kings to Joshua, he summoned all the men of Israel and said to the army commanders who had come with him, "Come here and put your feet on the necks of these kings." So they came forward and placed their feet on their necks.

²⁵Joshua said to them, "Do not be afraid; do not be discouraged. Be strong and courageous. This is what the LORD will do to all the enemies you are going to fight." ²⁶Then Joshua struck and killed the kings and hung them on five trees, and they were left hanging on the trees until evening.

²⁷At sunset Joshua gave the order and they took them down from the trees and threw them into the cave where they had been hiding. At the mouth of the cave they placed large rocks, which are there to this day.

Notice the contrast between 9:1,2, in which the kings of the land are coming together to oppose Joshua, and now. Those same kings have fled and are cringing in a cave. The cave is at Makkedah, a city mentioned earlier in verse 10. From that reference we can assume that Makkedah is in the vicinity of Azekah, but its exact location is unknown.

While the once-mighty kings are stopped up in the cave, like bugs in a corked bottle, the pursuit continues. The quote from the Book of Jashar may have made it sound like the battle account of that day had come to an end. But now the day's events continue.

Joshua sets up camp at Makkedah. He remains there as the army sweeps on to pursue and slay all but a few who reach their fortified cities. Then the whole army returns safely to the Makkedah camp.

The words "no one uttered a word against the Israelites" are fascinating. The Hebrew reads literally: "did not sharpen its tongue against the Israelites." The idea is that Israel is completely unopposed! This is what has come of all the mighty opposition. No one even dares speak anything against God's people, to say nothing of trying something. The Lord of the covenant has made good on his promise to the fullest extent: "I have given them into your hand. Not one of them will be able to withstand you" (10:8).

"Put your feet on the necks of these kings."

When the five kings are brought out of the cave, their cities are named for the third time in the chapter. This time, as the names are mentioned, the cities no longer sound unconquerable.

Joshua follows the usual practice of placing feet on the necks of the defeated kings bowing before him. Assyrian art illustrates this same ritual of war. This public display of the Amorites' defeat will inspire Israel to continue the conquest with courage. This is how all battles under the Lord will end. Joshua's words of encouragement in verse 25 show that this is his aim.

The execution of the kings is like that of the kings of Jericho and Ai. It is by God's command, and it is his judgment on those who opposed his people and tried to block the fulfillment of his promise.

Another stone memorial takes shape as the kings' bodies are put in the cave and large rocks are heaped up at its mouth. Like the previous memorials, this one also can be inspected by the first readers of Joshua, since it is there "to this day."

Southern cities conquered

²⁸That day Joshua took Makkedah. He put the city and its king to the sword and totally destroyed everyone in it. He left no survivors. And he did to the king of Makkedah as he had done to the king of Jericho.

²⁹Then Joshua and all Israel with him moved on from Makkedah to Libnah and attacked it. ³⁰The LORD also gave that city and its king into Israel's hand. The city and everyone in it Joshua put to the sword. He left no survivors there. And he did to its king as he had done to the king of Jericho.

³¹Then Joshua and all Israel with him moved on from Libnah to Lachish; he took up positions against it and attacked it. ³²The LORD handed Lachish over to Israel, and Joshua took it on the

second day. The city and everyone in it he put to the sword, just as he had done to Libnah. ³³Meanwhile, Horam king of Gezer had come up to help Lachish, but Joshua defeated him and his army—until no survivors were left.

³⁴Then Joshua and all Israel with him moved on from Lachish to Eglon; they took up positions against it and attacked it. ³⁵They captured it that same day and put it to the sword and totally destroyed everyone in it, just as they had done to Lachish.

³⁶Then Joshua and all Israel with him went up from Eglon to Hebron and attacked it. ³⁷They took the city and put it to the sword, together with its king, its villages and everyone in it. They left no survivors. Just as at Eglon, they totally destroyed it and everyone in it.

³⁸Then Joshua and all Israel with him turned around and attacked Debir. ³⁹They took the city, its king and its villages, and put them to the sword. Everyone in it they totally destroyed. They left no survivors. They did to Debir and its king as they had done to Libnah and its king and to Hebron.

Israel topples the major cities of the south in rapid succession. The quickened pace of the narrative helps emphasize the swift victories.

All of the conquered cities except Hebron are located in the *shephelah,* or western foothills. Hebron is located on the central ridge. The site of Debir is uncertain.

The names of seven cities appear. The number is perhaps significant. Its symbolic sense of completeness may be implied. Three of the cities—Lachish, Eglon, and Hebron—were part of the five-city league. The two other cities of that pact—Jerusalem and Jarmuth—are not mentioned.

Lachish does not fall until "the second day" of siege, evidence of its strength. Seven hundred years later, King Sennacherib of Assyria had trouble taking Lachish. In 586 B.C. it was one of the last cities to fall to Nebuchadnezzar of Babylonia. The famous Lachish Letters, written on broken pottery, are correspondence from the military commander of Lachish in the days when Nebuchadnezzar was closing in on Jerusalem. Joshua's victory at Lachish stresses the Lord's might against this strategic city.

Throughout the southern campaign, it is the Lord, the author makes clear, who is providing the total victory. "The LORD also gave [Libnah] and its king into Israel's hand. . . . The LORD handed Lachish over to Israel." At the same time, the author does not belittle Israel's actions in the conquest: "They took up positions . . . attacked . . . captured . . . totally

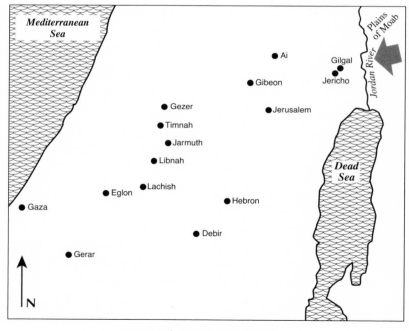

Southern campaign

destroyed." God wants his people, made confident by faith, to be active in his work. And he blesses their efforts.

Israel is careful to follow the Lord's orders. That is brought out by the repetition of the Hebrew word *cherem*. It appears four times in these verses, where it is translated as "totally destroyed." As noted in the NIV footnote, the word is a technical term that "refers to the irrevocable giving over of things or persons to the LORD, often by totally destroying them." The Lord had commanded the application of the cherem to Canaan's cities in Deuteronomy 20:16-18.

⁴⁰So Joshua subdued the whole region, including the hill country, the Negev, the western foothills and the mountain slopes, together with all their kings. He left no survivors. He totally destroyed all who breathed, just as the LORD, the God of Israel, had commanded. ⁴¹Joshua subdued them from Kadesh Barnea to Gaza and from the whole region of Goshen to Gibeon. ⁴²All these kings and their lands Joshua conquered in one campaign, because the LORD, the God of Israel, fought for Israel.

⁴³Then Joshua returned with all Israel to the camp at Gilgal.

These verses are a summary of the southern campaign. The area taken is described twice: once by its four geographical areas (verse 40) and again by its farthest points (verse 41). The hill country and western foothills have been mentioned before (9:1). The Negev, which literally means "dry" and came to mean "south," is the large southern area of rolling hills that leads into desert. The oasis of Beersheba is on the northern boundary of the Negev. The meaning of "the mountain slopes" is debated. They may be the slopes of the Judean mountains as they descend toward the Dead Sea, or they may be the slopes descending toward the west, leading to the western foothills.

The four points on the extreme borders of this area are *Kadesh Barnea,* deep in the Negev, about 50 miles south of Beersheba; *Gaza,* near the coast in the northwest of this southern area; *the region of Goshen,* evidently in the eastern Negev, not to be confused with the Goshen of Egypt, though perhaps named after it; and *Gibeon,* the northeastern boundary of the designated area, 8 miles northwest of Jerusalem. Kadesh Barnea to Gaza is the south to north line in the western section, and Goshen to Gibeon is the south to north line in the eastern part of the conquered territory.

The author stresses that Israel took all of this land *"in one campaign."* About a third of Canaan has been taken before Israel returns to camp at Gilgal. Apparently no occupation force is left behind to keep a tight grip on the new territory. Some areas will have to be recaptured when the land is distributed. Other sections of the south have not yet been taken (13:1-5). But that does not detract from the smashing success of this campaign in which "the LORD . . . fought for Israel."

Northern cities defeated

11 When Jabin king of Hazor heard of this, he sent word to Jobab king of Madon, to the kings of Shimron and Acshaph, ²and to the northern kings who were in the mountains, in the Arabah south of Kinnereth, in the western foothills and in Naphoth Dor on the west; ³to the Canaanites in the east and west; to the Amorites, Hittites, Perizzites and Jebusites in the hill country; and to the Hivites below Hermon in the region of Mizpah. ⁴They came out with all their troops and a large number of horses and chariots—a huge army, as numerous as the sand on the seashore. ⁵All these kings joined forces and made camp together at the Waters of Merom, to fight against Israel.

Chapters 10 and 11 begin the same way. A king hears of Israel's great victories and gathers a coalition force. This time the king is in the north. His city is the most impressive of all that Joshua has faced. The king is Jabin. The name is probably a title, like Pharaoh, since it is also used for a later king of Hazor (Judges 4).

Hazor is nine miles north of the Sea of Galilee and five miles southwest of Lake Huleh. Its strategic location on the Via Maris, or "Way of the Sea," an ancient superhighway, made it a commercial giant. Since it overlooked the approach to Canaan from the north, it also had major military significance. Hazor's area was much larger than the cities of the south. Excavations at the site have revealed a 30-acre "tell," or mound, for the city itself and a 175-acre plateau just to the north that was also inhabited. The site may have been home for 40,000 or more residents.

To add to his own great strength, Jabin gathers the combined forces of the kings of a wide area. Verses 4 and 5 underscore the amassed strength that Israel now faces. For the first time in Joshua, chariots are mentioned. Chariots were introduced to this part of the world about 1800 B.C. and by 1500 B.C. were a major element of military might. Since the next verses will speak of burning these chariots, their construction must have been mostly of wood. (It has been suggested that these iron chariots had only iron axles.) Iron chariots will be mentioned later in the book (17:16). The combined army is "huge." The historian Josephus offers these figures: 300,000 infantry, 10,000 cavalry, and 20,000 chariots. They gather at the Waters of Merom, thought to be near Meron on a 4,000-foot high plateau a few miles northwest of Hazor. This high terrain does not seem ideal for maneuvering chariots that are effective only on the plains.

⁶The LORD said to Joshua, "Do not be afraid of them, because by this time tomorrow I will hand all of them over to Israel, slain. You are to hamstring their horses and burn their chariots."

⁷So Joshua and his whole army came against them suddenly at the Waters of Merom and attacked them, ⁸and the LORD gave them into the hand of Israel. They defeated them and pursued them all the way to Greater Sidon, to Misrephoth Maim, and to the Valley of Mizpah on the east, until no survivors were left. ⁹Joshua did to them as the LORD had directed: He hamstrung their horses and burned their chariots.

As in 10:8, the Lord's encouragement comes just before battle. We are reminded again of our need to keep focused on the Lord's promises as we face life's many challenges.

Victory will be swift, says the Lord, in spite of what faces Israel. In 24 hours all will be accomplished.

At Ai the Lord had provided the tactic of ambush. Here again he gives specific orders concerning the battle: "Hamstring their horses and burn their chariots." Cutting the tendon at the joint of a horse's hind leg would render the animal useless for war but still suitable for domestic chores. The Lord does not want the defeated army to rise and fight again another day. He may also be keeping Israel from using these horses and chariots in the future. He wants them to rely on his promises rather than on instruments of war. Psalm 33:17 will later remind Israel, "A horse is a vain hope for deliverance; despite all its great strength it cannot save."

Joshua may have been on the move from Gilgal northward before the enemy gathered. It is possible that other unmentioned battles preceded this one. Yet the surprise element in Joshua's attack at the Waters of Merom is evident by the word *suddenly*.

The victory is total, because "the LORD gave them into the hand of Israel." The fleeing enemy is pursued to the northwest toward the Mediterranean ("to greater Sidon" and "to Misrephoth Maim") and to the northeast ("to the Valley of Mizpah on the east").

¹⁰**At that time Joshua turned back and captured Hazor and put its king to the sword. (Hazor had been the head of all these kingdoms.) ¹¹Everyone in it they put to the sword. They totally destroyed them, not sparing anything that breathed, and he burned up Hazor itself.**

¹²**Joshua took all these royal cities and their kings and put them to the sword. He totally destroyed them, as Moses the servant of the LORD had commanded. ¹³Yet Israel did not burn any of the cities built on their mounds—except Hazor, which Joshua burned. ¹⁴The Israelites carried off for themselves all the plunder and livestock of these cities, but all the people they put to the sword until they completely destroyed them, not sparing anyone that breathed. ¹⁵As the LORD commanded his servant Moses, so Moses commanded Joshua, and Joshua did it; he left nothing undone of all that the LORD commanded Moses.**

After the pursuit of the fleeing armies, Joshua turns toward the city whose king mustered the opposition. The great importance of Hazor is emphasized in this comment: "Hazor had been *the head* of all these kingdoms." Joshua applies the Lord's "cherem" and totally destroys this center of commerce and military might. Like Jericho and Ai, Hazor is burned up. Excavations at the site reveal destruction and burning at about 1400, 1300, and 1230 B.C. The 1400 B.C. evidence is in line with the early date of Joshua's conquest.

The "cherem" is also carried out on the other king-led cities of the north. But with a difference. Their mounds, or tells, are not burned like Hazor. Israel could inhabit these cities and fulfill the Lord's promise of living in "large, flourishing cities you did not build" (Deuteronomy 6:10). Of all the conquered cities, burning is mentioned only in connection with Jericho, Ai, and Hazor.

Joshua's total obedience to God's commands by Moses is highlighted in verse 15. The Lord's covenant promises are laid hold of as Joshua fully obeys those commands. Moses wrote of Joshua that, more than 40 years earlier, he

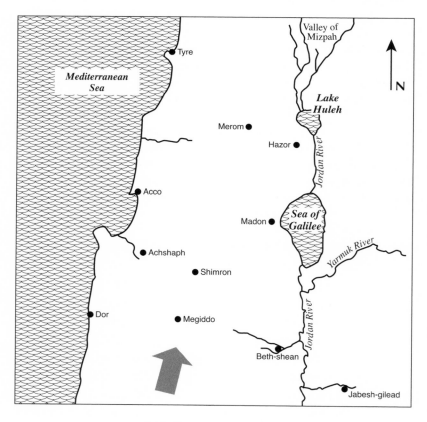

Northern campaign

"followed the LORD wholeheartedly" (Numbers 32:12). His obedience has not wavered. "He left nothing undone."

Victories reviewed

¹⁶**So Joshua took this entire land: the hill country, all the Negev, the whole region of Goshen, the western foothills, the Arabah and the mountains of Israel with their foothills, ¹⁷from Mount Halak, which rises toward Seir, to Baal Gad in the Valley of Lebanon below Mount Hermon. He captured all their kings and struck them down, putting them to death. ¹⁸Joshua waged war against all these kings for a long time. ¹⁹Except for the Hivites living in Gibeon, not one city made a treaty of peace with the Israelites, who took them all in battle. ²⁰For it was the LORD himself who hardened their hearts to wage war against Israel, so that he might destroy them totally, exterminating them without mercy, as the LORD had commanded Moses.**

²¹**At that time Joshua went and destroyed the Anakites from the hill country: from Hebron, Debir and Anab, from all the hill country of Judah, and from all the hill country of Israel. Joshua totally destroyed them and their towns. ²²No Anakites were left in Israelite territory; only in Gaza, Gath and Ashdod did any survive. ²³So Joshua took the entire land, just as the LORD had directed Moses, and he gave it as an inheritance to Israel according to their tribal divisions. Then the land had rest from war.**

These verses together with chapter 12 close out the conquest portion of Joshua. Not all battles have been related, only those that serve the Spirit's teaching aim. The author pauses to review the victories before moving on to the distribution of the land.

The geographical terms of verse 16 we have seen before. Verse 17 is a sweeping summary of the entire area taken from south to north. Mount Halak (bald mountain) is east of Kadesh Barnea and southwest of Beersheba. Seir is the mountain range south of the Dead Sea on the east side of the Arabah, or Great Rift. Those terms mark the southern extremity. The precise location of Baal Gad in the north is uncertain. It is somewhere in the Valley of Lebanon that separates the Lebanon and Anti-Lebanon mountains. Mount Hermon ends the Anti-Lebanon range.

Joshua's conquest has continued "for a long time." About seven years is an estimate based on references to Caleb's age. According to 14:7, Caleb was 40 years old when the 38 years of desert wandering began (Deuteronomy 2:14). That makes him 78 when Israel crossed the Jordan. According to 14:10, he is 85 when the years of intensive conquest seem to be over. Thus the seven years.

Just how Canaan's cities would react to Israel in those years was determined by God. "The Lord himself hardened their hearts to wage war against Israel." Forty years earlier he had hardened Pharaoh's heart (Exodus 4:21). The Lord did not predestine either the Canaanites or Pharaoh to destruction (Ezekiel 18:32; 2 Peter 3:9). God's hardening of their hearts was a later judgment on their utter refusal to respond to him. In their hardened attitude of hate toward God and his people, the Canaanites could do nothing else but fight. God used that attitude for the good of his people.

If the Canaanites had not fought, Israel might have spared them. Then all around the people of promise would be the seductive menace of Canaanite idolatry with its baals and Astartes and their rituals of sex and magic. Verse 20 stresses that the destruction of the Canaanites was by God's design, not by fate or because of the greed of land-hungry Israelites.

The destruction of the Anakites is underscored probably because they were the ones Israel had especially dreaded after the report of the 12 spies. Fear of those people of great size had caused the 38 years of desert wandering.

(See Numbers 13:28,33.) Those fears, the author now shows, were groundless because of God's promise. When Joshua acted under that promise, the Anakites were swept out of Israelite territory. Some survived only in three of the five Philistine cities: Gaza, Gath, and Ashdod.

Even giant fears vanish as we take God at his word and rest in his strength!

The land the Lord is giving as Israel's inheritance has rest from war. This does not mean that Israel has absolute control over all parts of the land, as chapter 13 will attest. It suggests that Joshua has "hamstrung" the Canaanites. They no longer have the might or the will to organize resistance. All the kings of the land that dared to fight have been crushed.

Chapter 12 gives a list of the defeated kings, beginning with the two kings east of the Jordan conquered under Moses.

12 **These are the kings of the land whom the Israelites had defeated and whose territory they took over east of the Jordan, from the Arnon Gorge to Mount Hermon, including all the eastern side of the Arabah:**

²Sihon king of the Amorites,
> **who reigned in Heshbon. He ruled from Aroer on the rim of the Arnon Gorge—from the middle of the gorge—to the Jabbok River, which is the border of the Ammonites. This included half of Gilead. ³He also ruled over the eastern Arabah from the Sea of Kinnereth to the Sea of the Arabah (the Salt Sea), to Beth Jeshimoth, and then southward below the slopes of Pisgah.**

⁴And the territory of Og king of Bashan,
> **one of the last of the Rephaites, who reigned in Ashtaroth and Edrei. ⁵He ruled over Mount Hermon, Salecah, all of Bashan to the border of the people of Geshur and Maacah, and half of Gilead to the border of Sihon king of Heshbon.**

⁶Moses, the servant of the LORD, and the Israelites conquered them. And Moses the servant of the LORD gave their land to the

Reubenites, the Gadites and the half-tribe of Manasseh to be their possession.

The combined territories of the kings Sihon and Og stretch from the Arnon Gorge in the south to Mount Hermon in the north. The Arnon Gorge runs east to west and empties its waters into the Sea of the Arabah (Dead Sea) at about its midpoint. The western limit of the kings' land is the Arabah, the rift that includes the Sea of Kinnereth (Galilee), the Jordan Valley, and the Dead Sea. The eastern boundary is marked by the Arabian desert. See the map on page 258 for the more specific place names.

Numbers 21:21-35 tells of Moses' defeat of Sihon and Og. Numbers chapter 32 relates how their land came under the possession of the Reubenites, Gadites, and the half-tribe of Manasseh.

⁷These are the kings of the land that Joshua and the Israelites conquered on the west side of the Jordan, from Baal Gad in the Valley of Lebanon to Mount Halak, which rises toward Seir (their lands Joshua gave as an inheritance to the tribes of Israel according to their tribal divisions—⁸the hill country, the western foothills, the Arabah, the mountain slopes, the desert and the Negev—the lands of the Hittites, Amorites, Canaanites, Perizzites, Hivites and Jebusites):

⁹ the king of Jericho	one
the king of Ai (near Bethel)	one
¹⁰ the king of Jerusalem	one
the king of Hebron	one
¹¹ the king of Jarmuth	one
the king of Lachish	one
¹² the king of Eglon	one
the king of Gezer	one
¹³ the king of Debir	one
the king of Geder	one

¹⁴ the king of Hormah	one
the king of Arad	one
¹⁵ the king of Libnah	one
the king of Adullam	one
¹⁶ the king of Makkeda	one
the king of Bethel	one
¹⁷ the king of Tappuah	one
the king of Hepher	one
¹⁸ the king of Aphek	one
the king of Lasharon	one
¹⁹ the king of Madon	one
the king of Hazor	one
²⁰ the king of Shimron Meron	one
the king of Acshaph	one
²¹ the king of Taanach	one
the king of Megiddo	one
²² the king of Kedesh	one
the king of Jokneam in Carmel	one
²³ the king of Dor (in Naphoth Dor)	one
the king of Goyim in Gilgal	one
²⁴ the king of Tirzah	one

thirty-one kings in all.

Most of these names we have seen before. Others are mentioned here for the first time, showing that the conquest narrative was not intended to be a complete record but, rather, a historical overview.

Why is this bare catalog of names included in the Bible? With one sweep of the eye, we are able to see that the Lord toppled a long list of Israel's foes to fulfill his promises. Not 31 kings, or even 31 million, can keep the King of kings from using this land, his land, to establish his eternal kingdom.

PART THREE

The Land Is Allotted
(13:1–21:45)

A summary of the geography of Canaan/Israel is helpful at the start of these nine chapters of boundary descriptions.

The shape and size of Canaan are comparable to the state of New Hampshire. Reaching from Mount Hermon to the Negev and from the Mediterranean to the edge of the Arabian Desert, the area covers approximately 10,000 square miles. About three-fifths of the land lies west of the Jordan.

The following are the natural geographical units as outlined in *The Geography of the Bible* by Denis Baly.

1. *The plains west of the Jordan:* coastal plains of Asher, Sharon, and Philistia; the central valleys of Jezreel and Esdraelon; and the *Shephelah,* or western foothills.

2. *The western highlands:* Upper and Lower Galilee, the basin of Manasseh, the Carmel range, the Dome of Ephraim, and the hill country of Judah.

3. *The Great Rift Valley:* the Huleh Basin, the Sea of Galilee, the Jordan Valley; the Dead Sea, and the Arabah south of the Dead Sea.

4. *The Plateau of Trans-Jordan:* area east of the Jordan divided by four rivers—the Yarmuk, the Jabbok, the Arnon, and the Zered; regions include from north to south Bashan, Gilead, Ammon, Moab, and Edom.

5. *The deserts:* eastern deserts and the Negev.

What spiritual value do nine chapters filled with boundary descriptions hold? A grateful psalmist who knows chapters 13 to 21 of Joshua relates some of their worth when he writes: "The boundary lines have fallen for me in pleasant places; surely I have a delightful inheritance. I will praise the LORD" (Psalm 16:6,7).

This same psalmist also prophesied of the One who gives the land its greatest meaning. After his life and death in the land, the Savior says to the Father through the psalmist, "You will not abandon me to the grave, nor will you let your Holy One see decay" (verse 10). For Christians, Israel's borders find their ultimate value as the place where Jesus gave himself to build his eternal kingdom. Jesus' sandals crossed Israel's turf. In its river he was baptized and on its lake he once walked. He died on one of its hills outside its greatest city. He stepped alive from one of its rock-hewn tombs and ascended to heaven from one of its mountains. With Jesus in focus, descriptions of his workplace are not dry details but living words that touch us. The whole book of Joshua with its conquests and descriptions steers toward Jesus' day.

Land still to be taken

13 When Joshua was old and well advanced in years, the LORD said to him, "You are very old, and there are still very large areas of land to be taken over.

²This is the land that remains: all the regions of the Philistines and Geshurites: ³from the Shihor River on the east of Egypt to the territory of Ekron on the north, all of it counted as Canaanite (the territory of the five Philistine rulers in Gaza, Ashdod, Ashkelon, Gath and Ekron— that of the Avvites); ⁴from the south, all the land of the Canaanites, from Arah of the Sidonians as far as Aphek, the region of the Amorites, ⁵the area of the Gebalites; and all

175

Lebanon to the east, from Baal Gad below Mount Hermon to Lebo Hamath.

⁶"As for all the inhabitants of the mountain regions from Lebanon to Misrephoth Maim, that is, all the Sidonians, I myself will drive them out before the Israelites. Be sure to allocate this land to Israel for an inheritance, as I have instructed you, ⁷and divide it as an inheritance among the nine tribes and half of the tribe of Manasseh."

Assuming that Joshua is somewhat older than Caleb, he may be in his 90s as the Lord speaks. Caleb is 85 (14:10). Joshua was already an old, but vigorous, man when the conquest began.

The Lord has given many victories. But "very large areas" in the southwest and far north are still unclaimed. Even these lands are to be allotted. The Lord is not now withdrawing his support. He is continuing to encourage Joshua and promises to keep on driving out the enemies.

The Philistines are mentioned in Joshua only here. At least some of them arrived on the southern coast of Canaan about 1200 B.C. as part of a later wave of Sea People from islands in the Aegean (Jeremiah 47:4; Amos 9:7). Their power in Canaan was concentrated in their five city-states on a narrow strip of coastland, the Philistine Plain. Palestine, the later name for all of Canaan, comes from the name Philistine. These people were a menace to Israel for many years and were not subdued until David's time. Goliath was one of their celebrated heroes.

The Geshurites are in the extreme southwest.

Verses 4 and 5 relate the unconquered northern territories. The Gebalites are inhabitants of the northern coastal city of Gebal near present-day Beirut. Another name for their city is Byblos (book) from which we get our word *Bible;*

writing material was exported from Byblos and provided its name.

The two and a half tribes east of the Jordan already possess their inheritance. New allotment involves only the remaining nine and a half tribes.

Division of the land east of the Jordan

⁸The other half of Manasseh, the Reubenites and the Gadites had received the inheritance that Moses had given them east of the Jordan, as he, the servant of the Lord, had assigned it to them.

> **⁹It extended from Aroer on the rim of the Arnon Gorge, and from the town in the middle of the gorge, and included the whole plateau of Medeba as far as Dibon, ¹⁰and all the towns of Sihon king of the Amorites, who ruled in Heshbon, out to the border of the Ammonites. ¹¹It also included Gilead, the territory of the people of Geshur and Maacah, all of Mount Hermon and all Bashan as far as Salecah—¹²that is, the whole kingdom of Og in Bashan, who had reigned in Ashtaroth and Edrei and had survived as one of the last of the Rephaites. Moses had defeated them and taken over their land. ¹³But the Israelites did not drive out the people of Geshur and Maacah, so they continue to live among the Israelites to this day.**

First, the eastern territory as a whole is delineated. The limits south to north are the city of Aroer on the Arnon River to the slopes of Mount Hermon.

¹⁴But to the tribe of Levi he gave no inheritance, since the offerings made by fire to the Lord, the God of Israel, are their inheritance, as he promised them.

Towns and pastures will be set aside for the Levites (Joshua 21). But the Levites will not receive a tribal inheritance, except the offerings promised them in Deuteronomy 18:1-8. They will be well provided for even without a land allotment. The same information about Levi is repeated in verses 13:33; 14:3,4; and 18:7. The repetition stresses the fact that though landless, Levi is not slighted and belongs to Israel as do the 12 tribes with land.

¹⁵**This is what Moses had given to the tribe of Reuben, clan by clan:**

¹⁶**The territory from Aroer on the rim of the Arnon Gorge, and from the town in the middle of the gorge, and the whole plateau past Medeba ¹⁷to Heshbon and all its towns on the plateau, including Dibon, Bamoth Baal, Beth Baal Meon, ¹⁸Jahaz, Kedemoth, Mephaath, ¹⁹Kiriathaim, Sibmah, Zereth Shahar on the hill in the valley, ²⁰Beth Peor, the slopes of Pisgah, and Beth Jeshimoth ²¹—all the towns on the plateau and the entire realm of Sihon king of the Amorites, who ruled at Heshbon. Moses had defeated him and the Midianite chiefs, Evi, Rekem, Zur, Hur and Reba— princes allied with Sihon—who lived in that country. ²²In addition to those slain in battle, the Israelites had put to the sword Balaam son of Beor, who practiced divination. ²³The boundary of the Reubenites was the bank of the Jordan. These towns and their villages were the inheritance of the Reubenites, clan by clan.**

Reuben holds the southern portion of the land east of the Jordan: from Aroer up to Heshbon, the former capital of King Sihon.

²⁴**This is what Moses had given to the tribe of Gad, clan by clan:**

²⁵**The territory of Jazer, all the towns of Gilead and half the Ammonite country as far as Aroer, near Rabbah; ²⁶and from Heshbon to Ramath Mizpah and Betonim, and from Mahanaim to the territory of Debir; ²⁷and in the valley, Beth Haram, Beth Nimrah, Succoth and Zaphon with the rest of the realm of Sihon king of Heshbon (the east side of the Jordan, the territory up to the end of the Sea of Kinnereth). ²⁸These towns and their villages were the inheritance of the Gadites, clan by clan.**

The middle section belongs to Gad. Its southern boundary begins where Reuben's ends. Its northern limits are difficult to determine with certainty because of problems locating some places named.

²⁹**This is what Moses had given to the half-tribe of Manasseh, that is, to half the family of the descendants of Manasseh, clan by clan:**

³⁰**The territory extending from Mahanaim and including all of Bashan, the entire realm of Og king of Bashan—all the settlements of Jair in Bashan, sixty towns, ³¹half of Gilead, and Ashtaroth and Edrei (the royal cities of Og in Bashan). This was for the descendants of Makir son of Manasseh—for half of the sons of Makir, clan by clan.**

³²**This is the inheritance Moses had given when he was in the plains of Moab across the Jordan east of Jericho. ³³But to the tribe of Levi, Moses had given no inheritance; the LORD, the God of Israel, is their inheritance, as he promised them.**

Half of Manasseh has received this northern part of Trans-Jordan. The rest of the tribe's land will be west of the river.

The author is careful to show that these eastern tribes received their lands through Moses. They have a legitimate claim on them and are not to be considered second-class citizens because their land is across the river from Canaan proper.

The three tribes have the same father, Jacob, but different mothers: Reuben was the son of Leah; Gad, of the maidservant Zilpah; and Manasseh, the grandson of Rachel through her son Joseph.

Division of the land west of the Jordan

14 Now these are the areas the Israelites received as an inheritance in the land of Canaan, which Eleazar the priest, Joshua son of Nun and the heads of the tribal clans of Israel allotted to them. ²Their inheritances were assigned by lot to the nine-and-a-half tribes, as the LORD had commanded through Moses. ³Moses had granted the two-and-a-half tribes their inheritance east of the Jordan but had not granted the Levites an inheritance among the rest, ⁴for the sons of Joseph had become two tribes—Manasseh and Ephraim. The Levites received no share of the land but only towns to live in, with pasturelands for their flocks and herds. ⁵So the Israelites divided the land, just as the LORD had commanded Moses.

The often repeated word *inheritance* emphasizes that the tribal lands are gifts from God because of his promise. Israel has not earned them.

The distribution "by lot" stresses that the Lord is guiding the whole procedure. Eleazar, the high priest who succeeded Aaron, was in charge of casting the lots. The Urim and Thummim in his priestly breastplate may have been used. (See Exodus 28:30 and Numbers 27:21.) Jewish tradition in the Talmud speaks of two urns, one containing the names of the tribes and the other containing boundary descriptions. After shaking each of them well, it is said, a tribe name and land description came up in Eleazar's hand. We can only speculate on the procedure.

Jacob had officially adopted his two grandsons, Ephraim and Manasseh (Genesis 48:5). That would have led to a 13-part division of the land if Levi had received an allotment.

The allotment account starts and ends with special grants of land to the two men who had been faithful spies 45 years earlier. The first grant is to Caleb (14:13); the latter, to Joshua (19:49,50).

Hebron given to Caleb

⁶Now the men of Judah approached Joshua at Gilgal, and Caleb son of Jephunneh the Kenizzite said to him, "You know

what the Lord said to Moses the man of God at Kadesh Barnea about you and me. ⁷I was forty years old when Moses the servant of the Lord sent me from Kadesh Barnea to explore the land. And I brought him back a report according to my convictions, ⁸but my brothers who went up with me made the hearts of the people melt with fear. I, however, followed the Lord my God wholeheartedly. ⁹So on that day Moses swore to me, 'The land on which your feet have walked will be your inheritance and that of your children forever, because you have followed the Lord my God wholeheartedly.'

¹⁰"Now then, just as the Lord promised, he has kept me alive for forty-five years since the time he said this to Moses, while Israel moved about in the desert. So here I am today, eighty-five years old! ¹¹I am still as strong today as the day Moses sent me out; I'm just as vigorous to go out to battle now as I was then. ¹²Now give me this hill country that the Lord promised me that day. You yourself heard then that the Anakites were there and their cities were large and fortified, but, the Lord helping me, I will drive them out just as he said."

¹³Then Joshua blessed Caleb son of Jephunneh and gave him Hebron as his inheritance. ¹⁴So Hebron has belonged to Caleb son of Jephunneh the Kenizzite ever since, because he followed the Lord, the God of Israel, wholeheartedly. ¹⁵(Hebron used to be called Kiriath Arba after Arba, who was the greatest man among the Anakites.)

Then the land had rest from war.

Joshua is still at Gilgal for this first part of the distribution, described in chapters 14 to 17. Later it will be from Shiloh that he gives the land (18:1).

Men of Judah approach Joshua when Caleb makes his request. Caleb himself is associated with the tribe of Judah (Numbers 13:6). But there is some question whether he is a Judahite by blood or by adoption. The Kenizzites, from whom he seems to come, were Canaanites (Genesis 15:19). Perhaps the name Kenizzite is used of various people and sometimes of a clan of Judah. The other men of Judah with Caleb probably come to support his request.

Caleb serves well as a focus of study on the character of a man of God. As a spy at age 40, he took God at his word, stood alone with Joshua, and urged the capture of Canaan (Numbers 13:30; 14:6-9). He followed the Lord "wholeheartedly" (Numbers 14:24; Deuteronomy 1:36) and acted on the convictions of his heart built up by the Lord's promises. As an 85-year-old man, he now gives full credit to God for his strength and vigor and wants a challenge to use his gifts. He requests for his inheritance not a secure and lazy valley but the hill country around Hebron where he will have to deal with the Anakites. His courage shines as he rests on God's promises. His words "the Lord helping me" show both his faith and his humility. He finds his strength in the Lord's help and promise of success.

Today, when real heroes are scarce, we should not fail to direct our children to men of faith like Caleb. His attitude is also a refreshing model for "seniors." By the year 2030, over one-fifth of the population of the United States. will be over age 65. Many will be in excellent health. What potential the church has if we, like Caleb, give productive retirement years to the Lord's service! If church leaders fail to tap the talents of seniors, how refreshing if seniors themselves step forward like Caleb and ask for a challenge!

Caleb's references to his age help us with a *chronology* of his life and of the years of conquest. He was 40 years old when sent out as a spy from Kadesh Barnea. Since the spies were deployed about two years after the exodus, Caleb was 38 when Israel left Egypt. If the exodus took place in 1446 B.C. (see the introduction), then Caleb was born in 1484 B.C. in Egypt. He would have been 78 when Israel crossed the Jordan, 40 years after the exodus. Since he is

85 when the land is allotted, Israel's conquest of Canaan must have lasted seven years, perhaps 1406–1399 B.C.

Moses' promise to Caleb is found in Deuteronomy 1:36. Caleb's words in verse 9 show that Moses also swore an oath with that promise.

Caleb's request does not directly mention Hebron, only the "hill country." When Joshua grants the request and gives him Hebron, we are to understand that this means "the fields and villages around the city" (21:12). Hebron itself will be a city for priests and a city of refuge (21:13).

Hebron is about 25 miles south of Jerusalem on the road to Beersheba in the hill country of Judah. It had historical significance already at Joshua's time. Abraham had purchased the cave of Machpelah near there as a burial vault for his family (Genesis 23:19,20).

Joshua had driven the Anakites from Hebron (11:21,22), but some must have filtered back into their old city and presented a challenge for Caleb. The other name for Hebron, Kiriath Arba, means "city of Arba," after the greatest of the Anakites.

As in Joshua 11:23, these verses close with the statement "Then the land had rest from war." The words provide a transition to the main distribution. There will be many new challenges coming up. But for now peace prevails for the allotting of the land.

Allotment for Judah

15 **The allotment for the tribe of Judah, clan by clan, extended down to the territory of Edom, to the Desert of Zin in the extreme south.**

²Their southern boundary started from the bay at the southern end of the Salt Sea, ³crossed south of Scorpion Pass, continued on to Zin and went over to the south of Kadesh Barnea. Then it ran past Hezron up to Addar and

curved around to Karka. ⁴It then passed along to Azmon and joined the Wadi of Egypt, ending at the sea. This is their southern boundary.

⁵The eastern boundary is the Salt Sea as far as the mouth of the Jordan.

The northern boundary started from the bay of the sea at the mouth of the Jordan, ⁶went up to Beth Hoglah and continued north of Beth Arabah to the Stone of Bohan son of Reuben. ⁷The boundary then went up to Debir from the Valley of Achor and turned north to Gilgal, which faces the Pass of Adummim south of the gorge. It continued along to the waters of En Shemesh and came out at En Rogel. ⁸Then it ran up the Valley of Ben Hinnom along the southern slope of the Jebusite city (that is, Jerusalem). From there it climbed to the top of the hill west of the Hinnom Valley at the northern end of the Valley of Rephaim. ⁹From the hilltop the boundary headed toward the spring of the waters of Nephtoah, came out at the towns of Mount Ephron and went down toward Baalah (that is, Kiriath Jearim). ¹⁰Then it curved westward from Baalah to Mount Seir, ran along the northern slope of Mount Jearim (that is, Kesalon), continued down to Beth Shemesh and crossed to Timnah. ¹¹It went to the northern slope of Ekron, turned toward Shikkeron, passed along to Mount Baalah and reached Jabneel. The boundary ended at the sea.

¹²The western boundary is the coastline of the Great Sea. These are the boundaries around the people of Judah by their clans.

The patriarch Jacob had given his son Judah the longest blessing (Genesis 49:8-12). Now Joshua gives Judah's offspring the first and largest territory. The census of Numbers chapter 26 shows that Judah is the most populous tribe and needs a wide area. Jacob's blessing called Judah a "lion," a symbol of strength and leadership. The tribe will give Israel its greatest kings and the world its King of kings. Judah was the fourth son of Jacob by his first wife, Leah.

In broad terms, Judah receives all the land west of the Dead Sea to the Mediterranean and south to Kadesh Barnea. Simeon will later get its allotment within this vast area.

These verses lay out Judah's boundaries on its four sides. When presented in a line, special features of the landscape like gorges, slopes, springs, and mountains mark the borders. Greater detail surrounds places of special interest, such as the area near Jerusalem in verse 8. Some names, like Debir and Mount Seir, should not be confused with other locations of the same name.

¹³In accordance with the LORD's command to him, Joshua gave to Caleb son of Jephunneh a portion in Judah—Kiriath Arba, that is, Hebron. (Arba was the forefather of Anak.) ¹⁴From Hebron Caleb drove out the three Anakites—Sheshai, Ahiman and Talmai—descendants of Anak. ¹⁵From there he marched against the people living in Debir (formerly called Kiriath Sepher). ¹⁶And Caleb said, "I will give my daughter Acsah in marriage to the man who attacks and captures Kiriath Sepher." ¹⁷Othniel son of Kenaz, Caleb's brother, took it; so Caleb gave his daughter Acsah to him in marriage.

¹⁸One day when she came to Othniel, she urged him to ask her father for a field. When she got off her donkey, Caleb asked her, "What can I do for you?"

¹⁹She replied, "Do me a special favor. Since you have given me land in the Negev, give me also springs of water." So Caleb gave her the upper and lower springs.

These seven verses provide details about the area given to Caleb and his son-in-law Othniel, one of the later judges (Judges 3:7-11). The desire for a challenge that 85-year-old Caleb expressed in 14:12 was not just a vain statement from an old man. He tackles the job, drives out the Anakites, and challenges others to capture Debir.

The towns of Judah are now listed in each of its four general areas: the Negev in verses 21-32; the Shephelah, or western foothills in verses 33-47; the hill country in verses 48-60; and the desert in verses 61 and 62.

²⁰**This is the inheritance of the tribe of Judah, clan by clan:**

²¹**The southernmost towns of the tribe of Judah in the Negev toward the boundary of Edom were:**

Kabzeel, Eder, Jagur, ²²Kinah, Dimonah, Adadah, ²³Kedesh, Hazor, Ithnan, ²⁴Ziph, Telem, Bealoth, ²⁵Hazor Hadattah, Kerioth Hezron (that is, Hazor), ²⁶Amam, Shema, Moladah, ²⁷Hazar Gaddah, Heshmon, Beth Pelet, ²⁸Hazar Shual, Beersheba, Biziothiah, ²⁹Baalah, Iim, Ezem, ³⁰Eltolad, Kesil, Hormah, ³¹Ziklag, Madmannah, Sansannah, ³²Lebaoth, Shilhim, Ain and Rimmon—a total of twenty-nine towns and their villages.

³³**In the western foothills:**

Eshtaol, Zorah, Ashnah, ³⁴Zanoah, En Gannim, Tappuah, Enam, ³⁵Jarmuth, Adullam, Socoh, Azekah, ³⁶Shaaraim, Adithaim and Gederah (or Gederothaim)— fourteen towns and their villages.

³⁷**Zenan, Hadashah, Migdal Gad, ³⁸Dilean, Mizpah, Joktheel, ³⁹Lachish, Bozkath, Eglon, ⁴⁰Cabbon, Lahmas, Kitlish, ⁴¹Gederoth, Beth Dagon, Naamah and Makkedah— sixteen towns and their villages.**

⁴²**Libnah, Ether, Ashan, ⁴³Iphtah, Ashnah, Nezib, ⁴⁴Keilah, Aczib and Mareshah—nine towns and their villages.**

⁴⁵**Ekron, with its surrounding settlements and villages; ⁴⁶west of Ekron, all that were in the vicinity of Ashdod, together with their villages; ⁴⁷Ashdod, its surrounding settlements and villages; and Gaza, its settlements and villages, as far as the Wadi of Egypt and the coastline of the Great Sea.**

⁴⁸**In the hill country:**

Shamir, Jattir, Socoh, ⁴⁹Dannah, Kiriath Sannah (that is, Debir), ⁵⁰Anab, Eshtemoh, Anim, ⁵¹Goshen, Holon and Giloh—eleven towns and their villages.

⁵²**Arab, Dumah, Eshan,** ⁵³**Janim, Beth Tappuah, Aphekah,** ⁵⁴**Humtah, Kiriath Arba (that is, Hebron) and Zior—nine towns and their villages.**
⁵⁵**Maon, Carmel, Ziph, Juttah,** ⁵⁶**Jezreel, Jokdeam, Zanoah,** ⁵⁷**Kain, Gibeah and Timnah–ten towns and their villages.**
⁵⁸**Halhul, Beth Zur, Gedor,** ⁵⁹**Maarath, Beth Anoth and Eltekon—six towns and their villages.**
⁶⁰**Kiriath Baal (that is, Kiriath Jearim) and Rabbah—two towns and their villages.**

⁶¹**In the desert:**
Beth Arabah, Middin, Secacah, ⁶²**Nibshan, the City of Salt and En Gedi—six towns and their villages.**
⁶³**Judah could not dislodge the Jebusites, who were living in Jerusalem; to this day the Jebusites live there with the people of Judah.**

The chapter closes with a special note on Jerusalem. Judah's northern border dipped just south of Jerusalem leaving most of the city in Benjamin's allotment. Neither Judah nor Benjamin can dislodge the Jebusites from Jerusalem. Success will wait for King David, a Judahite.

Allotment for Ephraim and Manasseh

16 **The allotment for Joseph began at the Jordan of Jericho, east of the waters of Jericho, and went up from there through the desert into the hill country of Bethel.** ²**It went on from Bethel (that is, Luz), crossed over to the territory of the Arkites in Ataroth,** ³**descended westward to the territory of the Japhletites as far as the region of Lower Beth Horon and on to Gezer, ending at the sea.** ⁴**So Manasseh and Ephraim, the descendants of Joseph, received their inheritance.**

These verses describe the entire territory of the two Joseph tribes west of the river. This general description is given by marking only the southern border of the two tribes. Between the Joseph tribes and Judah stretches the narrow Dan-Benjamin corridor.

Jacob had adopted Ephraim and Manasseh, his grandsons by Joseph (Genesis 48:5). They are therefore entitled to an allotment with Jacob's sons. Joseph was the 11th of the 12 sons and the first by Rachel. Like Judah, Joseph had received a long blessing, showing his importance and that of his sons in Israel's future. In keeping with Jacob's blessing, Ephraim has priority over Manasseh, though Ephraim was younger (Genesis 48:17-19). Half of Manasseh has already received its land east of the Jordan (13:29-31).

⁵This was the territory of Ephraim, clan by clan:
> **The boundary of their inheritance went from Ataroth Addar in the east to Upper Beth Horon ⁶and continued to the sea. From Micmethath on the north it curved eastward to Taanath Shiloh, passing by it to Janoah on the east. ⁷Then it went down from Janoah to Ataroth and Naarah, touched Jericho and came out at the Jordan. ⁸From Tappuah the border went west to the Kanah Ravine and ended at the sea. This was the inheritance of the tribe of the Ephraimites, clan by clan. ⁹It also included all the towns and their villages that were set aside for the Ephraimites within the inheritance of the Manassites.**

Listing Ephraim's land before Manasseh's indicates its greater importance. Jacob's blessing refers to Joseph as "a fruitful vine near a spring, whose branches climb over a wall" (Genesis 49:22). The description is a pun on the name Ephraim, which means "twice fruitful." The tribe will expand its territory. The blessing also says, "His bow remained steady" (Genesis 49:24), prophesying Ephraim's fighting prowess. Joshua, the nation's general, is from the tribe of Ephraim. Canaan's armies with their iron chariots are no match for Ephraim (17:18). Ephraim's later strength and importance is shown by the prophets referring to all the northern ten tribes by the name Ephraim (Isaiah 7:17; Hosea 5:3,5,11-14). "When Ephraim spoke, men trembled; he was exalted in Israel" (Hosea 13:1).

Many commentators admit difficulty in following the author's scheme of laying out Ephraim's borders in these verses.

¹⁰They did not dislodge the Canaanites living in Gezer; to this day the Canaanites live among the people of Ephraim but are required to do forced labor.

Gezer, the most powerful city of the area, merits a special note. Earlier Israel had defeated Gezer's king when he came to help Lachish in the southern campaign (10:33). But now, even powerful Ephraim meets solid resistance from Gezer. Later, the king of Egypt will take Gezer and turn it over to Solomon as a wedding gift (1 Kings 9:16). The note on Gezer, like the one on Jerusalem (15:63), emphasizes the continuing challenge following the seven-year intensive conquest.

17 **This was the allotment for the tribe of Manasseh as Joseph's firstborn, that is, for Makir, Manasseh's first-born. Makir was the ancestor of the Gileadites, who had received Gilead and Bashan because the Makirites were great soldiers. ²So this allotment was for the rest of the people of Manasseh—the clans of Abiezer, Helek, Asriel, Shechem, Hepher and Shemida. These are the other male descendants of Manasseh son of Joseph by their clans.**

These two verses are a reminder that part of Manasseh, the Makirites, have already received land east of the Jordan. The allotment that follows is for the rest of the tribe west of the river.

³Now Zelophehad son of Hepher, the son of Gilead, the son of Makir, the son of Manasseh, had no sons but only daughters,

whose names were Mahlah, Noah, Hoglah, Milcah and Tirzah. [4]They went to Eleazar the priest, Joshua son of Nun, and the leaders and said, "The LORD commanded Moses to give us an inheritance among our brothers." So Joshua gave them an inheritance along with the brothers of their father, according to the LORD's command. [5]Manasseh's share consisted of ten tracts of land besides Gilead and Bashan east of the Jordan, [6]because the daughters of the tribe of Manasseh received an inheritance among the sons. The land of Gilead belonged to the rest of the descendants of Manasseh.

A special provision is made for the five daughters of Zelophehad, a Manassite with no sons. Inheritance normally passed through sons. Since Zelophehad is sonless, his name will disappear from the clans of Manasseh unless his daughters receive his land. In Numbers 27:1-11, the Lord and Moses set a legal precedent from the case of the five sisters. Those verses are the background for the sisters' words before Eleazar the priest and Joshua: "The LORD commanded Moses to give us an inheritance among our brothers."

Manasseh gets "ten tracts of land" west of the river "besides Gilead and Bashan east of the Jordan." Those ten tracts consist of five portions for the daughters of Zelophehad and five for the clans named in verse 2 minus Hepher, grandfather of the five sisters.

[7]The territory of Manasseh extended from Asher to Micmethath east of Shechem. The boundary ran southward from there to include the people living at En Tappuah. [8](Manasseh had the land of Tappuah, but Tappuah itself, on the boundary of Manasseh, belonged to the Ephraimites.) [9]Then the boundary continued south to the Kanah Ravine. There were towns belonging to Ephraim lying among the towns of Manasseh, but the boundary of Manasseh was the northern side of the ravine and ended at the sea. [10]On the south the land belonged to

Ephraim, on the north to Manasseh. The territory of Manasseh reached the sea and bordered Asher on the north and Issachar on the east.

¹¹Within Issachar and Asher, Manasseh also had Beth Shan, Ibleam and the people of Dor, Endor, Taanach and Megiddo, together with their surrounding settlements (the third in the list is Naphoth).

These verses describe the territory of Manasseh's ten tracts of land west of the Jordan. Only Judah received a larger portion.

¹²Yet the Manassites were not able to occupy these towns, for the Canaanites were determined to live in that region. ¹³However, when the Israelites grew stronger, they subjected the Canaanites to forced labor but did not drive them out completely.

Like Judah and Ephraim, Manasseh has problems in occupying some of its towns. The words "did not drive [the Canaanites] out completely" have an ominous tone. Temptations and compromise are lurking.

¹⁴The people of Joseph said to Joshua, "Why have you given us only one allotment and one portion for an inheritance? We are a numerous people and the Lord has blessed us abundantly."

¹⁵"If you are so numerous," Joshua answered, "and if the hill country of Ephraim is too small for you, go up into the forest and clear land for yourselves there in the land of the Perizzites and Rephaites."

¹⁶The people of Joseph replied, "The hill country is not enough for us, and all the Canaanites who live in the plain have iron chariots, both those in Beth Shan and its settlements and those in the Valley of Jezreel."

¹⁷But Joshua said to the house of Joseph—to Ephraim and Manasseh—"You are numerous and very powerful. You will have not only one allotment ¹⁸but the forested hill country as

well. Clear it, and its farthest limits will be yours; though the Canaanites have iron chariots and though they are strong, you can drive them out."

The two Joseph tribes complain of too little land for too many people. Joshua's solution turns their own reasoning back toward them. If they are many, they have plenty of manpower to clear forest lands and to drive out iron-charioted Canaanites to expand their livable space. No one can accuse Joshua of tribalism. He is an Ephraimite. Yet he is fair and gives no special favors to his brothers.

Some time passes between chapters 12 and 18. The scene changes from Gilgal to Shiloh for the allotment to the remaining seven tribes.

Division of the rest of the land

18 **The whole assembly of the Israelites gathered at Shiloh and set up the Tent of Meeting there. The country was brought under their control, ²but there were still seven Israelite tribes who had not yet received their inheritance.**

³So Joshua said to the Israelites: "How long will you wait before you begin to take possession of the land that the LORD, the God of your fathers, has given you? ⁴Appoint three men from each tribe. I will send them out to make a survey of the land and to write a description of it, according to the inheritance of each. Then they will return to me. ⁵You are to divide the land into seven parts. Judah is to remain in its territory on the south and the house of Joseph in its territory on the north. ⁶After you have written descriptions of the seven parts of the land, bring them here to me and I will cast lots for you in the presence of the LORD our God. ⁷The Levites, however, do not get a portion among you, because the priestly service of the LORD is their inheritance. And Gad, Reuben and the half-tribe of Manasseh have already received their inheritance on the east

side of the Jordan. Moses the servant of the LORD gave it
to them."

⁸As the men started on their way to map out the land, Joshua
instructed them, "Go and make a survey of the land and write a
description of it. Then return to me, and I will cast lots for you
here at Shiloh in the presence of the LORD." ⁹So the men left and
went through the land. They wrote its description on a scroll,
town by town, in seven parts, and returned to Joshua in the camp
at Shiloh. ¹⁰Joshua then cast lots for them in Shiloh in the presence of the LORD, and there he distributed the land to the
Israelites according to their tribal divisions.

Shiloh is not just the site for dividing the rest of the land
for the remaining seven tribes. For nearly four hundred
years, it will also be the center for Israel's worship. Shiloh is
located within Ephraim, 12 miles south of Shechem and 10
miles northeast of Bethel. Its central location will make it
accessible to all 12 tribes. The initial conquest has made this
area a secure site for the whole nation to assemble. Like at
Mounts Gerizim and Ebal, the landscape around Shiloh provides natural acoustics for large gatherings.

The Tent of Meeting (or tabernacle), mentioned here for
the first time in Joshua, is set up at Shiloh. For a description
of this portable temple, see Exodus chapters 26 and 27. It
houses the ark of the covenant, the symbol of the Lord's
presence among Israel. The ark will remain at Shiloh until
the Philistines capture it in the days of the prophet Samuel
(1 Samuel 4:1-11).

Joshua's words in verse 3 are a firm reprimand as well as
an encouragement. Since the time of the loud "amens" from
Gerizim and Ebal and since the great victories, the tribes'
courage has weakened. They are slack in taking possession
of their lands. Do the tribes that have their land want to
delay further distribution so they can stop being soldiers
and start being farmers? Do the seven tribes without land

stall their allotment as they think of all the problems of taking possession? Are they getting satisfied with the nomadic life they have known for about half a century? The land gift and God's promises seem to be fading in Israel's thinking. The Lord's promises have not changed, but Israel's faith is faltering. Joshua's message is this: You fortunate people! The land God promised to your fathers, he has given to you. Now get moving and take possession of your gift! His words are like those of a coach at halftime, firing up a team that is getting lazy and starting to lose its lead.

These verses bring out the two phases of taking the land: the *conquest* by the whole nation and the *occupation* by each tribe. Taking God at his word will bring success in the second phase as it did in the first.

Joshua now does something new before allotting the land to the last seven tribes. He commissions a survey team to write up a description of the remaining land. Perhaps this new venture will make the seven tribes more bold to possess the land their surveyors have seen firsthand. After the seven-part description is given to Joshua, he will cast lots to distribute it. The lots will be cast in the Lord's presence, probably at the tabernacle before the ark.

The written report primarily describes the towns. Besides town names, other facts in the report would probably include such items as water supply, soil condition, type of terrain, access roads, and strength of the current residents.

With description in hand, Joshua now casts lots to distribute the rest of the land.

Allotment for Benjamin

¹¹The lot came up for the tribe of Benjamin, clan by clan. Their allotted territory lay between the tribes of Judah and Joseph:

¹²On the north side their boundary began at the Jordan, passed the northern slope of Jericho and headed west into the hill country, coming out at the desert of Beth Aven. ¹³From there it crossed to the south slope of Luz (that is, Bethel) and went down to Ataroth Addar on the hill south of Lower Beth Horon.

¹⁴From the hill facing Beth Horon on the south the boundary turned south along the western side and came out at Kiriath Baal (that is, Kiriath Jearim), a town of the people of Judah. This was the western side.

¹⁵The southern side began at the outskirts of Kiriath Jearim on the west, and the boundary came out at the spring of the waters of Nephtoah. ¹⁶The boundary went down to the foot of the hill facing the Valley of Ben Hinnom, north of the Valley of Rephaim. It continued down the Hinnom Valley along the southern slope of the Jebusite city and so to En Rogel. ¹⁷It then curved north, went to En Shemesh, continued to Geliloth, which faces the Pass of Adummim, and ran down to the Stone of Bohan son of Reuben. ¹⁸It continued to the northern slope of Beth Arabah and on down into the Arabah. ¹⁹It then went to the northern slope of Beth Hoglah and came out at the northern bay of the Salt Sea, at the mouth of the Jordan in the south. This was the southern boundary.

²⁰The Jordan formed the boundary on the eastern side. These were the boundaries that marked out the inheritance of the clans of Benjamin on all sides.

²¹The tribe of Benjamin, clan by clan, had the following cities:
Jericho, Beth Hoglah, Emek Keziz, ²²Beth Arabah, Zemaraim, Bethel, ²³Avvim, Parah, Ophrah, ²⁴Kephar Ammoni, Ophni and Geba—twelve towns and their villages.

²⁵Gibeon, Ramah, Beeroth, ²⁶Mizpah, Kephirah, Mozah, ²⁷Rekem, Irpeel, Taralah, ²⁸Zelah, Haeleph, the Jebusite city (that is, Jerusalem), Gibeah and Kiriath— fourteen towns and their villages.

This was the inheritance of Benjamin for its clans.

Benjamin was the youngest son of Jacob and the only son born in Canaan. His mother was Rachel, who died shortly after giving birth. Jacob's blessing in Genesis 49:27 speaks of Benjamin as a "ravenous wolf." The reference is perhaps to the exploits of such future Benjaminites as the judge Ehud, King Saul, and his son Jonathan.

Benjamin's allotment is a narrow corridor between Ephraim and Judah. Though one of the smallest of the tribal areas, it is militarily and commercially strategic.

Benjamin's northern boundary touches Ephraim's southern border. (Compare verses 12 and 13 with 16:1-3.) The southern border corresponds with Judah's northern limits. (Compare verses 15-19 with 15:5-9. The descriptions correspond, except they are given in opposite directions.) Benjamin's eastern boundary is formed by the last few miles of the Jordan River before it enters the Dead Sea.

Benjamin's cities are listed in two groups: 12 in the east and 14 in the west. The tribe's best known cities include Jericho, Gibeon, and Jerusalem, the Bible's most celebrated, if not the world's most famous, city. Most of the city of Jerusalem lay within the tribal territory of Benjamin, although part of it lay within the territory of Judah (15:63).

Allotment for Simeon

19 **The second lot came out for the tribe of Simeon, clan by clan. Their inheritance lay within the territory of Judah. ²It included:**

Beersheba (or Sheba), Moladah, ³Hazar Shual, Balah, Ezem, ⁴Eltolad, Bethul, Hormah, ⁵Ziklag, Beth Marcaboth, Hazar Susah, ⁶Beth Lebaoth and Sharuhen—thirteen towns and their villages;

⁷Ain, Rimmon, Ether and Ashan—four towns and their villages—⁸and all the villages around these towns as far as Baalath Beer (Ramah in the Negev).

This was the inheritance of the tribe of the Simeonites, clan by clan. ⁹The inheritance of the Simeonites was taken from the share of Judah, because Judah's portion was more than they needed. So the Simeonites received their inheritance within the territory of Judah.

The lot of Simeon is the second of the remaining seven. The order of allotment follows a pattern. The first lot falls to the son of Rachel (Benjamin); then lots to the three sons of Leah (Simeon, Zebulun, and Issachar); then the lot to the son of Zilpah, Leah's maidservant (Asher); and finally lots to the two sons of Bilhah, Rachel's maidservant (Naphtali and Dan). The arrangement in Jacob's house thus provided the pattern of land distribution.

Jacob's deathbed blessing of his sons had treated Simeon and Levi together (Genesis 49:5-7). He prophesied that they would be scattered and dispersed in Israel. His words, more like a curse than a blessing, now begin to be fulfilled as Simeon receives its allotment within the territory of Judah. Later Simeon will lose its separate identity and be absorbed into more powerful Judah. A comparison of Simeon's population from the first census to the second (Numbers 1 and 26) shows a sharp decline from 59,300 men to 22,200. The shrinking size of Simeon also comes out later in 1 Chronicles 4:27.

Therefore, no boundaries are named in Simeon's inheritance, but only cities, and they are listed in two groups. The first group of 13 are all in the hot, dry southern land known as the Negev. Of the second group of four, two are in the Negev and two in the western foothills (Ether and Ashan).

Many of the cities were named earlier among Judah's inheritance in 15:21 and following. Others may be the same cities as mentioned among Judah but with different names.

Simeon's most significant city is perhaps Beersheba. "From Dan to Beersheba" is the Bible's common phrase to refer to the whole land of Israel, from north to south.

Allotment for Zebulun

[10]The third lot came up for Zebulun, clan by clan:
The boundary of their inheritance went as far as Sarid. [11]Going west it ran to Maralah, touched Dabbesheth, and extended to the ravine near Jokneam. [12]It turned east from Sarid toward the sunrise to the territory of Kisloth Tabor and went on to Daberath and up to Japhia. [13]Then it continued eastward to Gath Hepher and Eth Kazin; it came out at Rimmon and turned toward Neah. [14]There the boundary went around on the north to Hannathon and ended at the Valley of Iphtah El. [15]Included were Kattath, Nahalal, Shimron, Idalah and Bethlehem. There were twelve towns and their villages.
[16]These towns and their villages were the inheritance of Zebulun, clan by clan.

Zebulun was the sixth and last son of Leah. Jacob's blessing speaks of him as living "by the seashore" and becoming "a haven for ships" (Genesis 49:13). Though landlocked, Zebulun's borders are only about ten miles from the Mediterranean and also close to the Sea of Galilee to the east. The tribe turned to the sea to become a commercial leader.

In general terms, Zebulun's allotment is a portion of lower Galilee between the Valley of Jezreel on the south and the mountains of Naphtali to the north. On the west it is separated from the Mediterranean by Asher's territory. On the east, Naphtali and Issachar end Zebulun's boundaries short of the Sea of Galilee and the Jordan Valley.

Many of the names on Zebulun's boundaries cannot be located with certainty. Inside Zebulun's borders 5 cities are named, but the whole allotment is made up of 12 cities. Some of the 12 may include the cities named in the boundary descriptions. Bethlehem (house of bread) in verse 15 is not to be confused with the more famous Bethlehem in Judah.

Nazareth, though not mentioned in the Old Testament, falls within Zebulun. That means that Jesus grew up within this tribal territory and carried on some of his ministry here. Isaiah prophesied of the Messiah's light-giving presence in this area:

> In the past he humbled the land of Zebulun and the land of Naphtali, but in the future he will honor Galilee of the Gentiles, by the way of the sea, along the Jordan—

> The people walking in darkness
>   have seen a great light;
> on those living in the land of the
>   shadow of death
> a light has dawned. (Isaiah 9:1,2)

Matthew shows that in Jesus the prophecy has been fulfilled (Matthew 4:12-16).

Allotment for Issachar

¹⁷The fourth lot came out for Issachar, clan by clan. ¹⁸Their territory included:
> **Jezreel, Kesulloth, Shunem, ¹⁹Hapharaim, Shion, Anaharath, ²⁰Rabbith, Kishion, Ebez, ²¹Remeth, En Gannim, En Haddah and Beth Pazzez. ²²The boundary touched Tabor, Shahazumah and Beth Shemesh, and ended at the Jordan. There were sixteen towns and their villages.**
²³These towns and their villages were the inheritance of the tribe of Issachar, clan by clan.

Issachar was the fifth son of Leah. His allotment comes after that of his younger brother Zebulun, reflecting his undistinguished role in Israel's history.

Issachar's land lies in Lower Galilee to the southwest of the Sea of Galilee. Mount Tabor is on its northern border. On the south, its area includes the Valley of Jezreel. The Jordan River marks the eastern limit. On the west its border is the same as Zebulun's eastern limit. The author does not attempt to trace all the boundaries. Instead he names the cities of Issachar.

The prize in Issachar's allotment is the large and fertile Valley of Jezreel. Besides its rich soil, the valley is important as a junction of major trade routes. The international highway, the Via Maris, passed through Jezreel. Jacob's blessing mentions Issachar's pleasant land and calls him "a rawboned donkey lying down between two saddlebags" (Genesis 49:14,15). Streams of donkeys and camels, the "ships" of the desert, would pass through Issachar's pleasant Valley of Jezreel with saddlebags loaded with merchandise.

Allotment for Asher

²⁴The fifth lot came out for the tribe of Asher, clan by clan. ²⁵Their territory included:

Helkath, Hali, Beten, Acshaph, ²⁶Allammelech, Amad and Mishal. On the west the boundary touched Carmel and Shihor Libnath. ²⁷It then turned east toward Beth Dagon, touched Zebulun and the Valley of Iphtah El, and went north to Beth Emek and Neiel, passing Cabul on the left. ²⁸It went to Abdon, Rehob, Hammon and Kanah, as far as Greater Sidon. ²⁹The boundary then turned back toward Ramah and went to the fortified city of Tyre, turned toward Hosah and came out at the sea in the region of Aczib, ³⁰Ummah, Aphek and Rehob. There were twenty-two towns and their villages.

³¹**These towns and their villages were the inheritance of the tribe of Asher, clan by clan.**

Asher was the second son of Zilpah, Leah's handmaid. Gad was his only full brother.

Many of the locations in the boundary description are uncertain. Yet Asher's territory can be definitely determined by key references. The Mediterranean Sea and Mount Carmel set the limits on the west and south. The city of Sidon and the lands of Naphtali and Zebulun mark the borders on the north and east.

Jacob's blessings said, "Asher's food will be rich; he will provide delicacies fit for a king" (Genesis 49:20). The coastal plains of Asher boast some of the country's richest soil. The magnificent Gulf of Acco just north of Mount Carmel (vineyard of God) is the best natural harbor south of Beirut. Asher's inheritance fulfills the blessing. He has natural riches surpassing the other tribes.

The first chapter of Judges reveals that Asher failed to drive out the Canaanites in the territory allotted to it and instead began to live among them (Judges 1:31,32). Among Asher's 22 towns are Ramah and Aphek. Both are common names for towns throughout Canaan and should not be confused with other places of the same name.

Allotment for Naphtali

³²**The sixth lot came out for Naphtali, clan by clan:**

³³**Their boundary went from Heleph and the large tree in Zaanannim, passing Adami Nekeb and Jabneel to Lakkum and ending at the Jordan.** ³⁴**The boundary ran west through Aznoth Tabor and came out at Hukkok. It touched Zebulun on the south, Asher on the west and the Jordan on the east.** ³⁵**The fortified cities were Ziddim, Zer, Hammath, Rakkath, Kinnereth,** ³⁶**Adamah, Ramah, Hazor,** ³⁷**Kedesh, Edrei, En Hazor,** ³⁸**Iron, Migdal El, Horem,**

Beth Anath and Beth Shemesh. There were nineteen towns and their villages.
³⁹These towns and their villages were the inheritance of the tribe of Naphtali, clan by clan.

The next-to-last lot falls to Naphtali, Jacob's son by Bilhah, Rachel's maidservant. Naphtali's inheritance is a long and rather narrow area. It lies between Lebanon on the north and Zebulun and Issachar on the south and between the northern Jordan and Sea of Galilee on the east and Asher on the west.

Though second last, Naphtali's allotment is not second-rate. The west shores of the Sea of Galilee are some of the most scenic and fertile land in the whole country. The Via Maris and other trade routes pass through Naphtali. The reference to the "large tree" hints at the dense forests that cover the mountains of Upper Galilee. The important fortress city of Hazor belongs to the inheritance of Naphtali.

Jacob's blessing says, "Naphtali is a doe set free that bears fruitful fawns" (Genesis 49:21). His words may refer to an independent spirit in Naphtali that comes from being set off to the north, somewhat removed from the other tribes.

Jesus' Galilean ministry often brought him to the area of Naphtali and its New Testament cities such as Capernaum and Tiberias. Isaiah's prophecy concerning Jesus' presence in Naphtali was quoted under Zebulun's allotment. Notice that Isaiah's words, "by the way of the sea" (Isaiah 9:1), are a probable reference to the Via Maris (Way of the Sea) that runs through Naphtali.

Allotment for Dan

⁴⁰The seventh lot came out for the tribe of Dan, clan by clan.
⁴¹The territory of their inheritance included:
Zorah, Eshtaol, Ir Shemesh, ⁴²Shaalabbin, Aijalon, Ithlah,
⁴³Elon, Timnah, Ekron, ⁴⁴Eltekeh, Gibbethon, Baalath, ⁴⁵Jehud,

Bene Berak, Gath Rimmon, ⁴⁶Me Jarkon and Rakkon, with the area facing Joppa.
⁴⁷(But the Danites had difficulty taking possession of their territory, so they went up and attacked Leshem, took it, put it to the sword and occupied it. They settled in Leshem and named it Dan after their forefather.)
⁴⁸These towns and their villages were the inheritance of the tribe of Dan, clan by clan.

The tribe of Dan receives the last and smallest allotment. Dan is the only full brother of Naphtali, the other son of Jacob by Bilhah, Rachel's maidservant.

The borders for Dan are not spelled out since its land touches on the already designated borders of Ephraim, Benjamin, and Judah. The area is indicated by listing Dan's cities, some of which are taken from the neighboring tribes. Dan's territory is a small elbow of land between the Plain of Sharon to the north and the Philistine Plain to the south. It rests between two rivers, the Yarkon in the north and the Sorek in the south. The Mediterranean coast north and south of Joppa marks the western border. "Small but fertile" describes Dan's inheritance.

The tribe of Dan later migrated to the far north, as verse 47 reveals. Dan's difficulty in possessing its original land may be related to the influx of the "sea peoples" of Egyptian writings. The Philistines are commonly identified with these sea people. Judges chapter 18 gives the full story of Dan's move north.

The city of Leshem is called Laish in Judges 18:29. Both names mean "lion." The Danites give it a third name after the patriarch of their tribe. The city of Dan sits at the southern foot of Mount Hermon where a powerful spring forms one of the main sources of the Jordan River. As Israel's northernmost city, Dan becomes part of the common phrase that covers the land's limits: "from Dan to Beersheba."

Tribal allotments

Jacob refers to Dan as "a serpent" in Genesis 49:17. His words may refer to the treachery involved in taking Leshem. One of the most famous Danites is the mighty Samson (Judges 13–16).

Allotment for Joshua

⁴⁹**When they had finished dividing the land into its allotted portions, the Israelites gave Joshua son of Nun an inheritance among them,** ⁵⁰**as the LORD had commanded. They gave him the town he asked for—Timnath Serah in the hill country of Ephraim. And he built up the town and settled there.**

⁵¹**These are the territories that Eleazar the priest, Joshua son of Nun and the heads of the tribal clans of Israel assigned by lot at Shiloh in the presence of the LORD at the entrance to the Tent of Meeting. And so they finished dividing the land.**

The author frames the allotment chapters by relating first the inheritance given to Caleb (14:6-15) and now that given to Joshua. These two men of courage have based their lives on the Lord's sure promises. Their faith is well-placed. The skeletons of all their contemporaries litter the barren desert. But Joshua and Caleb enjoy a portion of the land flowing with milk and honey.

A leader in it for himself would have grabbed the best portion of land before thinking of anyone else. Joshua's allotment at the very end is in keeping with his character. He is a servant of the Lord, not a self-centered tyrant. He does not demand and seize his land. He is patient until the Israelites give him what he has requested. Under the Lord there is no need to grab for it all now for fear we will never receive. The patient servant knows that at the proper time God opens his hands in blessing to satisfy every need (Psalm 145:15,16).

Joshua receives Timnath Serah, a town within the land of his tribe of Ephraim. The Lord had commanded that the

Israelites give this town to their leader, though the command is not recorded in Scripture. Timnath Serah means either "abundant portion" or "leftover portion." The site, known today as Tibnah, is 15 miles southwest of Shechem and 17 miles northwest of Jerusalem in Ephraim's hill country. Like Caleb, Joshua is an old, but energetic, man who gets busy and builds up his town before settling there.

The final verse rounds out the distribution chapters with a reminder of the procedure that has been followed and the place of this second phase of the allotment. The Lord has been directing everything. His presence, symbolized through the Tent of Meeting, shows this. His will has been carried out by means of the lot and through his agents: Eleazar, Joshua, and the heads of Israel's clans.

Cities of refuge

20 Then the LORD said to Joshua: ²"Tell the Israelites to designate the cities of refuge, as I instructed you through Moses, ³so that anyone who kills a person accidentally and unintentionally may flee there and find protection from the avenger of blood.

⁴"When he flees to one of these cities, he is to stand in the entrance of the city gate and state his case before the elders of that city. Then they are to admit him into their city and give him a place to live with them. ⁵If the avenger of blood pursues him, they must not surrender the one accused, because he killed his neighbor unintentionally and without malice aforethought. ⁶He is to stay in that city until he has stood trial before the assembly and until the death of the high priest who is serving at that time. Then he may go back to his own home in the town from which he fled."

⁷So they set apart Kedesh in Galilee in the hill country of Naphtali, Shechem in the hill country of Ephraim, and Kiriath

Arba (that is, Hebron) in the hill country of Judah. ⁸On the east side of the Jordan of Jericho they designated Bezer in the desert on the plateau in the tribe of Reuben, Ramoth in Gilead in the tribe of Gad, and Golan in Bashan in the tribe of Manasseh. ⁹Any of the Israelites or any alien living among them who killed someone accidentally could flee to these designated cities and not be killed by the avenger of blood prior to standing trial before the assembly.

Only two more arrangements specified by Moses remain to be put in place in the Promised Land. The first is the naming of special cities of refuge. A panic-stricken person who has accidently killed someone finds protection through God's appointment of six special cities of refuge. The arrangement keeps an avenger from acting in rage and killing someone who does not deserve to die. (The background for these provisions is Numbers 35:6-34; Deuteronomy 4:41-43; 19:1-14).

Moses had already set aside the three cities of refuge east of the Jordan (Deuteronomy 4:43). He also left instructions for designating three more refuge cities west of the Jordan, "if the LORD your God enlarges your territory" (Deuteronomy 19:8,9). The appointment of all six cities now hints at the Lord's faithfulness. He has enlarged Israel's land as promised so that this provision can now be put in place.

Three parallel expressions tell of who may flee to a city of refuge: one who has killed "accidentally," "unintentionally and without malice aforethought." Moses gives examples of such innocent taking of life: An ax head flies off while two men are cutting trees and a man is hit and dies (Deuteronomy 19:5). Someone innocently shoves another or throws something that accidentally hits another so that death results. Or an unseen person is hit and killed when a stone is dropped (Numbers 35:22,23). The one who caused the death can run to one of the six special cities with the confidence that upon his arrival he will be guaranteed the right to a trial.

The procedure at the city is carefully outlined by the Lord so that the person fleeing and the city elders know exactly what to do. If the man is being pursued, confusion at the city gate could cost him his life at the hands of his avenger. He is to halt at the gate entrance. The city elders are to give him a preliminary hearing there. Then they are to admit him and provide living quarters inside the city. The security of the city is to continue as the fugitive receives a

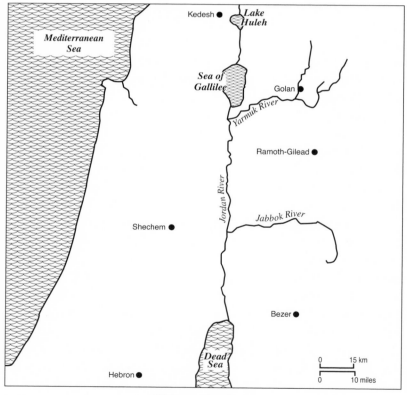

Cities of refuge

full trial before an assembly to determine whether the killing was unintentional.

The statement regarding the death of the high priest is open to several interpretations. Are both the full trial and the high priest's death necessary before an innocent fugitive can return home? Or is it a matter of one or the other? The high priest's death evidently signalled a general amnesty for the accused.

Excavations at some of Israel's cities have given us a sharper focus on "the entrance of the city gate" where the preliminary hearing takes place. "The town gate was an elaborate structure at least two stories high, with guardrooms flanking a tunnel-like opening, and bench-lined court(s) guarded by towers."[11] The Bible often refers to the city gate as the place where discussions take place, the elders meet, deals are struck, and hearings and trials are conducted. Security was only one of its functions. The entrance of the city gate was the town hall and courtroom.

The Israelites now "set apart" the six cities of refuge. The Hebrew says literally that they "sanctified" or "set apart for sacred use" the six. The expression shows that it is God's orders that are being carried out and that this is his sacred arrangement for protecting the innocent.

The six special cities are among those to be given to the Levites (Numbers 35:6). They are centrally located and are to have roads that make them accessible (Deuteronomy 19:2,3). Their locations make it possible for one fleeing to arrive at a city of refuge within a few hours from any point in the land. No matter where in Israel someone lived, he was within 30 miles of one of the cities of refuge. The cities are named in a U-shaped arrangement. West of the Jordan are Kedesh in the north, Shechem in the center, and Hebron in the south. East of the river are Bezer in the south, Ramoth in the center, and Golan in the north. In listing the cities, the author uses a more ancient and full name for the river: "the Jordan of Jericho." A look at the map on page 208 shows the cities' rather even distribution across the land.

The Lord who arranged for these special cities is our true refuge and strength. His six cities across the Promised Land protected the innocent. But he is the "ever-present help" of the guilty; "therefore we will not fear" (Psalm 46:1,2).

Now only one last provision of Moses remains to be put in place.

Towns for the Levites

21 Now the family heads of the Levites approached Eleazar the priest, Joshua son of Nun, and the heads of the other tribal families of Israel ²at Shiloh in Canaan and said to them, "The LORD commanded through Moses that you give us towns to live in, with pasturelands for our livestock." ³So, as the LORD had commanded, the Israelites gave the Levites the following towns and pasturelands out of their own inheritance:

⁴The first lot came out for the Kohathites, clan by clan. The Levites who were descendants of Aaron the priest were allotted thirteen towns from the tribes of Judah, Simeon and Benjamin. ⁵The rest of Kohath's descendants were allotted ten towns from the clans of the tribes of Ephraim, Dan and half of Manasseh.

⁶The descendants of Gershon were allotted thirteen towns from the clans of the tribes of Issachar, Asher, Naphtali and the half-tribe of Manasseh in Bashan.

⁷The descendants of Merari, clan by clan, received twelve towns from the tribes of Reuben, Gad and Zebulun.

⁸So the Israelites allotted to the Levites these towns and their pasturelands, as the LORD had commanded through Moses.

Shiloh, 20 miles north of Jerusalem, is now Israel's spiritual and administrative center. Present there are the Tent of Meeting with its Levite caretakers; Eleazar, the high priest; and Joshua, the chief administrator.

The Levites approach the leaders at Shiloh and ask that they now put in place what God commanded by Moses in Numbers 35:1-8. The arrangement called for 48 towns for the Levites with pasturelands extending three thousand feet in all directions from each city. Of the 48 towns, 6 are to be the cities of refuge just named.

We have seen four reminders in Joshua that the Levites received no allotment like the other tribes (13:14; 13:33; 14:3; 18:7). The Lord himself and Israel's offerings are their inheritance (Deuteronomy 18:1,2); the 48 cities and pasturelands are not their real inheritance.

Jacob had spoken of Levi being scattered and dispersed in Israel (Genesis 49:5-7). His words were a curse brought on by Simeon and Levi's fierce anger and cruelty. Jacob's prophecy finds fulfillment as the Levites receive their cities scattered among each of the 12 tribes.

Levi's curse becomes a blessing for all Israel. The Levites will be the nation's teachers who watch over the Word of the Lord and guard his covenant throughout the land (Deuteronomy 33:8-11; 2 Chronicles 17:8,9).

Levi had three sons: Gershon, Kohath, and Merari (Exodus 6:16). Moses and Aaron were from Kohath's line (Exodus 6:18,20). Aaron and his offspring were appointed to be the priests (Exodus 28,29). All priests therefore were Levites, but only those Levites who descended from Aaron's family were priests. In the desert the three branches of Levites were responsible for the care of the Tent of Meeting (tabernacle) and its furnishings (Numbers 3,4). David would later reorganize the Levites' duties for service at the permanent temple (1 Chronicles 23,26).

Because of the special status of the priests, the towns allotted to the Kohathites are in two groups. Thirteen towns go first to the priestly Kohathites of Aaron's line. Since their towns are in Judah, Simeon and Benjamin, they will be near Jerusalem for the later temple service. God's control over the lot with a view toward the future is obvious. The rest of the Kohathites receive ten towns in three tribes farther north.

The descendants of Gershon are given 13 towns among the tribes in Galilee and in the half of Manasseh east of the Jordan. Merari's descendants receive 12 towns, most of them east of the river and some of them in Zebulun.

The 48 towns are now listed by name:

⁹**From the tribes of Judah and Simeon they allotted the following towns by name ¹⁰(these towns were assigned to the descendants of Aaron who were from the Kohathite clans of the Levites, because the first lot fell to them):**

¹¹They gave them Kiriath Arba (that is, Hebron), with its surrounding pastureland, in the hill country of Judah. (Arba was the forefather of Anak.) ¹²But the fields and villages around the city they had given to Caleb son of Jephunneh as his possession.

¹³So to the descendants of Aaron the priest they gave Hebron (a city of refuge for one accused of murder), Libnah, ¹⁴Jattir, Eshtemoa, ¹⁵Holon, Debir, ¹⁶Ain, Juttah and Beth Shemesh, together with their pasturelands—nine towns from these two tribes.

¹⁷And from the tribe of Benjamin they gave them Gibeon, Geba, ¹⁸Anathoth and Almon, together with their pasturelands—four towns.

¹⁹**All the towns for the priests, the descendants of Aaron, were thirteen, together with their pasturelands.**

²⁰**The rest of the Kohathite clans of the Levites were allotted towns from the tribe of Ephraim:**

²¹In the hill country of Ephraim they were given Shechem (a city of refuge for one accused of murder) and Gezer, ²²Kibzaim and Beth Horon, together with their pasturelands—four towns.

²³Also from the tribe of Dan they received Eltekeh, Gibbethon, ²⁴Aijalon and Gath Rimmon, together with their pasturelands—four towns.

²⁵From half the tribe of Manasseh they received Taanach and Gath Rimmon, together with their pasturelands—two towns.
²⁶All these ten towns and their pasturelands were given to the rest of the Kohathite clans.

²⁷The Levite clans of the Gershonites were given:
from the half-tribe of Manasseh,
Golan in Bashan (a city of refuge for one accused of murder) and Be Eshtarah, together with their pasturelands—two towns;
²⁸from the tribe of Issachar,
Kishion, Daberath, ²⁹Jarmuth and En Gannim, together with their pasturelands—four towns;
³⁰from the tribe of Asher,
Mishal, Abdon, ³¹Helkath and Rehob, together with their pasturelands—four towns;
³²from the tribe of Naphtali,
Kedesh in Galilee (a city of refuge for one accused of murder), Hammoth Dor and Kartan, together with their pasturelands—three towns.
³³All the towns of the Gershonite clans were thirteen, together with their pasturelands.

³⁴The Merarite clans (the rest of the Levites) were given:
from the tribe of Zebulun,
Jokneam, Kartah, ³⁵Dimnah and Nahalal, together with their pasturelands—four towns;
³⁶from the tribe of Reuben,
Bezer, Jahaz, ³⁷Kedemoth and Mephaath, together with their pasturelands—four towns;
³⁸from the tribe of Gad,
Ramoth in Gilead (a city of refuge for one accused of murder), Mahanaim, ³⁹Heshbon and Jazer, together with their pasturelands—four towns in all.
⁴⁰All the towns allotted to the Merarite clans, who were the rest of the Levites, were twelve.
⁴¹The towns of the Levites in the territory held by the Israelites were forty-eight in all, together with their pasturelands. ⁴²Each of these towns had pasturelands surrounding it; this was true for all these towns.

This list of 48 cities may not hold us spellbound. But it is a part of the Bible at the Holy Spirit's direction and serves his purposes. Among his aims may be to show God's great care in providing teachers for his people. An arrangement is in place whereby Israelites in every corner of the land can be instructed in the Lord's covenant. The Lord's physical care for his Levite teachers is also impressed by the list of towns with their pasturelands. Though they own no tribal land, the Levites are well provided for as they do God's work and value him as their true inheritance.

The arrangement for the Levites also serves as a picture of our lives as "aliens and strangers on earth" (Hebrews 11:13). "Here we do not have an enduring city, but we are looking for the city that is to come" (Hebrews 13:14). While we use earthly things for a time and consider them God's gifts, we do not truly own them. The Lord and his salvation is our lasting inheritance (1 Peter 1:3-5). In a sense, the Levites were fortunate beyond the other tribes. They were not encumbered with the burden of land ownership and management. Fortunate is anyone who is released from undo attachment to mere things and finds joy in the Lord.

The author closes the distribution chapters with summary statements that cover the whole book of Joshua and emphasize its theme.

⁴³So the LORD gave Israel all the land he had sworn to give their forefathers, and they took possession of it and settled there. ⁴⁴The LORD gave them rest on every side, just as he had sworn to their forefathers. Not one of their enemies withstood them; the LORD handed all their enemies over to them. ⁴⁵Not one of all the LORD's good promises to the house of Israel failed; every one was fulfilled.

The Lord's name appears in each of these three verses and twice in verse 44, stressing that he is the cause of Israel's success. All credit goes to him. Long ago he made a promise. He remained faithful. He kept his word. He defeated

Israel's enemies. Israel enjoys "rest" in the Promised Land. For comments on the use of the key word *rest* in Joshua, see the remarks under 1:15.

This short but important section spells out the Spirit's purpose in producing this inspired book. He wants to assure readers that the Lord keeps his promises. Just as John's gospel pauses to say, "These are written that you may believe that Jesus is the Christ" (John 20:31), the inspired writer stops here to highlight his theme: The Lord fulfills his promise of the land.

The author is following up on the promises of chapter 1:2-6 and, still further back, on the original promises to Abraham (Genesis 12:2,3; 13:14-17). The author wants us to compare the old promises with the present reality and sing the Lord's praises. He wants readers to contrast the generous allotment just enumerated in chapters 13 to 21 with the time when the promises first were made. At that time Abraham owned "not even a foot of ground" in Canaan (Acts 7:5). Now Israel holds an expanse of land from Mount Hermon to the Negev and from the Mediterranean to the Arabian desert.

The fulfillment of God's land-promise is critical because it is a down payment on his Savior-promise. God is faithful! He delivers every good thing he has promised!

What Israel does from now on cannot detract from the Lord's faithfulness. Likewise, whether or not we take advantage of God's promises and collect their blessings does not affect the reality of his goodness.

A tone of praise and thanksgiving resounds through these verses. We get the feeling that the author is on the verge of bursting into a grateful doxology. Yet he saves that song for us thankful readers.

The last three chapters of Joshua reflect how Israel reacts to the Lord's fulfilled promise of the land.

Levite towns

PART FOUR

The Heirs of the Land Respond
(22:1–24:33)

A misunderstanding settled

22 Then Joshua summoned the Reubenites, the Gadites and the half-tribe of Manasseh ²and said to them, "You have done all that Moses the servant of the LORD commanded, and you have obeyed me in everything I commanded. ³For a long time now—to this very day—you have not deserted your brothers but have carried out the mission the LORD your God gave you. ⁴Now that the LORD your God has given your brothers rest as he promised, return to your homes in the land that Moses the servant of the LORD gave you on the other side of the Jordan. ⁵But be very careful to keep the commandment and the law that Moses the servant of the LORD gave you: to love the LORD your God, to walk in all his ways, to obey his commands, to hold fast to him and to serve him with all your heart and all your soul."

⁶Then Joshua blessed them and sent them away, and they went to their homes. ⁷(To the half-tribe of Manasseh Moses had given land in Bashan, and to the other half of the tribe Joshua gave land on the west side of the Jordan with their brothers.) When Joshua sent them home, he blessed them, ⁸saying, "Return to your homes with your great wealth—with large herds of livestock, with silver, gold, bronze and iron, and a great quantity of clothing—and divide with your brothers the plunder from your enemies."

⁹So the Reubenites, the Gadites and the half-tribe of Manasseh left the Israelites at Shiloh in Canaan to return to Gilead, their own land, which they had acquired in accordance with the command of the LORD through Moses.

Each of the last three chapters contains an address of Joshua. His concern as he speaks is to preserve Israel's unique covenant relationship with the Lord.

Joshua delivers the first of his three messages to the special armies of Reuben, Gad, and half of Manasseh gathered at Shiloh. He is dismissing them after faithful duty so that they may return to their homes east of the Jordan. They have been absent from their families during the many years of conquest. Yet they have not complained as they helped their brothers secure the Lord's "rest." Their day of "homecoming" is a day of great joy, especially as they listen to Joshua's words of kind compliment (verses 2-4), exhortation (verse 5), and blessing (verses 6-8).

Both Moses and Joshua had commanded the tribes east of the Jordan to help the other nine and a half tribes until the Lord gave them the same rest the eastern tribes already enjoyed (Numbers 32:20-24; Deuteronomy 3:18-20; Joshua 1:12-15). Through many victories the Lord has now provided that rest. There now is nothing to keep the eastern tribes from going home. The author is giving unity to his inspired book by concluding in these verses what he introduced in 1:12-18. All that the eastern tribes said they would do they have done. Joshua takes time to note their faithfulness. His words remind us to be quick to compliment Christian faithfulness and less quick to criticize.

Joshua not only knows the obedient service of the soldiers he is dismissing. He also knows human nature and adds urgent exhortation. They will be going home in long caravans heaped with plunder: silver, gold, bronze, iron, and stacks of clothing. They will also take with them large herds of livestock to add to the stock already in pens built back home years ago (Numbers 32:16). But all this is not their true treasure. The Lord and his holy contract with Israel is their unique wealth. So Joshua urges them to remain faithful to the Lord who will give the world its priceless Treasure through his covenant nation.

Joshua's encouragement shows urgency through the imperatives he uses: "be very careful to keep . . . love . . . walk . . . obey . . . hold fast . . . serve." Covenant faithfulness is not made up of mere outward obedience. Love for the Lord, who by grace established the covenant, is the very heart of faithfulness. The first and greatest commandment says, "Love the LORD your God with all your heart and with all your soul and with all your strength" (Deuteronomy 6:5; Matthew 22:37,38; Mark 12:30). The verb in the phrase "hold fast to" is the same Hebrew verb as in Genesis 2:24, where it is said that a man will "be united to" his wife. When the eastern tribes love and cleave to the Lord, willing service from the heart will follow. Separated from the rest of Israel by the river, the eastern tribes will feel strong temptations toward the religion of their neighbors. Joshua's words therefore throb with urgency.

Joshua is not a Levite. Yet he blesses the departing tribes like a priest. He is assuming the role of patriarchal father blessing his children as they leave home. His blessing includes some welcome commands. The eastern tribes will be blessed by the joy of giving as they return home and divide their wealth with their brothers and sisters across the river. From the battles after Jericho, Israel amassed this plunder and livestock (8:2).

The Israelites who stayed behind in Trans-Jordan to protect families and livestock are to receive their fair share. Moses made similar arrangements for dividing the booty of battle in Numbers 31:25-54. David would later make this ordinance regarding the spoils of war: "The share of the man who stayed with the supplies is to be the same as that of him who went down to the battle. All will share alike" (1 Samuel 30:24). No formal law is necessary now as the

Reubenites, Gadites, and the half-tribe of Manasseh head for home under Joshua's blessing, willing to share the plunder with their brothers.

¹⁰**When they came to Geliloth near the Jordan in the land of Canaan, the Reubenites, the Gadites and the half-tribe of Manasseh built an imposing altar there by the Jordan. ¹¹And when the Israelites heard that they had built the altar on the border of Canaan at Geliloth near the Jordan on the Israelite side, ¹²the whole assembly of Israel gathered at Shiloh to go to war against them.**

¹³**So the Israelites sent Phinehas son of Eleazar, the priest, to the land of Gilead—to Reuben, Gad and the half-tribe of Manasseh. ¹⁴With him they sent ten of the chief men, one for each of the tribes of Israel, each the head of a family division among the Israelite clans.**

¹⁵**When they went to Gilead—to Reuben, Gad and the half-tribe of Manasseh—they said to them: ¹⁶"The whole assembly of the LORD says: 'How could you break faith with the God of Israel like this? How could you turn away from the LORD and build yourselves an altar in rebellion against him now? ¹⁷Was not the sin of Peor enough for us? Up to this very day we have not cleansed ourselves from that sin, even though a plague fell on the community of the LORD! ¹⁸And are you now turning away from the LORD?**

"'If you rebel against the LORD today, tomorrow he will be angry with the whole community of Israel. ¹⁹If the land you possess is defiled, come over to the LORD's land, where the LORD's tabernacle stands, and share the land with us. But do not rebel against the LORD or against us by building an altar for yourselves, other than the altar of the LORD our God. ²⁰When Achan son of Zerah acted unfaithfully regarding the devoted things, did not wrath come upon the whole community of Israel? He was not the only one who died for his sin.'"

The brotherly spirit of the dismissal ceremony is violently strained when the two and a half tribes build an altar on the way home. What is the meaning of this altar? The eastern tribes have not consulted with Joshua before setting it up. Their action leads to suspicion. Are they cutting themselves off from the rest of the covenant nation? Have they built the altar as a rival to the central place of worship at Shiloh's tabernacle? Or, worse yet, are they preparing for sacrifices to Baal?

The NIV translation gives the location of the altar as Geliloth. Although the Hebrew word can be taken as a proper noun, it can also be translated as "region" or "circles," perhaps referring to a circle of stones at the site.

The place of the altar is near the Jordan east of Shiloh. Whether it is on the east or west side of the river is not clear from verse 11. The verse can mean either that the other Israelites *heard* about it on the Israelite or west side of the Jordan or that the altar was actually *built* there. Whatever the exact site, the altar is "imposing," literally, "big to look at." The eastern tribes are not trying to hide a secret altar.

The western tribes do not consider building the altar an innocent activity. Their dark suspicions are reflected in a swift assembly at Shiloh and readiness to go to war. Deuteronomy 13:12-15 provides the background for their serious action. There Moses commanded what Israel should do when it is heard that wicked men of a city are leading its people to worship other gods: "You must inquire, probe and investigate it thoroughly. And if it is true . . . you must certainly put to the sword all who live in that town."

To "inquire, probe and investigate," a high-powered delegation of 11 is dispatched to Gilead across the river. Chief men from each of the ten western tribes plus the future high priest, Phinehas, make up the committee of inquiry.

The presence of Phinehas, son of the high priest Eleazar, shows that the concern is not just political but spiritual. A breakaway threatens all Israel's existence as the Lord's covenant people. Phinehas, Aaron's grandson, already proved his zeal and faithfulness toward the Lord's covenant. During Israel's worship of the Baal of Peor with its sexual immorality, Phinehas had driven a spear through an adulterous Israelite man and Midianite woman (Numbers 25; Psalm 106:30,31).

This is a highly charged moment in Israel. The language of the committee, with Phinehas as the probable spokesman, shows this. The eastern tribes are accused of breaking faith with God, turning away from him and building the altar in rebellion against him and the rest of the covenant nation. They are charged with allowing the despicable sin of Peor to linger and fester in their hearts. Since the Lord deals with his nation as a unit, the whole community of Israel, it is said, will feel his rage if the two and a half tribes rebel against him. Didn't about 36 Israelites die when one man, Achan, broke one of God's covenant stipulations (7:1-5)? It can happen again, because the sin will be charged against the whole nation!

The delegation doesn't only accuse and condemn. It also makes a generous offer. If the eastern tribes consider their land unfit for the Lord's worship, they can come and live on the west side of the Jordan. That would shrink the territory of the western tribes. But what is losing some territory compared with the loss of the Lord's covenant?

The committee does not consider the alleged rebellion complete. There is still hope that things haven't gone too far. This is clear from their pleading: "But do not rebel against the LORD or against us."

Now it is the delegation's turn to listen. Could they have misinterpreted the altar?

²¹Then Reuben, Gad and the half-tribe of Manasseh replied to the heads of the clans of Israel: ²²"The Mighty One, God, the LORD! The Mighty One, God, the LORD! He knows! And let Israel know! If this has been in rebellion or disobedience to the LORD, do not spare us this day. ²³If we have built our own altar to turn away from the LORD and to offer burnt offerings and grain offerings, or to sacrifice fellowship offerings on it, may the LORD himself call us to account.

²⁴"No! We did it for fear that some day your descendants might say to ours, 'What do you have to do with the LORD, the God of Israel? ²⁵The LORD has made the Jordan a boundary between us and you—you Reubenites and Gadites! You have no share in the LORD.' So your descendants might cause ours to stop fearing the LORD.

²⁶"That is why we said, 'Let us get ready and build an altar—but not for burnt offerings or sacrifices.' ²⁷On the contrary, it is to be a witness between us and you and the generations that follow, that we will worship the LORD at his sanctuary with our burnt offerings, sacrifices and fellowship offerings. Then in the future your descendants will not be able to say to ours, 'You have no share in the LORD.'

²⁸"And we said, 'If they ever say this to us, or to our descendants, we will answer: Look at the replica of the LORD's altar, which our fathers built, not for burnt offerings and sacrifices, but as a witness between us and you.'

²⁹"Far be it from us to rebel against the LORD and turn away from him today by building an altar for burnt offerings, grain offerings and sacrifices, other than the altar of the LORD our God that stands before his tabernacle."

If the passions of the western delegation ran high, the response of the eastern tribes seems even more emotional. They utterly reject all the accusations. In their oath of denial they use three names for God: El (The Mighty One), Elohim (God), and Yahweh (The Covenant Lord Who Is!). Then they repeat the holy names. It is a solemn moment. If any of the accusations are true, they invite God to call them to account and encourage Israel to strike them dead.

Stated negatively, they say they have not built the altar in rebellion against Israel. Nor have they built it to turn away from the Lord or as a place of sacrifice to the Lord that rivals Shiloh. Worded positively, they have built the altar as a *replica* of the altar before the tabernacle at Shiloh, as witness to their *commitment* to keep on worshiping at the tabernacle with all Israel, and as testimony of their continuing *right* to share in the Lord's worship despite the river that separates them from the rest of Israel.

The intentions behind the altar are quite the opposite of all the suspicions. The altar stands for covenant unity, not division, for firm devotion to the Lord, not backsliding.

But will the delegation of the western tribes accept the explanation?

30When Phinehas the priest and the leaders of the community —the heads of the clans of the Israelites—heard what Reuben, Gad and Manasseh had to say, they were pleased. 31And Phinehas son of Eleazar, the priest, said to Reuben, Gad and Manasseh, "Today we know that the LORD is with us, because you have not acted unfaithfully toward the LORD in this matter. Now you have rescued the Israelites from the LORD's hand."

32Then Phinehas son of Eleazar, the priest, and the leaders returned to Canaan from their meeting with the Reubenites and Gadites in Gilead and reported to the Israelites. 33They were glad to hear the report and praised God. And they talked no more about going to war against them to devastate the country where the Reubenites and the Gadites lived.

34And the Reubenites and the Gadites gave the altar this name: A Witness Between Us that the LORD is God.

The zeal of Phinehas for the Lord is beyond question. And he is completely satisfied. The suspicions had been unfounded and all is well.

Some commentators seem to snicker at the explanation of the eastern tribes as if it were contrived and suspect. But there is nothing in the text that hints that the clarification is a quick invention.

The whole delegation and all the tribes in Canaan accept the explanation of their Trans-Jordanian brothers. They rejoice that there is harmony in Israel. The Lord's hand would not have to fall on Israel in judgment. Instead, the peaceful settlement proves that the Lord has been present with his hand raised in blessing over the whole nation. *He* receives the praise for keeping Israel faithful, for settling the problem, and for preserving the unity of his covenant nation.

Because human nature is what it is, at times misunderstandings are bound to flare up among Christians. Such misunderstandings may come about as a result of ill-advised actions and unfounded suspicions. The spirit and example of this chapter point the way to resolve such clashes. Love for the Lord and the unity he desires must guide us. We need to be willing to go and speak openly. Didn't a few frank words prevent civil war in Israel? We need to listen to explanations without allowing our suspicions to run wild. If our suspicions were wrong, we need to admit it humbly instead of stubbornly holding on to our pride at all cost. Finally, we will want to celebrate our God-given unity and praise the Lord for it.

False teaching always separates. But if Christians are going to be divided, let it not be over a simple misunderstanding that could have been talked out. The altar near the Jordan becomes another stone memorial in the Land of Promise. The eastern tribes give the monument a name that makes clear its purpose: "A Witness Between Us that the

Lord is God." The name is long but meaningful. The naming of altars was a common Old Testament practice. (See Genesis 33:20, 35:7; Judges 6:24.)

Joshua's farewell to the leaders

23 **After a long time had passed and the LORD had given Israel rest from all their enemies around them, Joshua, by then old and well advanced in years, ²summoned all Israel— their elders, leaders, judges and officials—and said to them: "I am old and well advanced in years. ³You yourselves have seen everything the LORD your God has done to all these nations for your sake; it was the LORD your God who fought for you. ⁴Remember how I have allotted as an inheritance for your tribes all the land of the nations that remain—the nations I conquered—between the Jordan and the Great Sea in the west. ⁵The LORD your God himself will drive them out of your way. He will push them out before you, and you will take possession of their land, as the LORD your God promised you.**

⁶"Be very strong; be careful to obey all that is written in the Book of the Law of Moses, without turning aside to the right or to the left. ⁷Do not associate with these nations that remain among you; do not invoke the names of their gods or swear by them. You must not serve them or bow down to them. ⁸But you are to hold fast to the LORD your God, as you have until now."

Joshua was well advanced in years when the intensive conquest was over and the land was distributed (13:1). After the allotment he retired to Timnath Serah in the hill country of Ephraim, built up the town, and settled there (19:49,50). Now, some 20 years later, he is very old, near the end of his 110 years (23:14; 24:29). Like Moses in his final days, Joshua speaks words of farewell, urging Israel to remain loyal to the Lord's covenant. The rest from enemies that the Lord has provided allows Joshua to summon Israel's leaders before him in security. The author does not specify the location. The two most likely sites are Shiloh before the tabernacle or Joshua's inheritance at Timnath Serah.

Later Joshua will address "all the tribes" (24:1). Here he speaks to Israel as represented by the leaders. *Elders* is the general term for all of Israel's representatives. The *leaders* are, literally, the heads of the tribes. The *judges* were mentioned earlier in connection with the covenant renewal at Mount Ebal (8:33). The *officials* are the same as the "officers" who mustered the people for the Jordan crossing (1:10; 3:2).

The address of the eloquent old general consists of three parts: verses 2-8, 9-13, and 14-16. Each section begins with a reminder of the Lord's faithful acts for his covenant nation and is followed by an appeal to remain faithful to him. Parts 2 and 3 build in power as Joshua spells out the tragic consequences of violating the covenant.

A clear-minded man just before his death speaks in earnest. By saying at the start "I am old and well advanced in years," Joshua gives his address the tone of a last will and testament.

At the start of his speech, Joshua credits the Lord for all Israel's victories. The *Lord* fought for his covenant people. The nation experienced his miraculous power at the Jordan, at Jericho, during the central, southern, and northern campaigns and when the sun stood still over the Aijalon. Israel's success everywhere was the Lord's success for his people. The Israelites know this well. Yet the fact needs to be repeated and deeply impressed so that loyalty to the Lord will come from the heart. We show faithfulness and love toward the Lord only after we are first convinced of his love and faithfulness toward us.

It may surprise us to hear Joshua speaking in the first person in verse 4 about his role during the past several decades: "I allotted . . . I conquered." His expression does not reflect conceit. Throughout his long life he has continued to be the Lord's humble servant, a Spirit-filled man of wholehearted obedience (Numbers 27:18; 32:12). Coming within the context of the Lord's acts for Israel, Joshua's words are not designed to call attention to himself. They boast of the deeds of the Lord. Joshua is grateful for his role as the Lord's special agent of victory.

The Lord's past acts over enemies furnish confidence for the *future*. Joshua impresses that God's covenant faithfulness and promises continue. "He *will* drive them out of your way and you will take possession of their land." Much work remains for Israel to possess and hold on to the land. But all along the future way, the old promises will deliver new blessings. The Lord will never leave nor forsake his people (1:5). It may be the end of an era with Joshua about to enter his eternal rest. But his departure will not mean the end of covenant blessings for Israel. Added to past promises fulfilled, knowing what the Lord *will continue to do* for us instills love and loyalty.

In verse 6 Joshua borrows the Lord's own language. He passes on in his "will" what the Lord first bequeathed to him (1:7,8). God's people will be strong as they meditate on the Book of the Law of Moses, that portion of the inspired Scriptures completed by Joshua's time. Faithfulness to the written Word of the Lord is essential for the nation's success. See the remarks under 1:8 for commentary on "the Book of the Law."

The most serious danger facing Israel involves the enemy nations that remain among them. The threat is not so much political as spiritual. Association with these nations will lead to contact with their gods, sacrifices, and fertility rites. Joshua will say more about the cancer of compromise in the next two sections of his address. Here he simply exhorts Israel to stay clear of any hint of Canaanite worship.

He names four outward forms of religious practice that the people of God are to avoid. First, Israel is not to "invoke" the names of Canaanite gods; the Hebrew says literally: Do not "bring to remembrance" or "make mention of" the names of their gods. In other words, he calls for total disassociation from them. Second, Israel is not to "swear by them"; calling them to be witnesses would imply that these gods are real. Third, Israel must not "serve them," probably referring to the service of sacrifices and offerings. Fourth, God's people are not to "bow down" to these false gods in prayers or incantations.

In contrast to the above, Israel is to "hold fast to the LORD." Joshua had used the same term to urge the departing eastern tribes to remain faithful (22:5). The expression refers to "cleaving to," or "being united with," the Lord as a man and woman are united in marriage (Genesis 2:24). By making a covenant, the Lord has taken Israel as his bride.

Joshua commends Israel for her faithfulness to the Lord "until now." Apart from the Achan episode, the pages of Joshua have pictured a refreshing era of covenant loyalty. There has been no mass "spiritual adultery" against the Lord, as in the golden calf incident or the Baal of Peor seduction (Exodus 32; Numbers 25). Joshua's compliment encourages more of the same.

⁹"The LORD has driven out before you great and powerful nations; to this day no one has been able to withstand you. ¹⁰One of you routs a thousand, because the LORD your God fights for you, just as he promised. ¹¹So be very careful to love the LORD your God.

¹²"But if you turn away and ally yourselves with the survivors of these nations that remain among you and if you inter-

marry with them and associate with them, ¹³then you may
be sure that the LORD your God will no longer drive out these
nations before you. Instead, they will become snares and traps
for you, whips on your backs and thorns in your eyes, until
you perish from this good land, which the LORD your God has
given you."

In beginning the second part of his address, Joshua
reminds Israel of the Lord's extraordinary acts in their
behalf. He cannot say too often or too strongly: "The
LORD your God fights for you, just as he promised."
Joshua aims to instill genuine love for the Lord.

God receives heartfelt service only after his people
are impressed with his saving actions for them. The New
Testament writers direct us to God's saving acts in Jesus
Christ: "We love because he first loved us" (1 John 4:19).
"He [Jesus] died for all, that those who live should no
longer live for themselves but for him who died for
them and was raised again" (2 Corinthians 5:15). What
he first did changes our hearts and then sets our lives in
grateful motion.

Sharp words of warning follow. Joshua sees potential
disaster brewing in the nations that remain. He uses a
thick cluster of metaphors to focus on the misery Israel
can experience: snares, traps, whips, and thorns! That is
what the Canaanites will be if Israel chooses to ally, inter-
marry, or generally associate with them. The Canaanite
girl who looks like a rose as she dances at one of Baal's
fertility rites will be a blinding thorn in the eye if taken as
a bride (see Exodus 34:15,16). Joshua borrows his
imagery from earlier warnings of the Lord: a snare (Exodus 23:33; 34:12) and barbs in your eyes and thorns in
your sides (Numbers 33:55). Israel has nothing to fear as
long as she rests on God's all-sufficient grace and cher-
ishes his covenant.

But Israel has everything to fear if Joshua's warning is ignored. Blessings and possession of the land are conditional. The chosen nation can "perish from this good land." The phrase "good land" stresses the dear loss Israel will experience if she is to discard the covenant.

Israel's later story shows that Joshua's warnings are right on target. Paul uses Israel's story to wake us up to temptations that can drag us from faith and salvation. Like Joshua, he warns, "So, if you think you are standing firm, be careful that you don't fall!" (1 Corinthians 10:12).

> [14]**"Now I am about to go the way of all the earth. You know with all your heart and soul that not one of all the good promises the LORD your God gave you has failed. Every promise has been fulfilled; not one has failed.** [15]**But just as every good promise of the LORD your God has come true, so the LORD will bring on you all the evil he has threatened, until he has destroyed you from this good land he has given you.** [16]**If you violate the covenant of the LORD your God, which he commanded you, and go and serve other gods and bow down to them, the LORD's anger will burn against you, and you will quickly perish from the good land he has given you."**

Joshua's preface to this third section accents his earnestness. It also calls attention to the last will and testament character of his address. He announces that he is about to go "the way of all the earth," an Old Testament euphemism for death (1 Kings 2:2). The statement is more gripping than his opening to part 1: "I am old and well advanced in years." The nation can inherit nothing better from their aged leader than his fatherly words that "correct, rebuke and encourage—with great patience and careful instruction" (2 Timothy 4:2).

Nothing will give Joshua's last days more joy than to know that the hearts and souls of his "children" rest solidly on the truth of God's covenant promises. He spends his last energies to that end. The spirit of his address is like that of the third letter of the aged apostle John: "I have no greater joy than to hear that my children are walking in the truth" (3 John 4).

Sharp warning closed out part 2. Joshua now returns to the welcome reminder that the Lord is totally trustworthy and keeps every one of his promises. Only that often-repeated "gospel" message can endear Israel more and more to her Lord and produce greater covenant loyalty. Solemn threats then follow again. Israel must see the tragic picture of life without the Lord's covenant. Joshua measures just the right amounts of gospel and law for people who love the Lord and yet can be tempted.

Apart from references to the ark of the covenant, we have seen the word *covenant* only twice before verse 16 (7:11,15). While the word itself is scarce in Joshua, the covenant concept fills the entire book. The holy contract between the Lord and Israel is the only thing that makes this nation different from any other. If the covenant is violated, Israel can expect to be treated just like the conquered Canaanites. The once-special people will "quickly perish from the good land" the Lord has given.

Joshua's sobering statement is obviously a solemn threat. But his words also call attention to God's covenant grace. They show that Israel's privileged position did not result from their own goodness. It came because God chose them by grace out of all the world's nations and covenanted with them for a saving purpose. The covenant needs careful guarding, otherwise the name Israelite will carry no more special meaning than Canaanite, Amorite, or Hittite. Israel's name could be added to the list of nations driven from the land as God's anger burned. Therefore guard your God-given status! Hold on to it! Keep the covenant!

That is the heart of Joshua's message here and in his final address in the closing chapter.

The covenant renewed at Shechem

24 Then Joshua assembled all the tribes of Israel at Shechem. He summoned the elders, leaders, judges and officials of Israel, and they presented themselves before God.

²Joshua said to all the people, "This is what the LORD, the God of Israel, says: 'Long ago your forefathers, including Terah the father of Abraham and Nahor, lived beyond the River and worshiped other gods. ³But I took your father Abraham from the land beyond the River and led him throughout Canaan and gave him many descendants. I gave him Isaac, ⁴and to Isaac I gave Jacob and Esau. I assigned the hill country of Seir to Esau, but Jacob and his sons went down to Egypt.

⁵"'Then I sent Moses and Aaron, and I afflicted the Egyptians by what I did there, and I brought you out. ⁶When I brought your fathers out of Egypt, you came to the sea, and the Egyptians pursued them with chariots and horsemen as far as the Red Sea. ⁷But they cried to the LORD for help, and he put darkness between you and the Egyptians; he brought the sea over them and covered them. You saw with your own eyes what I did to the Egyptians. Then you lived in the desert for a long time.

⁸"'I brought you to the land of the Amorites who lived east of the Jordan. They fought against you, but I gave them into your hands. I destroyed them from before you, and you took possession of their land. ⁹When Balak son of Zippor, the king of Moab, prepared to fight against Israel, he sent for Balaam son of Beor to put a curse on you. ¹⁰But I would not listen to Balaam, so he blessed you again and again, and I delivered you out of his hand.

¹¹"'Then you crossed the Jordan and came to Jericho. The citizens of Jericho fought against you, as did also the Amorites, Perizzites, Canaanites, Hittites, Girgashites, Hivites and Jebusites,

but I gave them into your hands. **¹²I sent the hornet ahead of you, which drove them out before you—also the two Amorite kings. You did not do it with your own sword and bow. ¹³So I gave you a land on which you did not toil and cities you did not build; and you live in them and eat from vineyards and olive groves that you did not plant.'"**

The event described in this chapter seems to be more official than that of the previous chapter. A formal renewal of the covenant is at the center of what takes place, as verses 25-27 show. The assembly also appears to be more general. "All the tribes of Israel" are now present, whereas in chapter 23 the nation may have been represented by its leaders.

For his last official act as God's servant, Joshua chooses the city of Shechem, in the dead center of Canaan. The town's name means "shoulder." The city's location on the slope, or shoulder, of the two surrounding mountains, Gerizim and Ebal, provides the name. Shechem, one of the cities of refuge (20:7), is about 35 miles due north of Jerusalem and about 12 miles north of Shiloh in the hill country of Ephraim. It is the present-day Arab city of Nablus.

Shechem was an appropriate place to renew the covenant. The site is rich in salvation history. It is the first place in Canaan mentioned after Abraham arrived in the land. Here the Lord first promised: "To your offspring I will give this land" (Genesis 12:7). Abraham responded by building the first altar to the Lord in Canaan. Jacob later settled at Shechem and bought a plot of ground from the sons of Hamor (Genesis 33:18,19; Joshua 24:32). At Shechem Jacob's sons were grazing their father's flocks when Joseph was sent to check on them. That event gives the background to the years of bondage in Egypt (Genesis 37:12-36). The covenant renewal of Joshua 8:30-35 took place near Shechem.

Thoughts of God's early promises and lasting faithfulness already fill the site as Israel assembles.

The people present themselves "before God." The phrase may hint that the ark of the covenant, or even the whole tabernacle, has been brought 12 miles north from Shiloh for the special ceremony.

To his function as general and chief administrator, Joshua now adds the role of prophet. He begins his message just like the great Old Testament prophets: "This is what the LORD, the God of Israel, says." His words are packed with power as he speaks for God while being carried along by the Spirit (2 Peter 1:21).

Many commentators see parallels between ancient suzerainty treaties and what now unfolds. Joshua may be following a covenant/treaty pattern known throughout the Middle East. One element of such treaty making was a review of past relationships between the suzerain, or overlord, and his subjects. Joshua reviews the relationship between the Lord and his chosen nation.

Joshua does not speak like a rambling preacher picking out snatches of Israel's history at random. Quoting the Lord directly, he recalls choice portions of history that punctuate God's undeserved love and powerful acts for his people. He knows exactly where he is going in his review. He aims to stir up every Israelite to personal renewal and commitment in light of the Lord's unswerving faithfulness.

In chapter 23 Joshua had recalled God's acts in the immediate past of the conquest years. Now his sweep is much broader. He goes back about five hundred years to God's selection of Abraham when he lived beyond the Euphrates River (Genesis 11:27–12:1).

It is clear that Abraham and his offspring became the chosen nation only by God's gracious choice and not because of some superior quality of their own. After all, Abraham came from a family of idol worshipers! Israel has no cause for personal pride but every reason to glory in the Lord. He chose their forefathers by pure grace when they were no different from their neighbors who worshiped the moon-god at Ur. The household gods, or "teraphim," that Jacob's uncle, Laban, clung to were a later vestige of that old idolatry (see Genesis 31:19). At Shechem, the very place where Israel is now assembled, Jacob had gathered up those foreign gods and buried them under an oak tree (Genesis 35:2-4).

Christians who speak with pride of coming from a long line of believers should go back a bit further. They also will find their ancestors steeped in dark superstitions, "without hope and without God in the world" (Ephesians 2:12). God alone deserves our boasting for calling us to Christ's salvation by the gospel. "For it is by grace you have been saved, through faith—and this not from yourselves, it is the gift of God—not by works, so that no one can boast" (Ephesians 2:8,9).

Joshua's review of salvation history continues as he reminds the nation of Abraham's "many descendants." The Lord has been faithful to his promise and produced millions of offspring from an old man and his seemingly barren wife, Sarah. The people need only look around now to see the landscape of Shechem packed with those descendants. Besides this throng, there is the nation that came from Jacob's brother Esau, Abraham's other grandson. Esau's offspring inhabit the land of Edom around Mount Seir, southeast of the Dead Sea.

The Lord's gracious guidance is accented in each episode of Israel's story: the sending of Moses and Aaron to prepare for Israel's release from Egypt (Exodus 3:10; 4:14-16); the ten plagues on the Egyptians (Exodus 7–11); the great day of the exodus (Exodus 12:31-51); the miracle when the Lord turned a section of the Red Sea into a corridor of dry land (Exodus 14);

the Lord's care for his often-grumbling people during the 40 long desert years (Exodus 15–Numbers 21); the defeat of Sihon and Og, the Amorite kings east of the Jordan (Numbers 21:21-35); the Lord's control over Balaam so that he blessed Israel when commanded by King Balak to curse (Numbers 22–24); the Jordan miracle and the victories related in the first 12 chapters of Joshua. What Israelite can keep loyalty to the Lord from welling up as these historical facts pass from Joshua's lips?

How can our faith and commitment do anything but grow as we hear again the story of our rescue by Jesus? As Joshua speaks to Israel, God has performed acts leading only to a gift of land for his Old Testament people. They enjoy physical fruits they did not win by their fighting or develop by their hard work. As we now read the Scriptures, God has finished every act leading to our gift of eternal life. We enjoy the undeserved fruits of forgiveness, peace with God, and eternal hope. The greater the gift, the greater the gratitude! The key for us is to review our gifts of grace.

A curious detail in verse 12 may invite questions. What does the Lord mean when he says, "I sent the *hornet* ahead of you"? In Exodus 23:27,28, the Lord first promised the hornet. That context speaks of the terror and confusion the Lord would send on Israel's enemies. There are several acceptable understandings of the verse before us:

1. "The hornet" may be a colorful metaphor for the dread that gripped the Canaanites. After the Lord stung Israel's enemies with defeat, the hornet of terror winged its way to future opponents to stun them. For references in Joshua to this terror, see 2:11; 5:1; and 9:24.

2. Some commentators point out that the hornet was a symbol of Lower Egypt. They suggest that

early incursions of Egyptian armies, which
weakened the Canaanites, may explain "the
hornet."

3. A completely literal interpretation of "the hornet" is also possible. The Lord who summoned
frogs, gnats, flies, and locusts to plague the
Egyptians (Exodus 8–10) could also gather
swarms of hornets to terrorize the Canaanites.

Having finished his review of God's salvation history,
Joshua now hits the target he has been aiming at.

¹⁴"**Now fear the LORD and serve him with all faithfulness.
Throw away the gods your forefathers worshiped beyond the River
and in Egypt, and serve the LORD. ¹⁵But if serving the LORD seems
undesirable to you, then choose for yourselves this day whom you
will serve, whether the gods your forefathers served beyond the
River, or the gods of the Amorites, in whose land you are living.
But as for me and my household, we will serve the LORD."**

As mentioned earlier, Joshua may be following a pattern
from Near Eastern treaty making. A study of Hittite treaties
shows elements that seem to have parallels in this chapter:

1. A preamble that introduces the king (verse 2).
2. The history of past relationships between the
   two parties making the treaty (verses 2-13).
3. Stipulations that govern the treaty relationship
   (verses 14,16,18,21,23,24).
4. Treaty witnesses; in the case of Hittite
   treaties, their gods were called on to witness
   (verses 22,27).
5. Blessings and curses (verses 19,20).

The word *now* that opens verse 14 indicates that Joshua
has come to the heart of the official business at hand. Israel

must continue to meet covenant requirements if the solemn pact is to remain in force. Joshua does not present a long list of regulations. The basic stipulation is summarized in the command "Fear the LORD and serve him with all faithfulness."

To *fear* the Lord means "to stand in awe of him, to honor him, to give him allegiance." *Fear* can include trust, love, and worship. Fear for the Lord in the case of his people is not the same as dread. This is obvious from Psalm 130:4: "But with you there is forgiveness; therefore you are feared." Forgiveness produces quite the opposite of dread.

To *serve* the Lord, in its general sense, includes worship, trust, love, and grateful obedience. The Hebrew word for serve is used seven times by Joshua in verses 14 and 15, indicating that serving the Lord is a basic covenant stipulation for Israel. "Fear and serve" sums up the whole covenant relationship toward the Lord.

The phrase "with all faithfulness" emphasizes that Israel's fear and serving is to be for the Lord alone. He will not share his people's affections with another. The Hebrew for "with all faithfulness" says literally "with completeness and in truth." Undivided allegiance is critical to the covenant relationship.

To fear the Lord *alone* means that all idols, whether attitudes of the heart or tangible objects, must be thrown away. If those gods are gone when discarded, what were they in the first place? Together with the gods Israel's forefathers worshiped beyond the Euphrates, Joshua now mentions gods served in Egypt. During the four hundred years in Egypt, at least some Israelites must have bent to social pressure and bowed before the sun-god Ra, the sky-goddess Nut, and the sacred bull Apis. The golden calf episode of Exodus chapter 32 demonstrated the influence of Egyptian religion, an elaborate system of local gods and celestial powers.

Does Israel cling to objects of wood, stone, or metal as Joshua speaks? While we cannot answer with certainty, the following suggest that he demands throwing away all false gods *of the heart,* anything that keeps Israel from giving the Lord undivided worship:

1. Joshua 23:8 and 24:31 emphasize Israel's faithfulness at this time. That emphasis would seem strange if outward idolatry were now being practiced.
2. God's blessings came to a jarring halt when Achan took some of the forbidden booty of Jericho (chapter 7). We would expect the same fierce anger from God if outright worship of idols were going on now.
3. No discarding of physical idols seems to take place after Joshua's words in verses 14 and 23.

The Canaanites and their gods are still in the vicinity. Those gods are of the same nature as the gods of Egypt and across the Euphrates. Any lurking tendency to assign reality and power to such idols must be rooted out of the heart. In the future, as they settle in former Canaanite territory, God's people must also physically throw away those gods of the land. By his demand, Joshua is repeating the First Commandment: "You shall have no other gods before me" (Exodus 20:3).

Secret trusting in the powers of the occult, haunting fears that chance and accident control life, seeking security in mere things, all such idolatrous attitudes need to be torn from the heart and thrown far away from those who belong to the Lord. He tolerates no rivals.

Israel faces a choice. When seen clearly, the choice is easy. It is between idols of wood, stone, and metal on the one hand and the living, powerful, gracious Lord on the other. It is between the gods who were powerless to help their worshipers keep their land and the Lord who has just given his people that same land. The gods who brought the Canaanites defeat or the God who brought you where you are today? Choose!

While the choice is very clear at Shechem, the author of Judges will tell of Israel's tragic choice not long in the future (Judges 2:11-13). Six hundred fifty years after Joshua, the prophet Hosea will write: "They consult a wooden idol and are answered by a stick of wood" (Hosea 4:12). "They offer human sacrifice and kiss the calf-idols" (Hosea 13:2). Human nature, the pressures of society, and the great deceiver, Satan, are hard at work to blur the obvious choice.

Joshua is not advocating the "decision theology" of many preachers today when he says, "Choose for yourselves." Modern decision theology claims that unconverted people have the power within themselves to choose the Lord and become believers. Sinful humanity has no such power of its own to turn from unbelief to faith in the Lord. That power comes from God (1 Corinthians 12:3). Joshua is here calling for a choice from people who already own the gift of faith from the Lord. They can choose to abandon the Lord or, by the power of the Spirit already given them, to confirm their God-given faith and renew the covenant he put in place. But if they reject the Lord, the only choice they can make is which worthless idol to serve. The spiritually dead can make only deadly choices.

Joshua's expression at the end of verse 15 is one of the best known statements of the entire Bible. Before all Israel he sounds this clear credal trumpet blast that has stirred God's people for almost three and a half millennia: "But as for me and my household, we will serve the LORD." His words are a bold and unashamed statement of personal commitment to the Lord. Even if he would have to stand alone, as he and Caleb did earlier (Numbers 14:1-9), he would serve the

Lord. At the same time, he uses his role as the head of his house to lead those under his care to serve the Lord.

Joshua, of course, hopes Israel will follow his lead. But sincerity precedes every good example. Even if no one would follow his lead, that would not change Joshua's stance. What the Lord said at the start of Joshua's service is still true at the end of his life: he follows the Lord "wholeheartedly" (Numbers 32:12).

What led Joshua to his bold creed commitment? It was the Lord's undeserved love, powerful acts of rescue, fulfilled promises, and covenant faithfulness—all those evidences of God's grace just reviewed in verses 2-13!

By his Spirit, the Lord leads us to the same firm statement of faith when the marvelous record of his love in Christ takes hold of our hearts. In love he chose us, redeemed us through the blood of Christ, called us to saving faith by the gospel, forgives us, and lavishes on us all the riches of his grace (Ephesians 1:3-14.). When we clearly see God's grace, nothing can keep us from singing out:

> Then here will I and mine today
> A solemn promise make and say:
> Though all the world forsake his Word,
> I and my house will serve the Lord! (CW 506:5)

[16]Then the people answered, "Far be it from us to forsake the LORD to serve other gods! [17]It was the LORD our God himself who brought us and our fathers up out of Egypt, from that land of slavery, and performed those great signs before our eyes. He protected us on our entire journey and among all the nations through which we traveled. [18]And the LORD drove out before us all the nations, including the Amorites, who lived in the land. We too will serve the LORD, because he is our God."

The people are horrified at the very idea that they could choose idols over the Lord. Their expression in the Hebrew is one of utter revulsion at the thought: "Far be it from us!" Woe be to us! God forbid!

In professing absolute loyalty to the Lord, they echo the Lord's own words attached to the First Commandment. Compare the first part of verse 17 with Exodus 20:2: "I am the LORD your God, who brought you out of Egypt, out of the land of slavery." In the light of his overwhelming faithfulness, his people can only pledge their total allegiance.

If Joshua had any doubts that the assembly was really listening to his sermon of verses 2-13, those doubts are soon removed. The people not only hung on his words; they took them to heart and then expand on them. They continue the story of God's faithful grace as they speak of the Lord's great signs, protection, and victories.

Teachers of God's Word, who may wonder if anyone is really paying attention, can take heart. Sometimes listeners are not only with the leader. They may be steps ahead, filling in what he or she has left out and already making personal applications from the message.

Joshua does not walk alone in serving the Lord. The people's words "we too" hark back to Joshua's personal pledge. Their commitment to the Lord is the same as his.

We expect Joshua to respond with total delight now that the nation has answered just the way he hoped.

[19]Joshua said to the people, "You are not able to serve the LORD. He is a holy God; he is a jealous God. He will not forgive your rebellion and your sins. [20]If you forsake the LORD and serve foreign gods, he will turn and bring disaster on you and make an end of you, after he has been good to you."

A totally surprising response! One writer calls Joshua's answer "perhaps the most shocking statement in the Old Testament."[12] Joshua appears to reject their bold statement of commitment, even though their response was just like his own and precisely what he should have wanted to hear. Why this bewildering response? One or more of the following reasons may give the answer:

1. Since words can be "cheap," Joshua is testing the sincerity of the Israelites' response. His aim is to strengthen and cement their commitment.

2. Joshua may be questioning the truthfulness of the response. His words may indicate that all along they were practicing idolatry, secretly worshiping other gods.

3. Anyone can be swept along by a mass movement and the emotion of a moment. Joshua wants the people to count the cost of their commitment. Loyalty will not be easy. Temptations to compromise will be overwhelming. And the holy, jealous Lord will settle for nothing less than total allegiance.

4. Joshua wants to break down all ideas that Israel can remain loyal by its own power. Self-confidence is tragic when it comes to spiritual matters. Confidence in God is critical for success, "for it is God who works in you to will and to act according to his good purpose" (Philippians 2:13). We can't by our own strength serve him.

5. Joshua wants to stress again that the grace of God, not the worthiness of his people, is their only hope. Israel must cling to God's grace and promises. While he is a holy God and a jealous God, he is also the loving and forgiving Lord.

6. Joshua is peering into the future and seeing the disastrous choice of future generations. That choice of foreign gods over the Lord will cause curses, captivity, dispersion, and death. Apart from the Lord there is no forgiveness.

The assembly seems to cut Joshua off, unable to hold back shouting its commitment again.

> ²¹**But the people said to Joshua, "No! We will serve the LORD."**
> ²²**Then Joshua said, "You are witnesses against yourselves that you have chosen to serve the LORD."**
> **"Yes, we are witnesses," they replied.**
> ²³**"Now then," said Joshua, "throw away the foreign gods that are among you and yield your hearts to the LORD, the God of Israel."**
> ²⁴**And the people said to Joshua, "We will serve the LORD our God and obey him."**

The people stick firmly to their resolve first voiced in verse 18. They repeat it two more times in verses 21 and 24. Their emphatic "No!" says it all in a word. They will not forsake the Lord to serve foreign gods!

The text casts no doubt on their sincerity. Neither should we. Celebrate the God-given commitment of this faithful generation in Israel, and praise God for it. Chapters with quite another picture are not far ahead or long past. It is scenes like this that set the book of Joshua apart as a refreshing oasis. God's grace is evident not only in his acts of conquest but also in the lives of his grateful people. Enjoy the scene while it lasts. God's faithfulness is lasting, but people's is not. (See 2 Timothy 2:13.)

For a second time Joshua commands to "throw away the foreign gods." This time the order hits closer to home. In verse 14 the gods to be discarded were the ones from beyond the Euphrates and in Egypt. Now they are the gods "that are among you." Are some Israelites confessing the Lord boldly yet trying to "cover all the bases" by reserving a soft spot in their hearts for the powers of Canaanite religion? Do some have objects of heathen worship hidden in their tents, lurking temptations for coming days of weakness? All gods, whether physical objects or niches of the heart kept for superstition, must be disposed of before the living Lord of the covenant.

The Lord is not like heathen gods. Such gods can be served when their worshipers "build images for them, dress them, perfume them, build a house for them, bring sacrifices to feed them, carry them in processions, even bury them in appropriate monuments."[13] But serving the Lord means loving him "with all your heart and with all your soul and with all your strength" (Deuteronomy 6:5). Reflecting those words of Moses, Joshua now says: "Yield your hearts to the LORD, the God of Israel." Joshua has already employed the power that causes people to give their hearts to God. That power is the message of the Lord's grace.

With the nation's loyalty sealed by another promise of commitment, Joshua is ready to complete the covenant reviewing ceremony.

²⁵On that day Joshua made a covenant for the people, and there at Shechem he drew up for them decrees and laws. ²⁶And Joshua recorded these things in the Book of the Law of God. Then he took a large stone and set it up there under the oak near the holy place of the LORD.

²⁷"See!" he said to all the people. "This stone will be a witness against us. It has heard all the words the LORD has said to us. It will be a witness against you if you are untrue to your God."

The whole chapter has centered on covenant renewal. But the word *covenant* itself appears for the first time in verse 25. The author now tells us that Joshua "made a covenant for the people" that day. The expression does not mean that this is a new contract. It is a *renewal* of the covenant first made at Mount Sinai.

The phrase "for the people" invites us to think not just of Joshua's act as the people's representative and not just of the people's covenant duties. "For the people" also suggests the nation's *covenant benefits* from their gracious King. The covenant is for the *people's* blessing. They have everything to gain by this generous arrangement. The covenant laws do not suggest that Israel must give up something to get something from God. Even keeping the covenant laws will bring blessings. Covenant benefits will spill over from Israel to all the world when the Lord makes good on his promise to give a special offspring, the Messiah, from his chosen nation.

Joshua writes down decrees and laws as part of the finalizing act. We are not told specifically what these are. We can say only that they are part or all of the terms that will keep the covenant in force. A summary of what joins Israel to God's covenant was given by Joshua in verse 14: "Now fear the LORD and serve him with all faithfulness." Joshua 8:32 says that at the earlier renewal ceremony, "Joshua copied on stones the law of Moses." Perhaps he does the same here.

Joshua then records "these things." What things? Again, the author does not specify. Are "these things" just the laws and decrees? Are they an account of the whole renewal ceremony together with those laws? Or still more generally, are they part of the book of Joshua itself? We will have to be content to speculate.

What is meant by the statement: "Joshua recorded these things in the Book of the Law of God"? At least two interpretations are possible:

1. Joshua may insert his document into the Book of the Law, or Torah, of Moses. Moses' Book of the Law is mentioned in Deuteronomy 31:26 and in Joshua 1:8. For remarks on the Book of the Law, see the commentary on page 23.

2. What Joshua now records may itself be called here "the Book of the Law of God."

Another stone memorial rises in the Promised Land as Joshua sets up a large stone as a covenant witness. The impressive stone will continue to remind the Israelites of this day. In verse 22 the people were their own covenant witnesses. Long after their shouts of commitment have faded, the stone can continue to stand as a witness. It will accuse any idolatrous Israelite of being "untrue" to God and of breaking the nation's vow. Its large size will not let the stone be removed by Israelites who do not want to be reminded of their unfaithfulness. It is as though this stone has heard and recorded the renewal ceremony long before the day of audio and video technology. To look at this stone would be the same as replaying a tape of this day's event.

The stone is placed "under *the* oak tree." The definite article *the* shows that this is a tree well known to first readers of the book of Joshua. That tree may be "the great tree of Moreh at Shechem," where the Lord appeared to Abraham and where Abraham built an altar to the Lord (Genesis 12:6,7). It may be the oak tree under which Jacob buried Israel's foreign gods and idolatrous earrings at Shechem (Genesis 35:1-4).

The stone's location is also described as "near the holy place of the LORD." Some think that this is a reference to the tabernacle that may have been brought 12 miles north from Shiloh for the ceremony. With or without the tabernacle, the Lord's appearance here to Abraham would certainly qualify this site as "the holy place of the LORD."

The land now receives three more memorials. Three graves will be emphatic reminders that the Lord has fully kept his promise of the land.

Buried in the Promised Land

²⁸Then Joshua sent the people away, each to his own inheritance.

²⁹After these things, Joshua son of Nun, the servant of the LORD, died at the age of a hundred and ten. ³⁰And they buried him in the land of his inheritance, at Timnath Serah in the hill country of Ephraim, north of Mount Gaash.

³¹Israel served the LORD throughout the lifetime of Joshua and of the elders who outlived him and who had experienced everything the LORD had done for Israel.

The word *inheritance* again stresses that the land is an outright gift from God. The book opened with the promise: "Get ready to cross the Jordan River into the land I am about to give to them—to the Israelites. I will give you every place where you set your foot" (1:2,3). What the Lord promised the whole nation, he has fulfilled for every individual. The people go home, "each to his own inheritance."

They can contemplate the advantages of being God's covenant people. At the end of their trip home, they will find tangible proof of the Lord's faithfulness. Their own personal inheritance of land is that proof.

If living under the Lord seems to have its drawbacks for us, we need only think about where we are walking and with whom we are traveling. We're on our way to collecting our inheritance (1 Peter 1:3,4). What are Christian "crosses" compared to the gift waiting for us? And all the while, we walk with the faithful One who will never leave us nor forsake us (Joshua 1:5; Hebrews 13:5).

Sometime after the people returned to their inheritances, Joshua died. The words surrounding his death announcement are solemn. But they also resound with a tone of *honor* and *fulfillment.*

At the start of the book, Joshua is known as "Moses' aide" (1:1). Now at the end he is called "the servant of the LORD." That is a title of high honor! The great Moses had carried that title (Joshua 1:1,2). Now, after a life of God-given faith, courage, and wholehearted obedience, Joshua receives it. In keeping with his humble character, Joshua never claimed that designation for himself. The inspired author confers it upon him. The title not only honors Joshua. It shows that the Lord has completely kept his promise to exalt Joshua in the eyes of Israel (Joshua 3:7). At Joshua's death, the author is telling us the same thing he said in 4:14: "And they revered him all the days of his life, just as they had revered Moses."

Joshua's long life of 110 years speaks of the Lord's blessings on him. Egyptian writings show that 110 was thought to be the ideal number of years on this earth. Joseph had also died at 110 in Egypt (Genesis 50:26).

Joshua's 110 years can be divided into three chapters: about 40 years in Egypt, 40 years in the desert, and 30 years in the Promised Land (7 conquest years and 23 at Timnath Serah). If Joshua was about 40 at the time of the exodus from Egypt (Caleb was 38), he may have been born around 1486 B.C. His death, then, would be about 1376 B.C. (To see how we arrive at these dates, see the introduction and the figures regarding Caleb's life in 14:7,10.)

The word *inheritance* is used again in connection with the place of Joshua's burial. Joshua lies not in Egypt, not in the desert, but in the very land the Lord said would be Israel's inheritance. Joshua's grave at Timnath Serah in the hill country of Ephraim therefore attests to the Lord's trustworthiness. The exact location of Mount Gaash is unknown.

"Joshua's epitaph was not written on a marble gravestone. It was written in the lives of the leaders he influenced and the people he led."[14] Those words are an excellent commentary on verse 31. Joshua did all he could to lead Israel to faithfulness. He obeyed the Lord, boldly conquered, reminded the nation of the Lord's gracious acts, and warned of the dangers to come. The Lord used Joshua's life effectively. What other era of Old Testament history can be characterized by such a glowing summary as this: "Israel served the LORD throughout the lifetime of Joshua and of the elders who outlived him"? Don't fail to notice the value of personal influence. Yet the glory goes to God, "for it is God who works in you to will and to act according to his good purpose" (Philippians 2:13).

As great as Joshua's service was, his achievements were only one step toward God's greatest day of fulfillment. What Joshua son of Nun could not begin to accomplish, Joshua (Jesus) Son of God did by his perfect life, redeeming death, and victorious resurrection. The body of Old Testament Joshua awaited that greater day. Today it rests in the sure promise of the resurrection to eternal life through his namesake (1 Corinthians 15:20-23).

When Moses died, the leadership passed to Joshua. At Joshua's death, no single leader receives his position. The Lord has set in place a system of leaders, judges, officials, and priests. That system, when applied faithfully, is sufficient for the nation's spiritual training and good order. Joshua's role had been unique for the exciting and fulfilling era of conquest.

Two more burial announcements conclude this book.

³²And Joseph's bones, which the Israelites had brought up from Egypt, were buried at Shechem in the tract of land that Jacob bought for a hundred pieces of silver from the sons of Hamor, the father of Shechem. This became the inheritance of Joseph's descendants.

³³And Eleazar son of Aaron died and was buried at Gibeah, which had been allotted to his son Phinehas in the hill country of Ephraim.

Joseph's deathbed instructions in Egypt are the background to verse 32. The book of Genesis ends this way: "And Joseph made the sons of Israel swear an oath and said, 'God will surely come to your aid, and then you must carry my bones up from this place.' So Joseph died at the age of a hundred and ten. And after they embalmed him, he was placed in a coffin in Egypt" (Genesis 50:25,26).

Joseph's instructions show his trust in God's promises, specifically his promise of the land. The writer of Hebrews calls attention to Joseph's faith: "By faith Joseph, when his end was near, spoke about the exodus of the Israelites from Egypt and gave instructions about his bones" (Hebrews 11:22). The preservation of those bones for four hundred years in Egypt was an act of Israel's faith. Exodus 13:19 tells us that Moses carried out Joseph's commands and took his bones from Egypt at the exodus. Moses' faith is evident in his action. Now the burial of those bones at Shechem stresses that faith in God's promises is never misplaced. God did come to his people's "aid" (Genesis 50:25) in Egypt. God did give his people the land he swore. When

God makes a promise, you can start making plans in keeping with its fulfillment. You can count on what he says.

Genesis 33:19 tells of Jacob's purchase of the plot of ground in which Joseph is now buried. In a sermon just before his stoning, Stephen calls attention to that purchase and Joseph's burial there (Acts 7:15,16). Joseph's resting place in the Promised Land was obviously significant both for Old Testament Jews and early Christians as proof that God delivers what he promises.

Joseph's bones rest at the center of the land allotted to his two sons, Ephraim and Manasseh. The actual burial may have taken place soon after the tribes received their land, years before Joshua's death. The author does not necessarily link the time of Joseph's interment with that of Joshua. He relates Joseph's burial here as part of his conclusion to the book's central theme of promises fulfilled.

Since Joshua was from the tribe of Ephraim, he was from the *physical* line of Joseph. As a man of faith in God's sure promises, he was also from Joseph's *spiritual* line.

Our final verse relates the death and burial of the high priest Eleazar. He had served Joshua just as his father, Aaron, had served Moses. His name appears eight times in the book of Joshua, three times in connection with his son Phinehas. Eleazar is especially important in the pages of Joshua as the person at the center of allotting the land (14:1; 17:4; 19:51; 21:1). His name, when associated with distributing God's land gift, once again stresses the book's theme of fulfillment. The precise location of Gibeah, his grave site, is unknown.

For Joshua, Joseph, Eleazar, and all the Old Testament faithful, the land of Canaan was not God's greatest gift. Through faith in God's continuing promises, they could see "from a distance" their far more valuable inheritance: "a better country—a heavenly one" (Hebrews 11:13-16).

Owning a grave in Canaan is insignificant compared to the enjoyment of life in God's eternal city.

Dark chapters of human unfaithfulness lie just ahead in the Old Testament. But when the time would fully come, the ever-faithful Lord would beam his glorious light through the gloom. A bright new day would dawn for all the world through the new "Joshua." He would open the heavenly Canaan and promise an eternal inheritance and citizenship.

The book of Joshua shows in a down-to-earth way that the Lord gives what he says he will. We can live in the confidence that "no matter how many promises God has made, they are 'Yes' in Christ" (2 Corinthians 1:20).

ENDNOTES

[1] Robert G. Boling, *Joshua: The Anchor Bible* (Garden City, New York: Doubleday & Company, 1982), p. 168.

[2] H. D. M. Spence and Joseph S. Exell, eds., *Joshua: The Pulpit Commentary* (New York: Funk & Wagnalls, 1913), p. 91.

[3] Clifford A. Wilson, *Rocks, Relics and Biblical Reliability* (Grand Rapids: The Zondervan Corporation, 1977), p. 65.

[4] Marten H. Woudstra, *The Book of Joshua* (Grand Rapids: William B. Eerdmans Publishing Company, 1981), p. 113.

[5] John L. McKenzie, *The World of the Judges* (Englewood Cliffs, New Jersey: Prentice-Hall, 1966), p. 43.

[6] Matthew Henry, *Matthew Henry's Commentary* (Mclean, Virginia: Macdonald).

[7] Wilson, *Rocks,* p. 62.

[8] Henry, *Matthew Henry's Commentary.*

[9] Woudstra, *The Book of Joshua,* p. 131.

[10] Denis Baly, *The Geography of the Bible* (New York: Harper & Brothers, 1957), p. 21.

[11] Boling, *Joshua,* p. 474.

[12] Trent C. Butler, *Joshua: Word Biblical Commentary,* Vol. 7 (Waco Texas: Word Books, 1983), p. 274.

[13] *Ibid.*

[14] Butler, *Joshua,* p. 283.

BIBLIOGRAPHY

Boling, Robert G. *Joshua: The Anchor Bible*. Garden City, New York: Doubleday & Company, 1982.

Bratcher, Robert G. *Handbook on the Book of Joshua*. New York: United Bible Societies, 1983.

Butler, Trent C. *Joshua: Word Biblical Commentary,* Vol. 7. Waco, Texas: Word Books, 1983.

Cohen, A., ed. *Joshua and Judges: Soncino Books of the Bible*. London: Soncino Press, 1950.

Harrison, R. K. *Introduction to the Old Testament*. Grand Rapids: William B. Eerdmans Publishing Company, 1969.

Harrison, R. K. *Old Testament Times*. Grand Rapids: William B. Eerdmans Publishing Company, 1970.

Henry, Matthew. *Matthew Henry's Commentary*. Mclean, Virginia: Macdonald.

Hoerber, Robert G., ed. *Concordia Self-Study Bible*. St. Louis: Concordia Publishing House, 1986.

Keil, C. F., and Delitzsch, Franz. *Old Testament Commentaries*—Grand Rapids: Associated Publishers and Authors, 1970.

Keller, Phillip W. *Joshua: Man of Fearless Faith*. Waco, Texas: Word Books, 1983.

Kretzmann, Paul E. *Popular Commentary of the Bible*. St. Louis: Concordia Publishing House, 1923.

McKenzie, John L. *The World Of The Judges*. Englewood Cliffs NJ: Prentice-Hall, 1966.

Roehrs, Walter R., and Franzmann, Martin H. *Concordia Self-Study Commentary*. St. Louis: Concordia Publishing House, 1979.

Schoville, Keith N. *Biblical Archaeology in Focus*. Grand Rapids MI: Baker Book House, 1978.

Spence, H. D. M., ed. *Joshua: The Pulpit Commentary.* New York: Funk & Wagnalls, 1913.

Tenny, Merrill C., ed. *The Zondervan Pictorial Bible Dictionary.* Grand Rapids: Zondervan, 1967.

Wilson, Clifford A. *Rocks, Relics, and Biblical Reliability.* Grand Rapids MI: The Zondervan Corporation, 1977.

Woudstra, Marten H. *The Book of Joshua.* Grand Rapids: William B. Eerdmans Publishing Company, 1981.

Young, Edward J. *An Introduction to the Old Testament.* Grand Rapids: William B. Eerdmans Publishing Company, 1965.

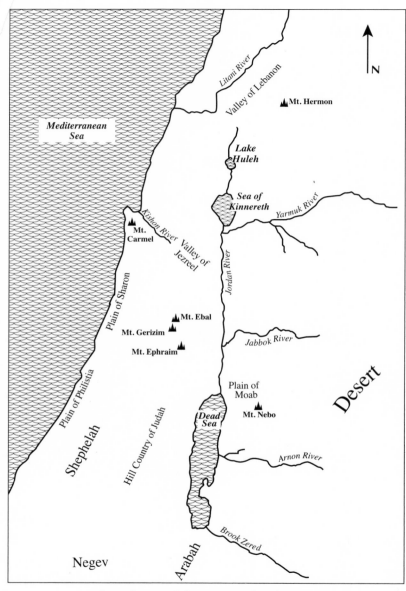

The physical features of Palestine